D0087654

American Vocal Chamber Music, 1945-1980

Recent Titles in the Music Reference Collection
Series Advisers: Donald L. Hixon
Adrienne Fried Block

Music for Oboe, Oboe D'Amore, and English Horn: A Bibliography of Materials at the Library of Congress
Compiled by Virginia Snodgrass Gifford

A Bibliography of Nineteenth-Century American Piano Music: With Location Sources and Composer Biography-Index
John Gillespie and Anna Gillespie

The Resource Book of Jewish Music: A Bibliographical and Topical Guide to the Book and Journal Literature and Program Materials
Compiled by Irene Heskes

American Vocal Chamber Music, 1945-1980

An Annotated Bibliography

Compiled by

PATRICIA LUST

Foreword by

Phyllis Bryn-Julson

The Music Reference Collection, Number 4

Greenwood Press
Westport, Connecticut • London, England

Library of Congress Cataloging in Publication Data

Lust, Patricia
American vocal chamber music, 1945-1980.

(Music reference collection, ISSN 0736-7740 ; no. 4)
Includes indexes.
1. Songs with instrumental ensemble—United States—20th century—Bibliography. 2. Vocal duets with instrumental ensemble—United States—20th century—Bibliography. I. Title. II. Series.
ML128.V7L8 1985 016.7843 84-25212
ISBN 0-313-24599-1 (lib. bdg.)

Library of Congress Catalog Card Number: 84-25212
ISBN: 0-313-24599-1
ISSN: 0736-7740

First published in 1985

Greenwood Press
A division of Congressional Information Service, Inc.
88 Post Road West, Westport, Connecticut 06881

Printed in the United States of America

10 9 8 7 6 5 4 3 2 1

Copyright acknowledgment is gratefully given to the following:

Babbitt, Milton. *Vision and Prayer*. New York: Associated Music Publishers, 1971.

Blank, Allan. *Four Poems of Emily Dickinson*. New York: American Composers Alliance, 1974.

Brings, Allen. *Tre Madrigali Concertati*. Copyright 1979 by Seesaw Music Corp: New York. Reprinted by permission.

Butler, Allen. *Plexus*. Reprinted by permission of the composer.

Cacciopo, George. *Bestiary I: Eingang*. Used for Permission, (c) 1976, Music For Percussion, Inc., Ft. Lauderdale, Florida 33334.

De Jong, Conrad. *hist whist*. New York: G. Schirmer, 1971.

Edwards, George. *Three Hopkins Songs*. Association for the Promotion of New Music

Feldman, Morton. *For Franz Kline*. Copyright 1962 by C. F. Peters Corporation. Used by permission.

James, Thomas S. *Four Poems of Michael Fried*. Hillsdale, N.Y.: Boelke-Bomart, 1975. Reprinted by permission.

Kavanaugh, Patrick. *Jubal*. New York: Carl Fischer, 1978. Reprinted by permission.

Lybbert, Donald. *Lines for the Fallen*. Copyright 1969 by C. F. Peters Corporation. Used by permission.

McNiel, Jan Pfischner. *Three Preludes to the Aureate Earth* New York: Carl Fischer, 1975. Reprinted by permission.

Schuller, Gunther. *Six Renaissance Lyrics*. New York: Associated Music Publishers, 1971.

Ung, Chinary. *Tall Wind*. Copyright 1975 by C. F. Peters Corporation. Used by permission.

Whittenberg, Charles. *Two Dylan Thomas Songs*. Permission given by Mary Whittenberg.

To Margaret Harshaw

Contents

Foreword

When Pat Lust told me of her ambitious task of compiling a list of chamber music for voice, published from 1945 to 1980, I enthusiastically endorsed her efforts. At last singers will have a source from which to choose repertoire and to further their knowledge of the wealth of lesser-known compositions written during this period. She has succeeded not only in giving us a thorough list of published works, but she has also included information about the music, the composer, and, most importantly, a short description of the vocal line.

In the past when a singer wanted to research contemporary compositions in our country, one began in the public library. This, unfortunately, was a limited source for even the early composers and their works, let alone the more contemporary literature.

Publishers have been another source for the inquisitive singer. But while publishers have proven to be helpful most of the time, one was still at the mercy of the sender as to the variety of styles seen, and it proved to be a costly and time-consuming adventure.

Another needless barrier to overcome is the common situation in which a student wishes to learn new repertoire but is faced with the attitude that such music cannot be included in the normal educational diet lest it "ruin the voice;" or, perhaps, the student is faced with a teacher who does not know the repertoire and therefore will not teach it.

FOREWORD

In my opinion an all-encompassing knowledge is a high priority in this field. The bibliography Pat Lust has furnished for our libraries and studios is invaluable as a means for closing the gaps in our education. I am grateful to her for spending the years of research required to compile such an in-depth catalogue, and I hope it is only the first of many volumes to come.

Phyllis Bryn-Julson

Phyllis Bryn-Julson

Preface

This book constitutes an extensive listing (544 entries) of the vocal chamber music written by American composers and published in the United States between 1945 and 1980. Vocal chamber music is here defined as music written for one or two voices and one to fifteen instruments, but excluding pieces for voice and keyboard.

The major sources of scores reviewed in this bibliography were the Library of Congress and the American Music Center in New York City. The following university libraries were also explored: Indiana University, The University of Cincinnati, Ohio State University, The Eastman School of Music, Indiana State University, Illinois State University, and The University of Illinois. Finally a systematic search of the OCLC holdings provided additional pieces not found in the above libraries. Items found in the OCLC search were obtained through interlibrary loan.

Foreign publications and American publications of works by foreign composers are excluded. In the case of a composer like Stravinsky (who became a naturalized American citizen in 1945), works published by an American company are included but foreign publications are not.

Each entry begins with a general bibliographic entry including composer, title, publisher, and publication date. Separate movements or titles of songs and the following details are listed before the annotation: text, instrumentation, duration, date of composition, commissions, grants, dedications, etc.

PREFACE

The text description names the poet or author and the translator when appropriate. All lyrics are in the same language as the title(s) unless otherwise noted here or in the annotation.

The vocal category is listed before the other instruments and appears as it does in the score, for example, "Soprano," "Voice," etc. Instruments noted in parenthesis indicate doublings. Optional and/or alternate arrangements are also listed.

Information about duration appears only when it has been supplied in the score. Otherwise, no attempt has been made to determine the length of a piece.

Since the reader may want to know if a piece was written a considerable time before publication, this information appears when the time lapse was four or more years (a median time gap).

The final item preceding the annotation provides information about commissions, grants, dedications, etc., and, in some cases the circumstances of the first performance (place, performers, conductor, etc.).

Each entry annotation includes information quoted directly from the score as well as a brief description of the piece. These descriptions focus on performance problems and are not intended to evaluate the quality of the music.

The first consideration of the annotation is identifying any unusual features of the piece. Descriptions of non-traditional notation appear when appropriate. In some pieces the composer gives the singer phonetic sounds instead of a text; some pieces require theatrical considerations such as speaking (on the part of instrumentalists as well as singer), movement around or off the stage as part of the performance, or the use of props; and multi-media considerations are also mentioned. Frequently singers are also required to play various percussion instruments.

Vocal range and tessitura have been examined in all cases. The annotations point out particular difficulties and problems as well as simplicity and narrow ranges. In cases where no mention of these elements is made, it may be assumed that range and tessitura are of moderate difficulty. When appropriate the outer limits of the range are defined in terms of the following chart:

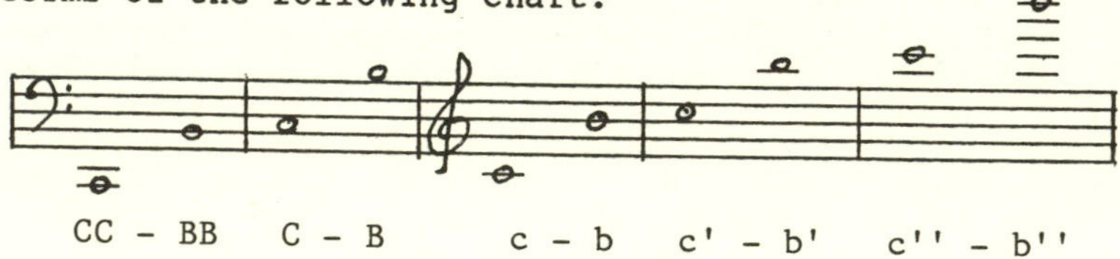

CC – BB   C – B   c – b   c' – b'   c'' – b''

Some pieces present no unusual pitch reference problems, and the vocal line relates closely to the instrumental parts. Distinguishing characteristics are doublings of vocal parts, consonant relationships between voice and instruments, and general consonance among instrumental parts. These pieces generally present little or no pitch reference problems to the singer. At the other extreme are those pieces in which the pitch reference is very difficult; the vocal line relates to the instruments only by large intervals, half steps, or other dissonant intervals. Often this remoteness is further complicated by rhythmic arrangement; when the tempo is fast and/or short notes are interspersed among rests, even consonant relationships may be difficult. Thickness of texture, timbre, and range relationships are also considered in discussing the accessibility of pitch reference for the singer.

Various shades of difficulty lie between these extremes. Often the singer can tune to frequent, isolated pitches by consonant interval or unison with the instruments. (Of course, a singer with absolute pitch may not be concerned with any of these comments about pitch problems.) Some pieces or parts of pieces have no pitch reference at all, for example those accompanied only by non-pitched percussion instruments. In some cases the composer has intended exact vocal pitches and in others he or she has not.

The annotations usually describe the vocal line as one of the following: lyric, angular, or non-traditional. Lyric lines usually move by steps (sometimes including chromaticism) and small consonant intervals; the pitch reference is usually less problematic. An angular line generally contains mostly large intervals, and often the movement of each leap is in the opposite direction from that of the previous leaps. The instrumental parts of these pieces usually move in angular lines as well. Generally the more angular pieces have more difficult pitch reference, and are more difficult to negotiate vocally. Pieces described as "somewhat angular" fall between the two above descriptions. In some pieces the singer uses predominantly or entirey non-traditional vocal techniques.

The rhythmic structure of the ensemble affects the difficulty of the piece. Frequently changing meter and tempo may present problems. Many rests interspersed among the notes, and especially rests between syllables of words, interfere with ensemble coordination. Diverse rhythmic figures superimposed within the various parts of a piece may cause more serious complications. Indications in the score for a conductor are also noted.

Some of the scores are printed, and some are published in manuscript. Several manuscript scores are nearly illegible, but most are easily readable. Some pieces may be purchased with score and parts; others are available only for rental. These facts are noted when appropriate.

No attempt is made to discuss or evaluate stylistic aspect of the pieces. Quotes by a composer on this subject are included, however, because they give insight into his or her thinking and best express his or her wishes for performance. The intent of the annotations is to describe the printed page so that any singer can decide which works are most appropriate in terms of interest, difficulty, and accessibility of resources.

The appendixes and indexes cross reference the information from the bibliography in several ways. The first appendix identifies pieces by the specific voice and instruments required, listing them in the following subdivisions:

Voice: Soprano; Mezzo-soprano and Contralto; Baritone; and Bass; Voice; High Voice; Medium Voice; Low Voice; Female Voice; Male Voice; Boy Soprano; Reciter, Speaker or Narrator (categorzed as stated by the composers on the scores).
Strings: Violin; Viola; Cello; Viols; Contrabass; Harp; Guitar and other Plucked Instruments.
Winds: Recorder; Flute and Piccolo; Clarinet; Saxophone; Oboe, English Horn and Hekelphone; Bassoon; Trumpet; French Horn; Trombone; Tuba, Euphonium and Baritone Horn.
Keyboard: Piano; Celesta; Harpsichord; Organ and Harmonium.
Percussion.
Tape, Synthesized Tape, Synthesizer.
Multimedia (Lights, Dancers, etc.).

This listing immediately leads one to the literature that is available for any desired voice or instrument.

Appendix II lists pieces according to the size of the ensemble, and Appendix III identifies pieces that fit standard instrumental ensembles, such as string quartet, woodwind quintet, etc. The General Index includes references to poets, authors of texts, performers, commissions, dedications, and other related information.

Many people have assisted in the collecting of materials and the writing of this bibliography. I am deeply indebted to two of my teachers at Indiana University for their influence: Margaret Harshaw encouraged me to pursue this subject, and David Fenske carefully guided me throughout the entire project. I am also extremely grateful for the support of my friends on Beech Street, especially Donald Stuart for writing the programs to sort the information in the appendixes, James Kidd for editing and advising, and Teri Kidd for helping with many tasks.

Introduction: Observations of Trends

Certain compositional techniques and conventions have arisen as indigenous to post World War II pieces. This essay will attempt to point out many of these and to discuss them, expecially in terms of vocal problems or other vocal considerations generated by them. Though many pieces reviewed in the bibliography are conventional scores with staves, clefs, time signatures, quarter notes, etc., this essay will focus only on innovative elements.

NOTATIONAL INNOVATIONS

New kinds of sounds have demanded new conventions of notation. For example, Kavanaugh used wiggly and short straight lines to indicate to the performers the desired sounds. Clarke notated glissandi to indicate an irregular slide from one note to another.

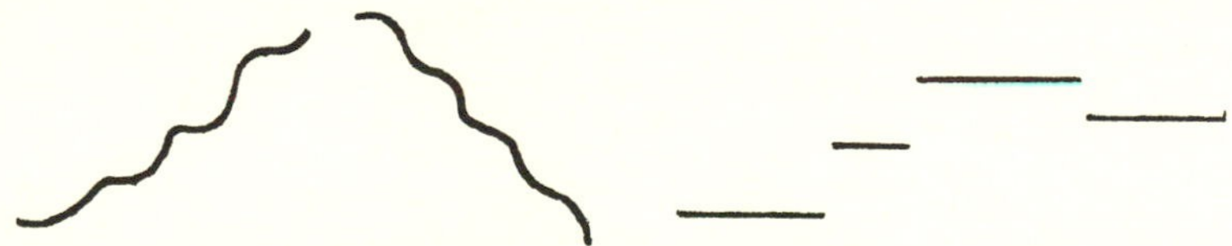

Example 1. Kavanaugh, Jubal.1

---

1. In cases where a piece is cited but no page number is noted, it may be assumed that the material is used to varying degrees throughout the piece.

INTRODUCTION

Some notational symbols unknown in 1945 have since become standard in non-traditional pieces. Examples two and three represent some that have become widely accepted among contemporary composers.

- Sprechstimme

- Sharped note played a quarter tone higher or lower (arrows also used with flats and naturals)

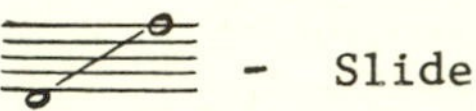
- Slide

Example 2.

- Approximate pitch, intoned or spoken

- as quickly as possible

- choice of pitch, non-diatonic, follow contour

- slow to fast

Example 3. De Jong, *hist whist*, p.2.

Unfortunately, some composers have used unusual notational symbols without adequately explaining them. Deciphering the notation is sometimes as difficult for the performer as learning the new techniques.

Visual impact of the score is significant in some. McNiel, in *Three Preludes To the Aureate Earth*, arranged the musical material in boxes: performers are to begin in any box and, when that material is finished, proceed to the next adjacent box. The composer stated that, when a performer reaches a field of silence (indicated by an arrow), he/she may continue in the same direction or change in the direction of the arrow.

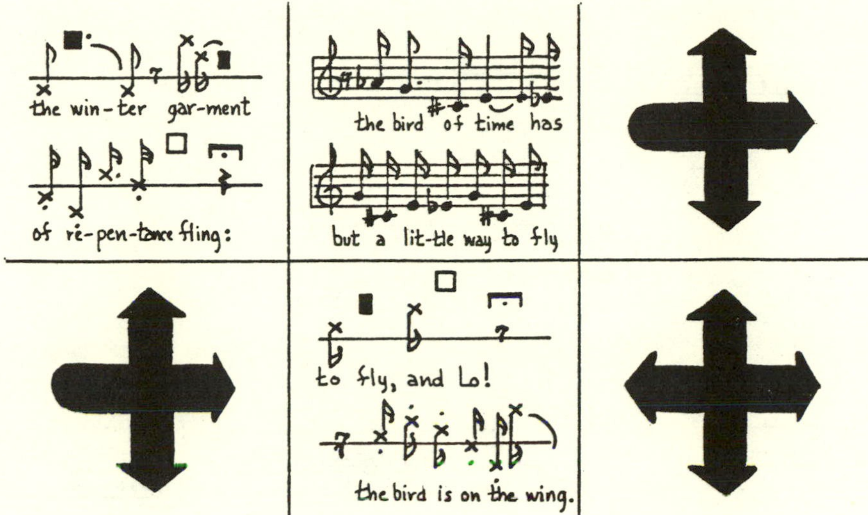

Example 4. McNiel, Three Preludes To the Aureate Earth

In Bestiary I: Eingang, Cacioppo uses measured and unmeasured segments. Unmeasured parts are notated in large boxes. "Time in these areas is a function of the decay characteristics of such instruments as piano, vibraphone, cymbal."2 In Serenade, Rosen notates "Improvisation II" in a graphic, pictorial maner.

Sometimes composers use various shapes and organizational techniques to prevent exact coordination. In Night Music I, Crumb notates the percussion and piano parts in circles segments and indicates that the performers may move in either direction around the circle. The soprano part is notated in a straight line. The composer states that "spacing of segments should be improvised. Ideally, one full turn of the circle will be made."3 Four cymbal strokes in the soprano part provide the only time reference for the instrumentalists.

Often composers remove the staff, leaving blank spaces where there are no notes. In some cases, this makes the score easier to read. In others it is used for its visual impact.

---

2. Cacioppo, George, Bestiary I: Eingang (New York: Music for percussion, 1976). n.p.

3. Crumb, George, Night Music I (Melville, NY: Belwin Mills, 1967), p.4.

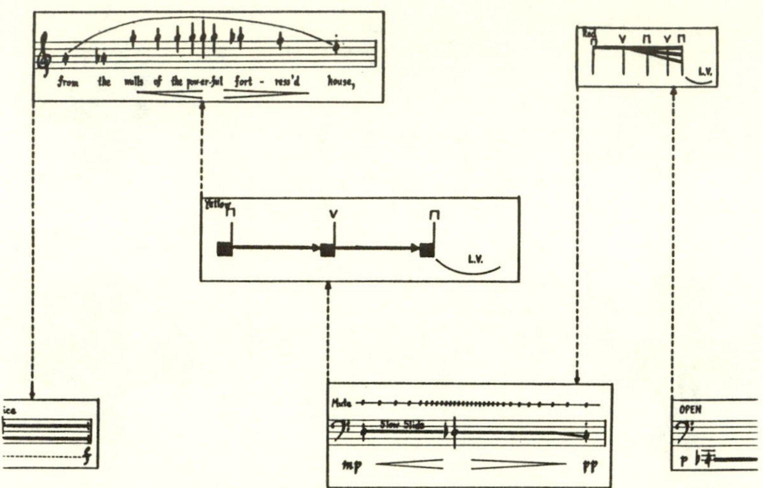

Example 5. Butler, Plexus, part 6, p. 3.

Shadows of an Orange Leaf by Zonn is printed on a very large page (about 2 1/2' by 3') with only one score printed on each page. The seven instrumental parts are in very large notation, creating an unusual ensemble problem. It is difficult to read one part and scan other parts as well.

Many modern pieces are notated conventionally in meters with metronome indications, whereas others employ various alternative methods of rhythmic notation. Movements ordered with time units, such as seconds, are popular, notated with visual units equivalent to the time units. (See e.g. 6.) De Jong has organized hist whist so that each bar has a duration of five seconds.

| 2" | 3" | etc.

Example. 6.

The time unit bars are sometimes interspersed with conventional metered notation. (See e.g. 7.) A metronome marking appears at the beginning of Hartway's Three Ways of Looking at a Blackbird, despite the fact that rests are indicated in numbers of seconds. Complete silences occur frequently in this song.

| 2" | 3/4 ♩=60 | 3" | 6/8 ♪=120 |

Example 7.

Some pieces measure continuously with timed check points, requiring use of a stop watch. (See e.g. 8.) Each segment, whatever its musical content, has the same duration.

0 10" 20" 30" 40"

| - - - | - - - | - - - | - - - |

Example 8.

Durational indications usually appear in conventional proportional notation (quarter notes, half notes, rests, etc.) or in segments of material defined in seconds. However, a few inovations should be noted. In <u>Her Drifting from Me These Days</u> St. John uses different shapes of noteheads to indicate the various durations: • = 1/2 second, ⁄ = 1 second, ■ = 2 seconds, ▲ = 3 seconds, □ = 4 seconds.

In several pieces, Feldman indicates the length of each note by the number of notes connected on the same pitch with a dotted line. (See e.g. 9.) Gaber, in <u>Voce II</u>, uses small marks above the staff to indicate beats of the metronome. The number of notes in each beat is irregular. (See e.g. 10.)

Example 9. Feldman, For Franz Kline, p.3.

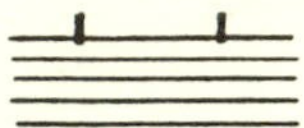

Example 10. Gaber, Voce II.

Various means have been devised to notate asymmetrical time relationships. In the prefatory notes of Speak Softly, Blickman states that "Time relationships are relative to spacial arrangements of notes on the page."[4] Moryl, in several pieces, states that the notation is proportional and does not always suggest a pulse or metric system.

The following is one of Steiner's explanatory notes for Three Poems. "In proportional notation, the entrances of instruments are lined up according to visual relationships. By the spatial distribution, the performers can coordinate their own parts with those of others."[5] Composers also give tempo indications in seconds or traditional tempo indications, such as Allegro, Andante, etc., or their English equivalents.

---

4. Blickhan, Tim, Speak Softly (New York: Seesaw Music, 1974), n.p.

5. Steiner, Gitta, Three Poems (New York: Seesaw Music, 1970), p.2.

Direct changes of tempo occur in many of these pieces, but gradual changes are usually notated conventionally with accelerando or decelerando or the English equivalents. Brings, however, in Tre Madrigali Concertati, devised a symbol to indicate graduated tempo change.

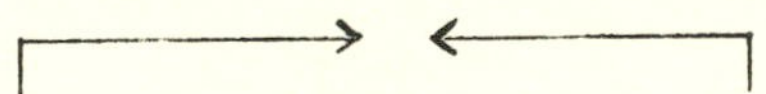

Example 11. Brings, Tre Madrigali Concertati.

In durationally-organized pieces, the tempo and sense of movement are controlled exactly by the seconds of a stop watch. Any effect of tempo change occurs automatically in that time framework.

SOUND MODIFICATIONS

Some pieces emphasize lateral movement of the sound in space rather than melody or thematic development. Portions of several pieces by Feldman consist of sequences of single pitches played by different instruments, each beginning with a soft attack as the previous pitch is fading.

In their exploration of possibilities in sounds, composers have used extremes in dynamics. Wernick, in A Prayer for Jerusalem, uses dynamics from pppp to fff. The most striking innovation in dynamics is the practice of moving rapidly from one dynamic extreme to the other. In a prefatory note to Tre Sonetti di Michalangelo Buonarroti, Brings expresses his wish for accurate observation of the specific dynamic markings which occur in every measure, or sometimes on every note. Babbitt indicates precise dynamic contrasts, sometimes note-for-note, in Vision and Prayer. (See e.g. 12.) Serialization of dynamics, however, is not a popular trend in this body of literature.

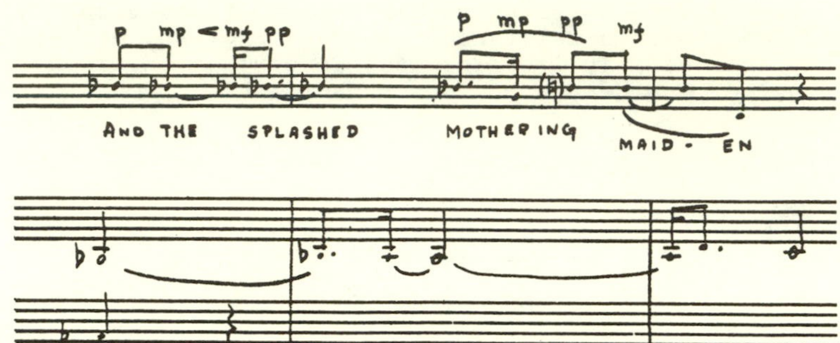

Example 12. Babbitt, Vision and Prayer, p.7.

Few composers have felt the need to devise new notation in dynamics. Lybbert uses unconventional dynamic indications in Lines for the Fallen.

Dynamics: + maximum volume and accent
x medium volume
z soft
- minimum volume

Example 13. Lybbert, Lines for the Fallen.

Many pieces use quarter-tones, in the instrumental parts, in the voice part, or both. Sims, in Celebration of Dead Ladies, notates 1/6-tone and 1/12-tone alterations as well as quarter-tones. Lines for the Fallen by Lybbert is scored for soprano and two pianos. One piano is tuned a quarter-tone lower than the other, and the soprano tunes to the upper of the two. In Johnston's Five Fragments, all instruments, as well as the voice, use microtones. The score includes an explanation of his microtonal music pitch notation, an extensive list of adjusted fingerings for oboe and bassoon microtones.

Some instructions for improvisation define performers' freedoms and limitations, some focusing on rhythm, and some on melody. Some call on the singer's imagination in vocal color and syllables. Crumb, in Night Music I, indicates different sorts of improvisation for all performers. The vocal part in number three is notated quite specifically with regard to rhythm, but the explanatory note states that "the pitches given in the soprano part are more or less approximate and merely suggest the melodic contour. The singer should 'realize' her part by improvisations. The rhythmic values can be followed more closely."6 Ran, in O the Chimneys, on the other hand, gives specific notes on which to improvise, but does not demand exact rhythmic coordina-

6. Crumb, Night Music I, p.4.

tion between performers unless specifically indicated. Perera, in Dove sta amore, indicates that the singer should improvise upon the general melodic contour of her vocal part.

EXTRA-MUSICAL EXPANSIONS

Many pieces in this group contain elements of chance; a few are based primarily on chance. The third movement of Crumb's Night Music I, with the percussion and piano parts in circular notation and the soprano part in a straight line, is not intended to be coordinated precisely. Sextet by Schwartz consists of eight pages (full score on each) which are performed in order three times for each movement. Each performer plays his own material only once during the movement and is silent during the other two performances of the page. It is arbitrarily arranged ahead of time so that there will be several solos and several dense pages. The second movement consists of the same players, same parts and same procedure, but in a different order. All performers in Peck's Automobile have cards which, except the first and last, are arranged in any order. At certain cues, all players shift from their parts to the appropriate cue card, then back to their parts. At the cue from the singer, all players abandon unfinished materials and perform the last card. In Aria, by Drew, the musicians perform several segments in order, then they perform the same segments in random order for four minutes. At a cue, all segments are again performed in the original order.

Many of these pieces involve unusual arrangements on the stage or around the hall as well as movement on the stage - sometimes for theatrical purposes and sometimes for sonorous, acoustic purposes. Zur states that The Affairs is a theatrical piece in which an attempt at communication is made between the singer and the ensemble. The singer is required to whistle extensively, and to use props, such as a newspaper. Druckman states that "Animus II is a concert-theatrical work for one female singer and two male percussion players. Its subject matter is the sensuality of ensemble playing amplified to the point of eroticism."7 Of the three parts of An Avalanche by Hiller, only number two contains musical events. Numbers one and three are theater events. The soprano sings parts of ten familiar songs, and her costume changes are an important part of the performance.

Movement on stage, as well as on and off the stage, contributes to the variety of sonority. For example, in Forms of Flight and Fancy by Diemente, the trumpet players move around the stage and off the stage in the various move-

---

7. Druckman, Jacob, Animus II (New York: MCA, 1973) n.p.

ments. At points in Reynolds' Again the musicians move while playing to different positions on the stage. The format of the printed score changes with this repositioning.

In addition to theatrical considerations and effects in sonority, stage movement also serves as an organizing factor. In McNiel's Three Preudes To The Aureate Earth, the soprano's movement from one part of the stage to another gives cues to coordinate the ensemble.

The spatial arrangement of the players in the hall, and the sound that results, is often a significant consideration. For example, a piece with electronic amplification and/or electronically generated sounds may require speakers in the four corners of the room. Adler, in Cantos V, specifies that the percussionists should be positioned on either side and at the back of the hall.

Few pieces specify lighting as part of the work's total effect. St. John's Her Drifting from Me These Days and Reynold's Again both have specific instructions for lighting. Kim indicated that a lighting cue sheet for Earthlight is available on request.

Going further, Moss combines projections, lights, tape and live performers in Unseen Leaves. It calls for mime, speaking, singing, Sprechstimme and imitation of the tape, as well as movement about and off the stage. Blank, in Finale: Mélange, indicates that both singers should function also as dancers and speakers. A solo dancer may perform in a "symbolic and ritualistic rather than expressionistic"[8] manner in several sections of Lux Aeterna by Crumb.

Amplificaion adds another dimension to the already wide variety of sounds. Ehle calls his Algorhythms an electronic song cycle and requires a microphone for the singer and for each instrument. He specifies adjustments in each microphone level and control over the tape reverberation. Fox, in Time Excursions, suggests microphones and speakers only for the soprano and reciter. In The Relativity of Icarus, Samuel indicates that the singer should use a directional microphone only for spoken and whispered passages.

USES OF INSTRUMENTS

Composers often require performers to produce unconventional sounds from their instruments. In the four books of Madrigals, Crumb asks the instrumentalists to make vocal sounds, usually singing. Amato, in Two Together, asks the tuba player to sing and play simultaneously. Often performers are required to hit or strike their instruments in various ways.

---

8. Crumb, George, Lux Aeterna (New York: C.F. Peters, 1972) n.p.

Many means are used to modify instrumental sounds. Chance in Duos I, asks both the singer and flutist for a slow pulsating effect which she calls "a slow heavy vibrato." In addition to flutter-tonguing and partials, Crumb, at various places, requires of flutist,"speak flute," which is speaking while fingering given pitches. Anderson indicated "choke tone" and "smear" for both the the trumpet and trombone in several pieces.

In a few pieces, instruments are required to play into the piano so that the pianist can catch sympathetic vibrations with the damper pedal. Also some pieces demand various types of prepared piano.

Mutes for instruments other than brass appear in the literature. In 5-4-3 by Ballou, the harpist uses a mute which is heavy paper approximately 1 1/2" wide and 19" long woven between the strings. Blank requires the clarinetist to use mutes in Coalition.

Schuman writes words under some of the flute part of In Sweet Music and gives the following instruction: "The words are given to enable the flutist to perform the melody with the clarity of a singer's projection."[9]

Performers not in the percussion section are often given percussion assignments. All performers in Reck's Night Sounds play percussion instruments and should be grouped in a cluster within reach of the appropriate instruments. Fox requires all performers to play a set of wind chimes in Time Excursions.

Most often, the singer is assigned percussion instruments to play. In Crumb's Night of Four Moons, the singer plays several percussion instruments, in Wernick's A Prayer for Jerusalem she plays the chimes, and in Chance's Duos I she plays finger cymbals. The finger cymbal strikes, played by the soprano in Crumb's Night Music I, provide a time-frame reference for the instrumentalists by dividing the song into four equal segments. In Crystals by Molineux, the singer performs a section of hand-clapping and plays the maracas, but never while singing.

Many pieces require instrumentalists to play more than one instrument. For example, a flutist may also have to play an alto flute and/or a piccolo in the piece. In Ancient Voices of Children, Crumb calls for some unusual instrumental doublings, such as the oboist also playing the harmonica.

The types and uses of tape parts vary widely. Melby states that "most of the music in the tape part is written out in the score." He warns, however, that "due to the

9. Schuman, William, In Sweet Music (Bryn Mawr, PA: Merion Music 1978), p. 5.

richness of the harmonic spectra on some of the notes, the pitches of these notes may be either partially or totally obscured."10 In another piece he combines pre-recorded speaking voice and computer-synthesized sounds on the tape.

In Animus IV by Druckman, the tape is not continuous. The score gives 3", 4" or 5" leader cues for tape entrances. Likewise, in Three Songs of Night by Ivey, the tape plays intermittently as indicated.

Pinkham states in notes for Safe in Their Alabaster Chambers, "The sounds (of the tape) are intended to be affective. They set the mood and give occasional pitches. They are not, however, meant as accompaniment, but rather a non-synchronous theatrical adjunct like scenery or lighting enhancing the effect of the otherwise unaccompanied vocal line."11

Some pieces are scored for a voice and a standard instrumental ensemble such as a string quartet, woodwind quintet, etc. The most popular ensemble, however, is voice with piano and one other instrument, most often clarinet or flute (see Appendix IV).

Two of the pieces in this bibliography are scored for self-accompanied singer. Kavanaugh's Jubal requires the singer to play violin, harpsichord, piano, harp and percussion, most often playing and singing simultaneously. In Sim's Cantata 3, the mezzo-soprano plays castanets and tabla. However, Sims allows the percussion part to be entrusted to a second performer.

Most of the ensembles contain mixed instrumentation, but some set the voice with instruments of one genre. Of these percussion is the most popular and multiple pianos or piano four hands wins second place.

With few exceptions, a work's instrumentation is explicit. But McNiel's Three Preludes to the Aureate Earth is scored for soprano and six unspecified instruments. Henry Clark calls for medium voice and any medium instrument in Puget Sound Cinquain, and in A Woman of Virtue, he specified only voice, reed and percussion.

Schwartz indicates that the instrumentation for Septet is voice, piano and any five of the following:

Woodwind I - any treble woodwind instrument
Woodwind II - any other woodwind instrument
Brass - any brass instrument
String I - Violin (or Viola or Cello)
String II - any other bowed instrument

---

10. Melby, John, Two Stevens Songs (New York: American Composers Alliance, 1975), n.p.

11. Pinkham, Daniel, Safe in Their Alabaster Chambers (Boston: Ione Press, 1974), n.p.

Percussion I
Percussion II

SPECIAL VOCAL CONSIDERATIONS

There are few limitations in the kinds of vocalisms and other sounds that composers demand of singers. Several composers ask the singer to lean into the piano and sing or hum. In Lux Aeterna, Crumb uses a symbol (——>) which means to modulate very gradually from one vowel sound to the next.

Deviations from traditional singing techniques are numerous. Druckman, in Animus II, indicates such special vocal effects as "choke" and "lingual trill," and special character interpretations such as "surprised," "embarrassed" and "sensually."12 Chance asks for a vocal flutter tongue and special trills. Silsbee's instructions for the soprano include "senza vibrato - bleak, heavy and monotonous."13 Gaburo requires distinctions among several vocal qualities: "normale, falsetto sotto voce, breathy."14 Boehnlein indicates that the soprano should sing in a pop music style with little vibrato.

Non-singing demands include whistling, whispering, shouting, humming, clapping hands, snapping fingers, etc. Colgrass asks for an "hysterical whisper," laughter and whispering double tongue (ta-ka-ta-ka). Reynolds specifies many effects for the singers: "voiceless flutter, multiphonic speech, husky purr and glottal amplitude modulation."

Sprechstimme usually functions as an expressive alternative to other sounds rather than throughout a piece. In one instance, Anderson calls for Sprechstimme while the singer breathes in.

The style and vocal demands of spoken parts vary widely. Nowak in Maiden's Song indicates that the spoken part should be like a recitation. He notates specific rhythms but leaves the soprano to choose the speech-pitch and nuance. In Finale: Melange, Blank gives the following instructions for the spoken parts: "Approximate rhythms. Always recite rather rapidly and a little breathlessly. The general rise and fall of the line should follow what seems

12. Druckman, Jacob, Animus II (New York: MCA, 1973) p. 7, 14 & 17.

13. Silsbee, Ann, Scroll (New York: American Composers Alliance, n.d.) p. 2.

14. Gaburo, Kenneth, Two (Bryn Mawr, PA: Theodore Presser, 1971) p. 3, 4 & 7.

natural to the speaker."15

In a few pieces, composers demand that singers function as instruments, or in an instrumental manner, rather than as vocalist and bearer of the text. Peck states that in the first movement of Automobile the voice should generally participate as an instrument, that is, on an equal footing with the other players. A rather lengthy section of Fox"s Time Excursions is to be sung in vocalise style marked "blend instrumentally." Chance wishes the voice to function instrumentally in Duos I. She even asks that the flute and voice try to match their timbre and articulation of tone. Childs stated that Lanterns and Candlelight is primarily a solo for marimba, accompanied throughout by the soprano.

Pitch reference is the most serious problem for singers in music of this period. In some pieces, the vocal line fits into a fairly simple harmonic structure. However, other pieces have no simple harmonic reference for the voice in the instrumental parts, and no doubling of the vocal part by the instruments. Often a singer must get a pitch in isolation, or find it among a dissonant group of notes. Lang, in a work for percussion and soprano, allows the soprano to start on whatever pitch is comfortable. He insists, however, that the relationships between the pitches must be sung as written. Forever and Sunsmell by John Cage is scored for voice and two non-tuned percussion. The composer asks the singer to transpose the vocal line so that the highest note will have an intense forced quality. In Brant's Encephalograms, the singer maintains a different tempo from the other instrumentalisis. Due to the variability in performances, the singer may have trouble finding any pitch references. The composer suggests that she stand by a xylophone and lightly play the first note of each entrance. In Schwarts's Septet, the vocal part is notated predominantly in non-specifically pitched sounds: hum, whisper, whistle, etc. A few pitched notes appear on the staff with instructions to insert any appropriate clef. Stewart states, in The First Joy of Marriage, that "Pitches are to be considered as being approximations. There may be places where the vocalist will need more of a spoken sound, rather than a sung sound."16

An angular vocal line, in contrast to a lyrical vocal line, contains many large leaps; it is jagged rather than smooth. Most often an irregularly shaped line is accompanied by complex rhythmic figures, including rests of short value interspersed. (See e.g. 14.) Many angular vocal lines also contain grace notes at a large interval, and multiple grace notes a large intervals from the goal tone. (See e.g. 15.) The speed at which these must be performed

15. Blank, Allan, Finale: Mélange (New York: American Composers Alliance, 1980), n.p.
16. Stewart, Frank, The First Joy of Marriage (New York: Seesaw Music, 1976), n.p.

makes it difficult to keep all the pitches in tune. Because there are few scalar or triadic patterns in this type of melodic line, it has very little harmonic relationsip to the other parts, and pitch reference can be difficult. The singer must rely on isolated pitches for tuning.

Example 14. Ung, Tall Wind, p. 15.

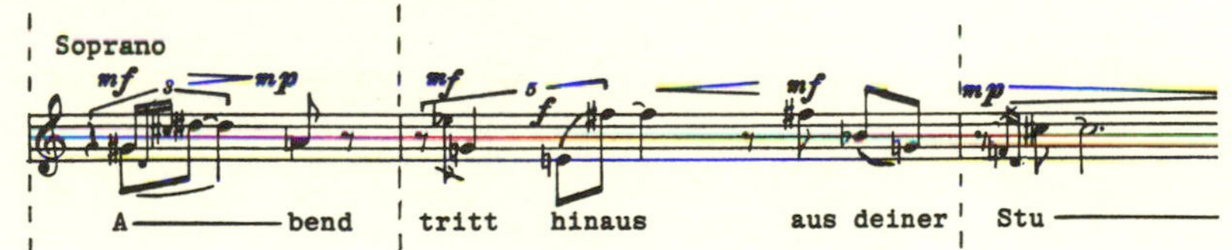

Example 15. G. Cacioppo, Bestiary I: Eingang, p.4.

The texts of some of these pieces come from unusual sources, such as The New York Times and the J.C. Penney Catalog. A few are set in foreign languages, and Trimble's Four Fragments from the Canterbury Tales is in Middle English. Rouse sets eight poems in eight different languages in Aphrodite Cantos.

A few pieces use I.P.A. (International Phonetic Alphabet) symbols rather than a text. Some use consonants for their percussive effects. In Motet and Madrigal by Pleskow, some words are begun by one singer and completed by the other. Reynolds divided words of the text in unconventional ways, e.g. day and night = da-ya-ndni-ght. Cowell writes several pieces as a vocalise on "ah".

Lerdahl, in *Eros* uses a poem in its entirety, fragments of the poem, words of the poem in retrograde order, and repetitions of several words. Uttrehyus uses the text and its retrograde as source materials in *Angstwagen*.

RHYTHMIC COMPLEXITIES

A prominent characteristic of music since 1945 is the increase in rhythmic complexity. Borrowed rhythms (or irregular subdivisions of beats) such as triplets in duple meter have been carried to extremes in complexity. Sometimes these irregular subdivisions are spread across several beats, and sometimes they cross bar lines. The addition of small-value rests to these already irregular figures further complicates the rhythmic problems. For example, Mel Powel used not only , but also and .

Superimposition of non-congruent rhythmic figures is common. (See e.g. 16.) Several layers of non-congruent figures create ensemble problems, and a conductor is usually specified in these cases.

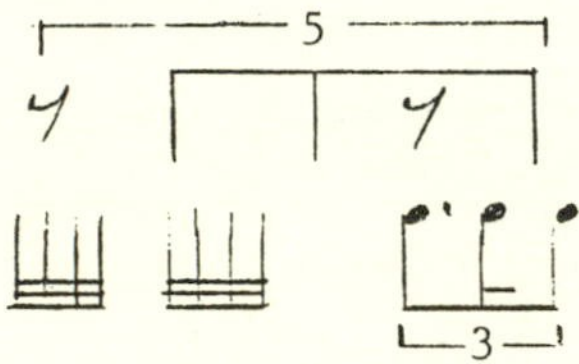

Example 16. C. Whittenberg, *Two Dylan Thomas Songs*.

A few pieces consist mostly of irregular rhythms; that is, dotted notes, ties across beats and bar lines, and small-value rests predominate. (See e.g. 17.) Sometimes, as in Babbitt's *Two Sonnets*, the attacks and pitch changes occur most often off the beats.

Example 17. T. James, *Four Poems of Michael Fried*.

In A. Blank's *Being: Three Vignettes*, the sound is tossed back and forth between the two performers with many rests interspersed. A number of pieces are constructed with a sparse texture, one or several instruments sounding only a note or a few notes, then resting while another instrument sounds (see e.g. 18). That these short bursts of sound must pass around from player to player contributes to problems of ensemble coordination.

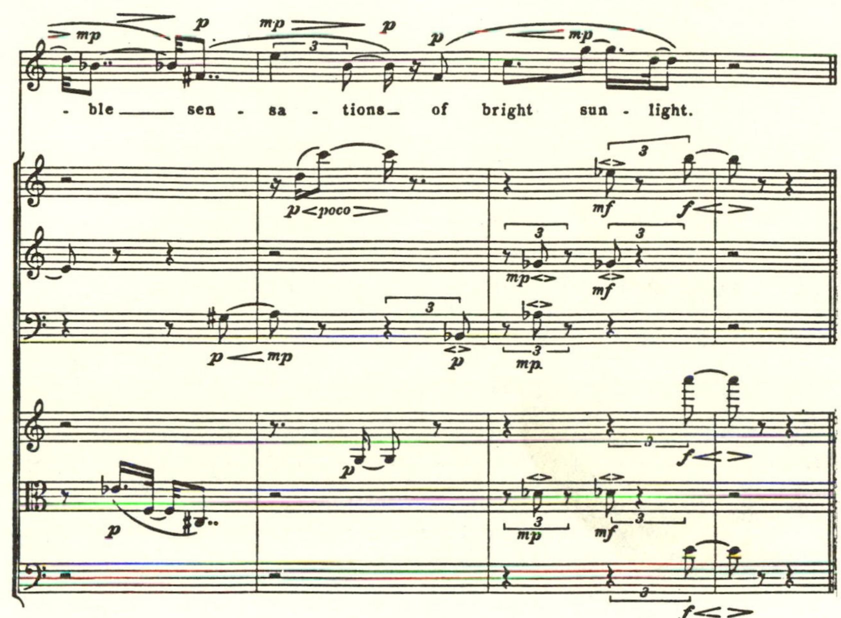

Example 18. T. James, Four Poems of Michael Fried, P.14.

In some pieces, e.g. the Time Cycle by Foss, the meter changes often, sometimes in each bar. In Incantations by Shapey, the meter shifts continuously: 1/4, 3/16, 4/4, 3/32, 1/8.

Many pieces combine meters and other indications for movement (see e.g. 19). In a piece such as Songs before an Adieu by Kolb, some parts are metered, some indicated in seconds, and some free. One of the more complex phrases in Gaburo's Two is guided alternately between seconds and conventional meter. 2/8 and 7/16 are the usual meter markings in Rochberg's Blake Songs. In Crumb's Night of Four Moons, 3/ is the most common meter in one piece and 7/ remains constant throughout another. Stewart uses four and a half over four, but only in single, isolated bars. Schuller begins one of the Six Renaissance Lyrics with three different meters simultaneously (see e.g. 20).

| 4" | 2" | ♩. = 60 | 3" | 𝅗𝅥 ♪ = 108 | 4" |

Example 19.

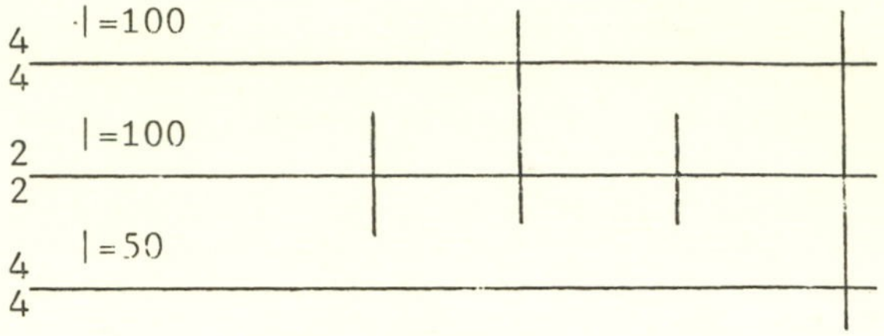

4/4 ♩=100

2/2 ♩=100

4/4 ♩=50

Example 20. Schuller, *Six Renaissance Lyrics*.

INFLUENTIAL PUBLISHERS AND SINGERS

American Composers Alliance has made more contemporary American chamber music available than any other single publisher. Boosey & Hawkes, C.F. Peters, Carl Fischer and Seesaw Music have also made major contributions in promoting new music. The reader will notice, however, that many of the American Composers Allinace publications are not discussed in this bibliography. A spokesperson from ACA explained that review copies are available only if the composers have made provisions for them. When composers do provide review copies, ACA sends them to the American Music Center, but otherwise, review copies literally are not available.

A few singers have taken the lead in introducing new pieces, and many pieces have been dedicated to them. Some who have been especially significant on the American scene are Phyllis Bryn-Julson, Phyllis Curtin, Adele Addison, Elaine Bonazzi and the late Bethany Beardslee.

The interest in vocal chamber music has grown steadily since 1945. The years between 1945 and 1950 produced less than five publications each. Average years in the 1970's offer at least 25 publications.

Bibliography

001. ADLER, Samuel. Canto V. New York, Carl Fischer, 1980.

1. The Importance of Poetry or the Coming forth from Eternity into Time
2. If Casuality Is Impossible, Genesis Is Recurrent.

Text: Hyam Plutzik, from Apples from Shinar.
Instrumentation: Soprano, Flute, Cello, Percussion (3).
Commissioned for the Dedication of the Interfaith Chapel of the University of Rochester, October, 1970.

The angular vocal line covers a wide range and approaches most notes above the staff by large leaps. Pitch reference is remote at best; doubling by an instrument almost never occurs. The composer wishes the percussionists to be positioned on either side and the back of the hall. He gives an alternate arrangement for use when this is not possible. A conductor is indicated in the score.

002. ADLER, Samuel. The Passionate Sword. New York: Carl Fischer, 1979.

Text: Jean Starr Untermeyer, Louis Untermeyer.
Instrumentation: Baritone, Flute, Clarinet, Violin, Cello, Percussion.
Composed: 1974.
Commissioned to commemorate the 150th Anniversary of Bexley hall school of theology.

Though this is not a theater piece, some movement is indicated. Tempo and meter remain fairly constant throughout except for an unmetered section at the beginning. Vocal pitches sometimes relate to the instrumental parts by a third or fifth, and occasionally the instruments double the vocal part. Often, however, the parts do not relate so easily. Large intervals are frequent.

003. ADLER, Samuel. Sixth String Quartet: A Whitman Serenade For Medium Voice and String Quartet. New York: Carl Fischer, 1977.

- Dearest Thou Now O Soul
- Quicksand Years
- That Music Always 'round Me
- The Last Invocation

Text: Walt Whitman, poems from the section of Leaves of Grass entitled "Whisers of Heavenly Death."
Commissioned by the Fine Arts Foundation of Chicago for Jan DeGaetani and the Fine Arts Quartet.

Though organized as a single piece, the four poems are separated by lengthy string quartet interludes and require some special effects. A complete set of string parts is available separately. In some sections the meter changes frequently and irregular subdivisions of beats are common. The angular vocal part lies mostly in the middle part of the range. The range encompasses G - a'.

004. ADOLPHUS, Milton. Lilacs. New York: American Composers Alliance, n.d.

Instrumentation: Voice, Clarinet, Piano.

Score not available for review.

005. ALBERT, Stephen. To Wake the Dead. New York: Carl Fischer, 1978, 1980.

Six Sentimental Songs and an Interlude After Finnegan's Wake
1. How it ends
2. Riverrun (ballad of Persse O'Rielly)
3. Pray your prayers
4. Instruments
5. Forget, Remember
6. Sod's brood,
7. Passing Out

Text: Fragments from James Joyce.
Instrumentation: Soprano, Flute, (Alto flute), Clarinet, (Bass Clarinet), Violin (Viola), Cello, Piano, Harmonium.
Duration: ca. 25 minutes.

Composed with the aid of a grant from the National Endowment for the Arts (1978).
Dedication: to the composer's Wife.

The soprano's entrance pitches relate to the instrumental parts usually by unison or small interval. The vocal line moves mostly by steps and small leaps except in the last two pieces (expecially #6)which are more angular. In most cases the tessitura is generally high; in a few cases it is generally low. The composer provides interpretative instructions, such as "childlike and artless" and "growing coarse" for the singer. Fairly frequent tempo and meter changes occur. Performance materials are available on rental.

006. AMATO, Bruno. Two Together. New York: Seesaw Music, 1973.

Six Short Untitled Pieces
Text: Walt Whitman.
Instrumentation: Soprano, Tuba.

The composer states very specific dynamic markings, requiring many shadings, fast changes and extremes. The tempo remains constant in each movemment, but the meter changes frequently in all but number three. The angular vocal line is labeled "chest Tone" or "normal" in various places. Entrances often appear at a half tone interval with the tuba. The tuba player sometimes sings and plays simultaneously and a short section bears the instruction "senza tone." The score also requires him to make some quarter tone changes and to hit the tuba.

007. AMES, William. Among the Gods. New York: American Composers Allinace, n.d.

Instrumentation: Soprano, Clarnet, Violin (2), Viola.

Score not available for review.

008. AMRAM, David. Three Songs for America. New York: C.F. Peters, 1974.

Text: I. first two sentences: from Profiles in Courage by John F. Kennedy
remainder: J.F.K.'s Inaugural Address.
II. from Strength of Love by Martin Luther King, Jr.
III. from public speeches by Robert F. Kennedy.
Instrumentation: Bass, Flute, English Horn, Clarinet, French Horn, Bassoon, String Quartet, Double Bass.
Duration: ca. 8 1/2 Minutes.
Completed: 1969.

The meter remains fairly constant throughout each piece. Some tempo changes and dynamic extremes occur. The vocal part moves mostly in steps and small leaps. Pitches at vocal entrances are not always easily related to those of the instruments, but sometimes doubling occurs. Range: FF(EE)-e. Three Songs for America is published with a score and parts for the instruments.

009. ANDERSON, T.J. Beyond Silence. New York: American Composers Alliance, 1973.

Text: Pauline Hanson.
Instrumentation: Tenor, Clarinet, Trombone, Viola, Cello, Piano.
Duration: ca. 15 Minutes.

In a section marked "cadenza, tempo ad lib." the tenor, moving in exact pitches but non-specific rhythm, performs in alternation with the instruments. The tempo remains constant before the cadenza, but changes frequently in the section immediately after it. Beyond Silence requires dynamic extremes and quick dynamic changes. The following are some of the instrumental instructions: "shake," "smear," "flutter tongue," "col legno, battuta, sul A." The angular vocal line often relates to the instrumental parts by half step intervals, especially at vocal entrances. Special requirements include Sprechstimme, humming and an alternation of Sprechstimme and Sprechstimme while breathing in.

010. ANDERSON, T.J. Block Songs. New York: American Composers Alliance, n.d.

Text: Perl Lomak.
Instrumentation: Medium Voice, Childrens Toys.

Score not available for review.

011. ANDERSON T.J. Variations on a Theme by M.B. Tolson. New York: Composers Facsimile Edition, 1969.

Text: M.B. Tolson.
Instrumentation: Soprano, Violin, Cello, Eb Alto Sax, Trumpet, Trombone, Piano.
Duration: ca. 16 Minutes.

The composer designates dynamic extremes (frequent ppp) and quick dynamic changes. The following indications appear in the trumpet and trombone parts: "choke tone" and "smear." In a section marked "Cadenza, tempo ad libitum," five unaccompanied spoken bits appear, each followed by a short instrumental bit. Special vocal requirements include speaking, Sprechstimme, humming and speaking while breathing in. The angular vocal line relates remotely to the pitches in the instrumental parts: few doublings, even of isolated pitches, occur.

012. ARGENTO, Dominick. Letters from Composers. New York: Boosey and Hawkes, 1971.

Frederic Chopin (to a friend)
Wolfgang Amadeus Mozart (to his father)
Franz Schubert (to a friend)
Johann Sebastian Bach (to the Town Council)
Claude Debussy (to a friend)
Giacomo Puccini (to a friend)
Robert Schumann (to his fiancee)

Instrumentation: High voice, Guitar.
Commissioned by Vern Sutton and Jeffery Van "to whom it is happily dedicated."
Guitar part edited by Mr. Van.

The vocal line moves mostly by steps and small leaps and some sevenths, and frequently the guitar doubles isolated vocal pitches. The composer places no demands on the extremes of the vocal range. The meter remains fairly constant throughout each song. Tempo changes occur more frequently. Some dynamic extremes are indicated.

013. ARGENTO, Dominick. To be Sung Upon the Water. New York: Boosey & Hawkes, 1974.

I. Prologue: Shadow and Substance
II. The Lake At Evening
III. Music On the Water
IV. Fair Is the Swan
V. In Remembrance of Schubert
VI. Hymn Near the Rapids
VII. The Lake At Night
VIII. Epilogue: De Profundis

Text: William Wordsworth.
Instrumentation: High Voice, Piano, Clarinet (Bass Clarinet).
Duration: 25 Minutes.

The tempo and meter are fairly constant within each movement except Number IV, in which the changing meter and placement of rests and tied notes may cause ensemble problems. This set requires extremes in dynamics, especially ppp. Vocal pitches, including wide intervals, clearly relate to the instrumental parts. Number V contains a melodic quote from the Schubert song of the same title as this set, and is scored for piano and voice only.

014. AUSTIN, Larry. Homecoming: A Cantata for Soprano and Jazz Quintet. Davis CA: Composer Performer Edition, n.d.

In two movements
Text: Peter Viereck.
Instrumentation: Soprano, Trumpet, Tenor Sax, Piano, Contrabass, Percussion.
Composed: 1959.

The vocal line includes some large leaps, somes chromaticism, repeated pitches and frequent glissandi. Pitch reference is remote at best. Half-tone relationships with the instruments exist, but doublings are rare. The second movement begins with a duet between the soprano and non-tuned percussion. All performers' parts indicate a variety of improvisation. Meter changes occur frequently in some sections.

015. AVISHALOMOV, Jacob. The Little Clay Cart. New York: American Composers Alliance, n.d.

Text: Ancient Hindu.
Instrumentation: Voice, Flute (Piccolo), Clarinet, Banjo

Score not available for review.

016. AVSHALOMOV, Jacob. Two Little Birds. New :York: American Composers Alliance, n.d.

Text: Katherine Hoskins.
Instrumentation: Soprano, Clarinet, Piano.

Score not available for review.

017. BABBITT, Milton. Two Sonnets. Hillsdale, New York: Bolke-Bomart, n.d.

Spelt from Sybil's Leaves
That Nature is a Heraclitean Fire

Text: Gerard Manley Hopkins.
Instrumentation: Baritone, Carinet, Viola, Cello.
Duration: ca. 7 1/2 Minutes.
Dedication: The Julliard School of Music.

Diverse rhythmic figures including small note values tied across the beats are common. Most frequently attacks and pitch changes occur off the beats. Vocal pitches relate remotely to the instrumental parts with little doubling, even of isolated pitches. Range: GG - ab. The tempo remains constant through each movement. Some meter changes occur with the quarter note always the basic unit.

018. BABBIT, Milton. Vision & Prayer for Soprano & Synthesized Accompaniment. New York: Associated Music Publishers, 1971.

12 Parts. Not specified as movements, but each identified by a new metronomic marking.
Text: Dylan Thomas.
Instrumentation: Soprano, Tape.

Part 1 and the end of 12 are spoken. Part 2 and the beginning of 12 are Sprechstimme. All parts between these are sung, and the angular line contains complex rhythmic figures. Precise dynamic contrasts are indicated, in some places one for each note. The score provides a reduction of tape (cues) on two staves for use with piano. Accompanying performance notes state that "The 'instrumental' cues are, in no sense, a complete indication of the content of the synthesized tape tracks, but merely those pitch and rhythmic events which may assist the singer." The tape includes interludes of about a minute between some sections and a short coda at the end. It is available on rental from the publisher.

019. BALAZS, Frederic, Sonnets After Elizabeth Barrett Browning. New York: American Composers Alliance, n.d.

Instrumentation: High Voice, String Quartet.

Score not available for review.

020. BALLOU, Esther. 5-4-3. New York: Composers Facsimile Edition, 1966.

I. all which isn't singing is mere talking
II. who is this
III. may i be gay
IV. ! hope

Text: e e cummings.
Instrumentation: Voice, Viola, Harp.
Commissioned by the Kindler Foundation.

Though the vocal line is somewhat angular, many small leaps and repeated intervals appear. The viola frequently doubles the vocal line. Some segments are spoken or whispered. Ballou gives instructions to raise the pitch of a few notes slightly. The harpist uses a mute, "heavy paper approximately 1 1/2" wide and 19" long woven between the strings." Frequent tempo and meter changes occur.

021. BARAB, Seymour. Bagatelles. New York: Galaxy Music, 1979.

1. Prelude
2. Roundelay (John Dryden)
3. Prue (Thomas Moore)
4. The Fly (William Blake)
5. If Love Were What the Rose Is (Charles Algernon Swinburne)
6. Tom (Thomas Moore)
7. The Owl (Alfred Tennyson)
8. The Pigtail (William Makepeace Thackeray)

Instrumentation: High Voice, Recorder, Guitar.
To the Conviviorum Deliciae.

The recorder frequently doubles or plays thirds with the lyric voice part. Within each song the tempo remains fairly constant, but the meter changes frequently. The recorder player uses both soprano and tenor instruments.

022. BARAB, Seymour. Moments Macabre. New York: Galaxy Music, n.d.

1. Prelude
2. Old Roger
3. Down by the Green Wood Shady
4. The Wald
5. A Man of Words and not of Deeds
6. Gypsies in the Wood
7. Elegy for Frederick the Great
8. Mama had a Baby

Text: Songs on Traditional Counting Rhymes of London Children (compiled by W.H. Auden).
Instrumentation: Voice, Flute, Oboe, Clarinet, String Quartet, Double Bass.
For the Mohawk Trail Festival.

The folk and folk-like tunes, moving mostly in steps and small leaps, usually encompass a small vocal range. Instrumental parts double isolated vocal notes, figures and full phrases. The tempo and meter are fairly constant within each song. Rhythmic unity appears within groups of instruments. The score includes a piano reduction.

023. BEALE, James. Lamentations, Op 35. New York: American Composers Alliance, n.d.

Text: Psalms.
Instrumentation: Soprano, Flute, Piano.

Score not available for review.

024. BEALE, James. Proverbs, Op. 28. New York: Pioneer Editions, 1960.

I. on wisdom
II. on truth
III. on slander
IV. on laziness

Instrumentation: Baritone, English Horn, Vibraphone, Piano (Celesta).
Duration: 8 Minutes.

Some parts of the vocal line are angular, some are recitative-like and some move by steps and small skips. Pitch reference is remote at best; doubling, even of isolated pitches, is rare. Most of the vocal part lies on the bass clef staff. Meter changes and tempo fluctuations occur frequently.

025. BEALE, James. Three Songs, Op, 33. New York: American Composers Alliance, n.d.

Text: Herrick, Dickenson, W. Morris.
Instrumentation: Soprano, Violin, Viola.

Score not available for review.

026. BEERMAN, Burton. Consort and Song. New York: American Composers Alliance, n.d.

Instrumentation: Soprano, Clarinet, Percussion, Harp, Tape.

Score not available for review.

027. BEERMAN, Burton. Mass. New York: American Composers Alliance, n.d.

Instrumentation: Tenor, Flute, Percussion, Harp, Tape.

Score not available for review.

028. BEESON, Jack. A Creole Mystery. New York: Boosey & Hawkes, 1979.

Text: Lafcadio Hern, from The Item. Adapted by the composer.
Instrumentation: Medium Voice, String Quartet.
Duration: 9-10 Minutes.
Dedication: Zelda Manacher.

The vocal line, moving generally by steps and small leaps, lies mostly on the treble staff. Pitches relate to the quartet, with some doubling. Occasional bits of recitative appear. The work is published in a piano-vocal reduction. Score and parts are available on rental from the publisher.

029. BEESON, Jack. *The Day's No Rounder Than its Angles Are*. New York: Boosey & Hawkes, 1979.

1. Why Can't I Live Forever?
2. Dance of the Haemophiliacs
3. The Day's No Rounder Than Its Angles Are

Text: Peter Viereck.
Instrumentation: Middle Voice, String Quartet.
Duration: 12 Minutes.

In a few sections the meter changes frequently, but rhythmic figures are generally quite simple. The lyric vocal line includes many triadic and scalar patterns, and vocal pitches relate to those of the string quartet by consonant intervals.

030. BENSON, Warren. *Nara*. New York: Carl Fischer, 1978.

I. Song - Response
II. Song - Response
III. Consequent Response
IV. Song - Response
V. Wind Chimes in a Temple Ruin

Text: Earl Birney, from "Wind Chimes In A Temple Ruin".
Instrumentation: Soprano, Flute, Piano, Percussion (2).
Duration: 16 Minutes.
Composed: 1970.
Dedication: Lyric Arts Trio, Toronto.

In the first part of number I, which is a dialog between flute and soprano, the soprano sings only two phrases, both unaccompanied. The first pitch of each relates easily to the last pitch of the flute's previous phrase. In number V, which is rhythmically free, only non-tuned percussion instruments accompany the angular vocal line. Numbers II, III and IV are scored for instruments only. The vocal range encompasses A to b'.

031. BENTON, Daniel. *Love Song*. New York: Seesaw Music, 1975.

Text: Jessica Hogedorn.
Instrumentation: Woman's Voice, Flute, Harp.

The vocal part moves mostly in small intervals within a low range (A - c#'). Vocal entrance pitches relate to previous instrumental material by unisons and small intervals. Little actual doubling occurs, however. The tempo is constant, but the meter changes frequently.

032. BENVENUTI, Arrigo. *Cantus, Gemellus*. Newton Centre, MA: Margun Music, n.d.

Instrumentation: Voice, Flute.
Composed: 1961.
Duration: Indefinite.

Score not available for review.

033. BERGER, Arthur. *Three Poems of Yeats from "Words for Music Perhaps."* New York: New Music Edition, 1950.

I. Crazy Jane on the Day of Judgement
II. His Confidence
III. Girl's Song

Instrumentation: Voice, Flute, Clarinet in A, Cello.

The composer gives extensive instructions with regard to dyamics, accents and other expressive marks. Rhythmic figures are not complex, but the positioning of rests, accents, ties across barlines, etc. pose possible ensemble problems. The vocal part moves mostly in steps and small leaps. Solos are passed back and forth between instruments.

034. BERGER, Jean. *Five Songs*. Boulder, CA: John Sheppard Music Press, 1965.

Pour lui j'ay méprisé
Car c'est le seul désir
Sans cesse mon coeur sent
Vouc n'estimez légère
O domine Deus

Text: Poems by Mary Stuart, Queen of Scots.
Instrumentation: Medium Voice, Flute, Viola, Cello.

The vocal line moves mostly by steps and small leaps within a moderate range (B - f#'). Instrumental parts often double the vocal pitches. Meter and tempo changes occur, but not frequently.

035. BERGER, Jean. Six Rondeau. Boulder, CO: John Sheppard Music Press, 1968.

Le premier jour du mois de Mai
Guardez le trait de la fênetre
Fuyez le trait de Doux Regard
Hiver, yous n'êtes qu'un vilain
C'est fait il m'en faut plus parler
Puis ça, puis Lá

Text: Charles d'Orléans.
Instrumentation: Voice, Viola.

The vocal part lies generally low (G - f') and moves mostly by steps, small leaps and triadic figures. Entrance pitches usually relate to the viola by a consonant interval, and many consonant intervals and doublings occur throughout.

036. BERGER, Jean. Tres Canciones. Boulder, CO: John Sheppard Music Press, 1968.

I. Ninguno cierre las puertas
II. Ay triste, que vengo
III. Ya cantan los gallos

Text: Anonymous poems from the Court of Ferdinand and Isabella (ca. 1500).
Instrumentation: Medium Voice, Viola, Cello (or Voice and Piano).

The lyric vocal line moves mostly in steps and small leaps. Instruments frequently double isolated vocal pitches, but not complete phrases. The meter and tempo remain fairly constant throughout each piece.

037. BIALOSKY, Marshall. Six Riddles from Symphosius. New York: Seesaw Music, 1976.

Prelude
Hobnail
Mother of Twins
Onion
Interlude
Saw
Stairs
Chicks in the Shell
Postlude

Text: Translations by Richard Wilbur.
Instrumentation: Voice, Cello, Trombone (or Bassoon).

Instrumental parts occasionally double the vocal pitches, but a relationship of a half tone or whole tone is far more frequent. The vocal part is generally middle range but extends from A to ab'. The meter changes frequently in some of these short pieces.

038. BIALOSKY, Marshall. Three Songs. New York: Seesaw Music, 1975.

A Stone by the shore
A Shell
The Mirror

Text: Howard Nemeror.
Instrumentation: Soprano, Clarinet.
Dedication: Luigi Dallapiccola.

The two parts relate frequently by an interval of a second, but sometimes fall into unison. The songs lie fairly low for soprano (A - g#'). The meter changes frequently in the first and third songs, but no complex rhythmic figures occur. The composer provides many dynamic and other interpretive marks.

039. BINKERD, Gordon. Portrait Intérieur. New York: Boosey & Hawkes, 1973.

1. Le Sublime est un depart
   (The sublime is a departure)
2. Ce ne pas des souvenirs
   (It is not Memories)
3. Comment encore reconnâitre
   (How might I again recall)
4. Tel cheval qui boit à la fontaine
   (A Certain horse drinking at the fountain)

Text: Rainer Maria Rilke, set in French.
Instrumentation: Mezzo-soprano, Violin, Cello,

The meter remains generally constant throughout each piece, except in number four where it changes in nearly every measure. Extended sections of glissandi appear in the string parts. The vocal line is sometimes angular, but usually lyric. Pitches relate directly to the string parts, but fall among much dissonance. Portrait is published with parts for violin and cello. A mini score is available separately.

040. BINKERD, Gordon. Secret-Love. New York: Boosey & Hawkes, 1977.

Text: John Dryden.
Instrumentation: Voice, Cello, Harp.

Secret-Love is published with a score and parts for cello and harp. The lyric vocal part lies mostly on the treble staff and relates clearly to the pitches of the instruments. The tempo changes several times, but the meter remains constant and no complex rhythmic figures appear.

041. BINKERD, Gordon. Three Songs For Mezzo-soprano and String Quartet. New York: Boosey & Hawkes, 1971.

1. Never the Nightingale (A.C.)
2. How Lilies Came White (R.H.)
3. Upon Parting (R.H.)

Text: Adelaide Crapsey, Robert Herrick.

The meter changes frequently, sometimes in every measure. Further ensemble complexities arise from the shifting accents. The vocal part encompases a wide range, G - bb'), but lies mostly on the treble staff. Pitches clearly relate to the quartet, though often falling among much dissonance. The score includes four parts, for the strings, and a mini-score. Each string part also includes the vocal part. A version for voice and piano has been prepared by the composer and is available for sale.

042. BISCARDI, Chester. Turning. New York: American Composers Alliance, 1973.

Text: Chester Biscardi.
Instrumentation: Soprano, Violin, String Trio.
Dedication: Irene Steiner.

The basic structure of the piece is a duet for voice and violin accompanied by the trio. The pitches of the angular vocal line very often relate to the violin by a half tone interval; doublings are rare.

043. BLACKWOOD, Easley. Un Voyage à Cythère, Op 20. New York: G. Schirmer, 1967.

Text: Charles Baudilaire, set in French.
Instrumentation: Soprano, Flute, Piccolo (also Second Flute), Oboe, Clarinet in A (also Eb Clarinet), Bass Clarinet in Bb (also Clarinet in A), Bassoon, Trumpet in C (or Bb), French Horn, Trombone, Contrabass.
Duration: 14 Minutes.
Commissioned by University of Chicago for the 75th Anniversary.
Written for the Contemporary Chamber Players, Ralph Shapey, music director.

The composer wishes the given metronomic indications to be observed within a tolerance range of plus or minus five percent. The meter changes frequently, sometimes every measure. Irregular subdivisions of beats,

e.g. 4/8 , 7/8 ,

are prominent. Ensemble coordination may be a problem. Blackwood uses traditional techniques, but some parts require virtuosic playing. The soprano must often relate pitches to tone clusters in the instruments. The vocal line is sometimes recitative-like and other times quite angular.

044. BLANK, Allan. Being: Three Vignettes for Soprano and Clarinet in A. Northampton, MA: Smith Publications, 1977.

In propinquity
Tantalized by new gaps
The past indubitable

Text: Margot Blank.
Composed: 1973.

The clarinet and soprano relate most often by an interval of a second or ninth, with little, if any, doubling. The two parts rarely move in similar rhythmic figures. Often the sound is tossed back and forth between the two with many rests interspersed. The meter changes frequently in these short pieces.

045. BLANK, Allan. Coalitions. New York: American Composers Alliance, 1975.

i. Wild and Agressive
ii. Playthings (Extension i)
iii. Introspection
iv. From the Past (Extension ii)
v. The Heart is the Capitol of the Mind
vi. Conclusion

Text: Based on a poem by Emily Dickinson.
Instrumentation: Soprano, Clarinet (2), Trombone, Piano, Percussion (2).
Commissioned by and dedicated to the American Artists Series.

Though the vocal line contains few large leaps, it is somewhat angular. Most of the entrance pitches appear in previous instrumental material. Coalitions is mainly an instrumental piece. The voice is used only in number V, which is very short. The composer indicated, however, that the singer may participate as an additional performer where necessary. The score includes a stage arrangement diagram. The composer uses some spacial notation and specifies the use of clarinet mutes.

046. BLANK, Allan. Don't let that horse eat that violin. New York: Composers Facsimile Edition, 1965.

Text: Lawrence Ferlinghetti.
Instrumentation: Voice, Bassoon, Violin.

The somewhat angular vocal line lies mostly on the treble staff. Pitch reference is remote, but occasional doublings occur. The tempo and meter change frequently. Irregular subdivisions occur in all parts and within the changing meter. The notation for harmonics appears frequently in the violin part.

047. BLANK, Allan. Esther's Monologue. New York: American Composers Alliance. 1970.

Text: Margot Blank.
Instrumentation: Soprano, Oboe, Viola, Cello.
Written for and dedicated to Stephen and Marlee Colburn.

The vocal line is distributed fairly evenly across a range of Bb - bb'. Wide leaps are not uncommon. Entrance pitches sometimes appear in previous instrumental material, but little doubling occurs. Relationships of a half or whole tone are frequent. The meter changes frequently. Some tempo changes appear.

048. BLANK, Allan. Finale: Mélange. New York: American Composers Allinace, 1980.

Text: drawn from "Problems and Other Stories," and "How to be Uncle Sam" by John Updike; Miscellaneous words and phrases by the composer.
Instrumentation: Soprano (Dancer/Speaker), Baritone (Dancer/Speaker), Tuba, Percussion, Piano.

Though the composer provides some suggestions, the singers are expected to improvise movements. Much of the vocal part is spoken and the two voices generally move in unison when singing. The composer gives the following instruction for the spoken parts: "Approximate rhythms. Always recite rather rapidly and a little breathlessly. The general rise and fall of the line should follow what seems natural to the speaker."

049. BLANK, Allan. Four Dream Poems. New York: American Composers Alliance, 1976.

i. The Harlequin of Dreams (Sidney Lanier)
ii. Bereft She Thinks She Dreams (Thomas Hardy)
iii. What Did I Dream (Robert Graves)
iv. i'll tell you a dream i had once i was away up in the (e e cummings)

Instrumentation: Soprano, Clarinet, Trumpet, Piano.

Vocal entrance pitches rarely appear in the previous instrumental material but often relate to it by a small interval. Not much doubling of pitches occurs. Pitch reference for the singer is strained. The tempo and meter change frequently. Irregular subdivisions of beats are common, and the rhythmic coordination of the ensemble is generally complex.

050. BLANK, Allan. Four Poems by Emily Dickinson. New York: American Composers Alliance, 1974.

How Happy is the Little Stone
In This Short Life
Surgeons must be very careful
"Nature" is what we see

Instrumentation: Soprano, Flute, Clarinet.
In celebration of the 1976 Bicentennial.
Dedication: Les Nouveaux Jongleurs.

The vocal part contains some large leaps. Doubling of pitches is uncommon. The meter changes frequently. Sometimes irregular subdivisions of beats further complicate the ensemble: e.g.,

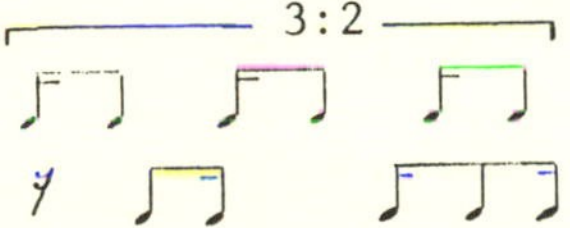

051. BLANK, Allan. I Missed His Book, But I Read His Name. New York: American Composers Alliance, 1980.

Text: John Updike, from Telephone Poles and Other Poems.
Instrumentation: Soprano, Baritone, Piano. Percussion and Trombone are optional.

In most of the song the soprano and baritone parts move in unison. The vocal line contains mostly steps and small leaps and the range is moderate. Vocal pitches are usually doubled by the piano. If the piece is performed without a percussionist, the singers assume minor percussion assignments. An instruction at the beginning states "create movement and bustle until vocal entrance."

052. BLANK, Allan. The pennycandystore beyond the El. New York: Composers Facsimile Edition, 1965.

Text: Lawrence Ferlinghetti.
Instrumentation: Voice, Bassoon.

The vocal line is angular and disjunct with rests between syllables of words. Pitches relate to the bassoon part by large and/or dissonant intervals. No unisons, thirds or other easily accessible intervals occur. Complex rhythmic figures include many short value rests and irregular subdivisions of beats. The measures are of varying lengths; no meter signatures appear.

053. BLANK, Allan. Poem. New York: American Composers Alliance, n.d.

Text: e e cummings.
Instrumentation: Voice, Clarinet, Harp, Cello.
Composed: 1963.

The vocal line moves mostly by leaps, but not especially large leaps. The instruments double the voice part infrequently. Pitch reference is remote. Some tempo changes occur, but the meter changes fairly frequently. The rhythmic coordination of the ensemble includes some irregular subdivisions of beats, and is generally complex.

054. BLANK, Allan. Recital. New York: American Composers Alliance, 1980.

Text: John Updike, from Telephone Poles.
Instrumentation: Soprano, Tuba, Piano.

Some tempo changes occur, but the meter changes fairly frequently. The vocal line contains some large leaps, but most are a fifth or less. The instruments double the vocal line only occasionally.

055. BLANK, Allan. Two Holy Sonnets by John Donne. New York: American Composers Alliance, n.d.

Death Be Not Proud
Batter My Heart

Instrumentation: Alto, English Horn/Oboe, Viola, Harp.

Vocal entrance pitches appear in or relate by a small interval to the previous instrumental material. The instruments frequently double isolated vocal pitches. Second relationships are prominent, also. The vocal line spans a range of E - eb' and contains some large leaps, though rarely over an octave. The rhythmic complexity of the ensemble results from diverse rhythmic figures in the various parts, irregular subdivisions of beats and small value rests interspersed. The meter changes frequently and some tempo fluctuations occur.

056. BLANK, Allan. Two Parables by Franz Kafka. New York: American Composers Alliance, 1965.

Die Sirenen (The Sirens)
Kuriere (Couriers)

Text: Translated by Clement Greenberg, set in German.
Instrumentation: Voice, Violin, Viola.

The pitch references of the angular vocal line are remote at best; doublings are rare. The composer indicates a section of humming and open sound (no vowel is specified). Irregular subdivisions of beats are prominent. The tempo changes or fluctuates frequently. Some meter chages occur.

057. BLANK, Allan. Zulus Live in Land Without a Square. New York: American Composers Alliance, 1980.

Text: John Updike, from Telephone Poles and other stories.
Instrumentation: Soprano, Percussion, Piano, Dancer.

Some but not extensive doublings of vocal pitches occur. A pitch often sounds in the instruments after it appears in the voice. Leaps of a fifth and an octave are common. The final phrase bears the marking, "stage whisper, quasi glissando." The composer asks for a few other vocal effects.

058. BLICKHAN, Tim. Speak Softly. New York: Seesaw Music, 1974.

Fall of the Evening Star
Interlude
O New the Drenched Land Wakes
Interlude
This Room Has Mystery Like a Trance

Text: Kenneth Patchen.
Instrumentation:; Soprano, Flute, Vibraphone.
Duration: 12-15 Minutes.

The composer explains the special effects and gives brief general explanations of the notation. He states, "Time relationships are relative to spacial arrangements of notes on the page." The staff lines are removed when a part is silent. Vocal entrances relate to instrumental parts mostly by unison or half step. The movement of the vocal line includes some repeated pitches, but mostly small intervals and some augmented octaves.

059. BOEHNLEIN, Frank. From the J.C. Penney Catalog, Spring and Summer, 1973. Pendleton, OR: Manuscript Publications, 1974.

1. What do the Symbols Mean? pg. 561
2. What is Mailable and What is Not? pg. 562
3. The Weight Loser's Bra and Girdle with Expand-A-Thigh, pg. 223
4. Penney's Fine Quality Underwear. Greater Comfort and Roominess for Men with Average Builds, pg. 472-3
5. Penney's Helps you Work at Getting the Body You Want, pg. 239
6. If You Can Count, You Can Play! pg. 524
7. Last, But Not Least! pg. 573

Text: from the 1973 J.C. Penney Spring and Summer Catalog.
Instrumentation: Soprano, Flute, Clarinet, Oboe, Bassoon, Trumpet, French Horn, Trombone, Percussion, Double String Quartet.
Also published in a soprano-piano version for easier programing and increased stage theatrics.
Dedication: Sherry Ingles Boehnlein.

The composer calls this a diversion for soprano and chamber ensemble. The following are excerpts from his notes: "These pieces are to be considered as frameworks for a few moments of fun." "...the soprano should sing in a popular music style with little vibrato." Some sections have frequently changing meter; some are free, with no meter; some fragments are indicated in seconds. Rhythmic figurations are simple. The vocal pitches relate directly to the instrumental pitches, but problems of timbre and range must be considered; sometimes the vocal pitch is related only to the timpani. The singer must also do a great deal of speaking.

060. BOND, Victoria. Cornography. New York: Seesaw Music, 1975.

I. Recitative
II. Aria Obnoxious
III. Buffoonery (to Jack Marsh)
IV. Cornography
V. Finale

Instrumentation: Soprano, French Horn, Bassoon.

The angular vocal line generally relates to the instrumental parts by a half or whole step. In number two, which is unaccompanied, the repetition of the word "aria" provides the entire text. Number three is a duet for voice and bassoon, number four a duet for voice and horn.

061. BOTTJE, Will Gay. In a word. New York: American Composers Alliance, n.d.

Instrumentation: Soprano, Piano, Oboe, French Horn, Trumpet.

Score not available for review.

062. BOTTJE, Will Gay. In Praise of Music. New York: American Composers Alliance, n.d.

I. Prologue (Shakespeare, Merchant of Venice)
II. When to her lute Corinna Sings (T. Campion)
III. Celia Singing (T. Carew)
IV. O, Care Thou Wilt Despatch Me (Madrigal, unknown)
V. Hark! Hark How the minstrels 'gin to Shrill Aloud (E. Spenser, from Epithalamion)

Instrumentation: Soprano, String Quartet.
Composed: 1958.

The vocal part lies mostly in the middle range, but stays below midde c for one short section. Entrance pitches frequently relate to the previous instrumental material by a small interval. The relationship of a half tone or a whole tone between the voice and instruments is frequent, but doubling is rare. Some meter and/or tempo changes occur in each piece. This may also be performed with piano instead of strings.

063. BRANT, Henry. Encephalograms. New York: Composers Facsimile Edition, 1955.

Instrumentation: High Voice, French Horn (8), Piano, Harp, Xylophone, Glockenspiel, Vibraphone, Timpani.

The following instruction appears at the singer's first entrance: "Voice begins each entrance on cue from the conductor and thereafter maintains her own tempo, as steadily as possible, ignoring both conductor and instrumentalists. In case of any difficulty in finding each opening pitch the singer should stand beside the xylophone... indicate each entrance's first note very lightly." The sometimes percussion-like vocal part utilizes phonetic syllables. Some sections lie very high. The range encompasses c - f". The conductor sometimes just gives cues and sometimes coordinates the ensemble metrically. A variety of different tempi appear, often proceeding simultaneously.

064. BREHM, Alvin. *A Cycle of Six Songs*. n.p.: Piedmont Music, 1976.

I. Fable (trans. Roy Campbell)
II. Night (trans. Jaime Anhulo)
III. Adam (trans. Roy Campbell)
IV. The Little Mute Boy (trans. W.S. Merwin)
V. He Died at Dawn (trans. Greville Texidor)
VI. Song of the Barren Orange Tree (trans. W.S. Merwin)

Text: Frederico Garcia Lorca, set in English.
Instrumentation: Soprano, String Quartet, Double Bass, Woodwind Quintet.
Duration: ca. 14 Minutes, 40 Seconds.

Though the vocal line is sometimes angular, large leaps appear infrequently. Often it moves by steps and small leaps with chromatic alterations. Isolated pitches are doubled by the instruments. Meter changes appear frequently in some areas. The tempo remains fairly constant within each movement. It is published in a piano-vocal score. Instrumental parts are available on rental.

065. BRINGS, Allen. *Tre Madrigali Concertati*. New York: Seesaw Music, 1978.

I. Ahi, despietata morte! (Petrarch)
(Ah, pitiless death!)
II. Come la notte ogni fiamelle (Ariosto)
(As each flame is bright at night)
III. Or che'l ciel e la terra d'l vento tace (Petrarch)
(Now that heaven and earth and the wind are silent)

Instrumentation: Soprano, Harpsichord, Cello.

Gradual changes in tempo, indicated ┌——→ ←——┐, appear frequently, sometimes within short spaces of time. Meter changes are also prominent. Frequent changes in dynamics are specifically indicated. The vocal line is sometimes angular, but does not exploit the extremes of the range. Pitches relate to the instrumental parts by half tones or sevenths or ninths; doublings are infrequent.

066. BRINGS, Allen. *Tre Sonetti di Michelangelo Buonarroti*. New York: Seesaw Music, 1975.

I. Sì amico all freddo sasso è'l foco interno
(So friendly is the fire to flinty stone)
II. I'mi credetti, il primo giorno ch'io
(I deemed upon that day when first I knew)
III. Al cor zolfo, alla carne di stoppa
(A heart of flaming sulphur, fresh of tow)

Instrumentation: Soprano, Flute, Clarinet, Violin, Cello, Double Bass, Piano, Percussion.
Duration: ca. 8 Minutes.
Dedication: The Forum Players and their director James Dashow.

In a prefatory note the composer expresses his wish for accurate observation of the specific dynamic markings which occur in every measure, or sometimes on every note. The meter changes frequently, often in every bar. Pitches of the angular vocal line relate to the instrumental parts most often by a half tone or a whole tone. Doubling is rare. The range includes Ab - ab'.

067. BROOKS, Richard. Last Night I Was the Wind. New York: American Composers Alliance, n.d.

Text: no credit given in the score.
Instrumentation: Baritone, Flute, Oboe, Clarinet, French Horn, Bassoon.
Composed: 1976.

In addition to singing, the vocal part includes. Sprechstimme, quasi recitativo and sections in the upper range labeled falsetto. The vocal line is angular with some fast moving parts. Pitch reference is remote at best; doubling is rare. The range includes BBb - g#. This piece is cast in sections with a new tempo and/or meter for each. The ensemble sometimes moves in similar rhythmic figuration and sometimes diverse irregular subdivisions of beats are superimposed.

068. CACIOPPO, George. Bestiary I: Eingang. New York: Music for Percussion, 1976.

Text: Rilke, set in German.
Instrumentation: Soprano, Percussion (6), Piano.
Duration: ca. 7 Minutes.

The following are notes by the composer:

"This song is conceived as a contrast between the lyric qualities of the human voice and the clangorous percussive qualities of the instrumental ensemble. These instruments not only support the vocal line, but comment on the text of the poem, between phrases."

" Two aspects of time are involved in the song: measured and unmeasured. Unmeasured time is repre-sented by large square boxes. Time in these areas is a function of the decay characteristics of such instruments as piano, vibraphone, cymbal."

The vocal line is extremely angular with many grace notes. Isolated pitches are sometimes doubled by an instrument. Specific dynamic markings appear almost continuously. The stage placement diagram indicates a conductor.

069. CAGE, John. Forever and Sunsmell. New York: Henmar Press, 1960.

Text: e e cummings
Instrumentation: Voice, Percussion (2).
Composed: 1944.
Music written for the dance by Jean Erdman.

The voice part appears in the bass clef in numbers one and five and in the treble clef in numbers two, three and four. Since both percussionists are playing non-tuned instruments, the singer has no pitch reference. The following instructions appear: "The singer may make any transposition that will give the written high E a forced intense quality. Avoid vibrato, especially in the low register." Rhythmic figures are generally not complex; the vocal part contains mostly quarter and half notes and triplets. The piece begins and ends with a section for solo voice.

070. CALDWELL, Mary E. A Christmas Triptych. n.p.: Gentry Publications, 1975.

In the Bleak Midwinter (Christina Rossetti)
It Was a Night of Stars (Mary E. Caldwell)
A Child Shall be Born (Mary E. Caldwell)

Instrumentation: Medium Voice, Piano, Flute.

The vocal line moves mostly by steps, small leaps and some octave leaps within a moderate range. The piano usually doubles the vocal pitches. Numbers one and two are for voice and piano alone. The flute joins in number three.

071. CALDWELL, Mary E. A Lute Caroll. Melville, New York: H.W. Gray, 1964.

Text: Robert Herrick.
Instrumentation: Medium Voice, Optional Flute (Violin), Accompaniment (Probably Piano).

The rolled chords of the accompaniment always include the vocal pitches. The optional obbligato is consonant with the voice and accompaniment. The lyric vocal line encompasses a moderately small range: db - f'. The short piece contains no complex rhythmic figures. This is also published for S.A.B.

072. CARTER, Elliott. A Mirror on Which to Dwell. New York: Associated Music Publishers, 1977.

1. Anaphora
2. Argument
3. Sandpiper
4. Insomnia
5. View of the Capitol from the Library of Congress
6. O Breath

Text: Elizabeth Bishop.
Instrumentation: Soprano, Flute (Piccolo, Alto Flute), Oboe, (English Horn), Clarinet (Clarinet in Eb, Bass Clarinet),Percussion, Piano, Violin, Viola, Cello, Contrabass.
Duration: 19 Minutes.
Commissioned by Speculum Musicae in honor of the United States' Bicentennial.
Dedication: Susan Daveny Wyner and Speculum Musicae.

Though the vocal line is angular, most leaps are not extremely large. Pitch reference is remote, with occasional doublings of isolated passing pitches. Some meter changes occur, but the tempo remains fairly constant withih each movement. Diverse complex rhythmic figures are superimposed. These include irregular subdivisions.

073. CARTER, Elliott. Tell Me where is Fancy Bred. New York: Associated Music Publishers, 1972,73.

Text: Shakespeare.
Instrumentation: Voice, Guitar.
Composed: 1938.

This short song encompasses a fairly low and narrow range: B - c#. The lyric vocal line moves mostly by steps and small leaps. Pitches are usually doubled by the guitar either by single pitches or within the chords. The guitar part was edited by Stanley Silverman.

074. CHAJES, Julius. By the Rivers of Babylon. New York: Transcontinental Music Publications, n.d.

Text: Psalm 137.
Instrumentation: Voice, Cello, Piano (or Organ).
Composed: 1942.

This is published with a score and a cello part which includes the entire vocal line. Few tempo and meter changes and no complex rhythmic figures appear. Vocal pitches relate closely to the instrumental parts, with much doubling. The range, g - ab', is modest for a high voice.

075. CHANCE, Nancy. *Darksong*. New York: Seesaw Music, 1976.

Text: Nancy Chance.
Instrumentation: Soprano, Flute (2), Clarinet (2), French Horn (2), Harp, Guitar, Piano, Percussion (5).

Much of the piano part consists of glissandi played with the fingertips on the strings with the damper pedal down. The meter remains constant and the tempo changes infrequently. The vocal part moves mostly in steps and small intervals. Pitch references and cues for the soprano exist, but are often obscured by the density of the ensemble. One segment lies very low in the range which encompasses Ab - ab'.

076. CHANCE, Nancy. *Duos I*. New York: Seesaw Music, 1976.

Instrumentation: Soprano, Flute.

The composer's note at the beginning states, "It is the intent of this piece to use the voice only instrumentally, and to this end it is desirable that flute and voice attempt insofar as possible to achieve a similarity of timbre and articulation of tone." The voice performs the entire piece on an open "ah" and in one instance fluttering the tongue while singing the open "ah." The composer asks both instruments for a pulsating effect which she calls a "slow and heavy vibrato." Half step dissonance between the parts is common, often with the pulsating effect. Both parts alternate among no vibrato, molto vibrato, normal vibrato and smorzato vibrato (pulsating effect). Trills appear frequently in both parts. The soprano also plays finger cymbals. The vocal pitch cues are obvious though often dissonant. Generally both parts fall within an octave of each other.

077. CHANCE, Nancy. *Edensong*. New York: Seesaw Music, 1973.

Text: Elizabeth Barrett Browning.
Instrumentation: Soprano, Flute, Clarinet, Cello, Harp, Vibraphone, Marimba, Percussion (3).
Dedication: for David.

The composer includes special performance notes on the use of flutter tongue and trill. The following is required of the singer and some instrumentalists: "dry flutter tongue, breath only, no voice - not through the mouthpiece." The soprano begins about a third of the way into the piece with a vocalise, then later sings the text. The fairly angular vocal line contains many wide intervals. Pitch reference is sometimes clear (second or third relationship), but more often is lost in the density or obscured by other sounds.

078. CHANCE, Nancy. Three Poems by Rilke. New York: Seesaw Music, 1976.

1. O dieses ist das Tier...
2. Nur wer die Leier...
3. Ein Gott vermags...

Text: Poems by Rainer Maria Rilke, set in German, no translation included.
Instrumentation: Soprano, Flute, French Horn, Cello.
Composed: 1966.

The meter remains mostly constant throughout each movement. Few tempo changes occur, but markings of ritardando and stretto appear fairly often. The piece is rhythmically simple except for triplets in duple meter and notes tied over bar lines. The angular vocal line includes many sevenths. Pitches relate closely to the instrumental parts.

079. CHILDS, Barney. Lanterns and Candlelight. Northampton, MA: Smith Publications, 1976.

Text: Orlando Gibbons, "The Cries of London."
Instrumentation: Soprano, Marimba.

The vocal part includes phonetic syllables as well as text. The range is mostly moderate, but narrow with repeated notes where the text is set. In one place the following appears: "If you can't do the given pitches, approximate them." This piece is primarily for solo marimba. The composer states, "Soprano is accompanying throughout. She sits... behind and stage left of marimba."

080. CHILDS, Barney. Seven Epigrams. Hattiesburg, MS: Tritone Press, 1964.

1. Dreams
2. Upon Bunce
3. Upon Cuffe
4. The Meane
5. Great boast, small rost
6. Upon Batt
7. His wish

Text: Robert Herrick.
Instrumentation: Soprano, Clarinet.
Composed: 1955.

The vocal entrance pitches often relate to the clarinet by a unison, step or third, but sometimes less closely. No demands are made on the extremes of the vocal range. The seven short pieces each begin and end with a clarinet solo. A few instances of shifting meters and complex rhythmic figures appear.

081. CHOU, Wen-Chung. Seven Poems of T'ang Dynasty. New York: New Music Edition, 1952.

Texts: Wang-Wei, Liu Yü-hsi, Chia Tao, Li Po, Liu Tsung-yuan, Liu Ch'ang-ch'ing. Translated by Louise Varese in collaboration with the composer.
Instrumentation: Tenor, Flute (piccolo), Oboe, Clarinet, Bassoon, French Horn, Trumpet, Trombone, Percussion, (2),Piano.
Duration: ca. 10 Minutes.
Dedication: Louise Varèse.

Dynamic extremes and quick changes in dynamics occur regularly. Tempo changes and fluctuations appear frequently. The meter remains constant throughout each section until near the end of the piece where changes are frequent. Few doublings of pitches occur. The singer takes the pitch of the first entrance from a nearly full chromatic cluster, and then is accompanied by non-tuned percussion for nine bars before any pitch reference appears. The vocal line frequently consists of triplet subdivisions while the instrumental parts are duple.

082. CIRONE, Anthony. Five Items. Meleno Park, CA: Cirone Publications, 1973.

I. At the Pinnacles
II. The Triple Refrain At Yang-Kuan Pass -- After Wang Wei
III. Spring in Nak Yang
IV. (untitled)
V. To a Gikuyu Musician

Text: Lou Harrison.
Instrumentation: Soprano, Percussion Quintet.

The vocal entrances relate to the tuned percussion by various intervals - sometimes half steps or major sevenths. The angular vocal line includes some staccati, glissandi and trills. The score specifies a soprano, but the vocal line generally lies quite low with some excursions into the upper range. Number five lies more in the soprano range. Few meter changes occur. The percussion parts include many ostinato patterns.

083. CLAFLIN, Avery. Finale. New York: American Composers Alliance, n.d.

Text: Pope.
Instrumentation: Contralto, String Quartet.

Score not available for review.

084. CLARK, Henry. Emily Dickinson Canons. New York: American Composers Alliance, n.d.

Instrumentation: Medium Voice, Viola.

Score not available for review.

085. CLARK, Henry Leland. Four Elements. New York: Composers Facsimile Edition, 1962.

1. Earth-Song (Ralph Waldo Emerson, from Hametreya)
2. "Song I" (Genevieve Taggard, from Slow Music)
3. Sea Slant (Carl Sandburg, from Slabs of Sunburnt West)
4. Shine! Shine! Shine! (Walt Whitman, from Out of the Cradle Endlessly Rocking)

Instrumentation: Soprano, Cello.

The angular vocal line includes many large intervals. However, pitches relate closely to the cello part with much doubling. Most of the vocal line lies on the treble staff; a few phrases lie below. Range: A - g'. The tempo and meter remain constant within each song.

086. CLARK, Henry Leland. Life in Ghana. New York: American Composers Allinace, 1966.

Text: Matei Markwei.
Instrumentation: Voice, Flute, Piano.

The vocal part moves mostly by steps and small leaps and encompasses a moderate range. Entrance pitches are sounded in the previous instrumental material and doublings are prominant. Few meter changes occur. The tempo is constant throughout the piece.

087. CLARK, Henry Leland. The Lord Is My Shepherd. New York: American Composers Alliance, 1972.

Text: Psalm 23 with versets.
Instrumentation: Voice, Flute, Timpani (or String Bass).
Dedication: Felix Skowronek.

The flute often doubles or plays in third or fifth relationship with the voice. The indication "subtones" appears for the flute. The tempo and meter are constant and rhythmic figures are mostly simple. The vocal range is moderate.

088. CLARK, Henry. Puget Sound Cinquain. New York: American Composers Alliance. n.d.

Text: W. Bartholomew.
Instrumentation: Medium Voice, Any Medium Instrument.

Score not available for review.

089. CLARK, Henry Leland. Rondeau Redoublé. New York: Composers Facsimile Edition, 1955.

Text: Dorothy Parker.
Instrumentation: Baritone (or Mezzo-soprano), Clarinet, Bassoon, Cello.

The lyric vocal line moves mostly by steps and small leaps. Pitches relate clearly to the instrumental parts with frequent doubling. The meter and tempo remain generally constant and rhythmic figures are simple. This short piece is published with a score and parts.

090. CLARK,Henry Leland. Song to a Young Pianist. New York: Composers Facsimile Edition, 1961.

Text: Ethelyn Miller Hartwich.
Instrumentation: Medium Voice, Flute.

The vocal line moves mostly by steps and small leaps. Pitches relate clearly to the flute part with doublings of pitches or short sequences of pitches. The range is modest: c - e'.

091. CLARK, Henry Leland. A Woman of Virtue. New York: Composers Facsimile Edition, 1955.

Text: Paraphrase from Proverbs by Irving Finemen.
Instrumentation: Voice, Reed, Percussion.

The entire short piece consists of alternation between the reed and the voice, punctuated by percussion. The percussion instrument (not specified) should be non-pitched. The first pitch of each vocal line relates clearly to the last pitch of the reed part. All melodies are unaccompanied. The vocal part lies generally low and encompasses a moderate range: A - d'.

092. CLARKE, Rosemary. Suite of Changes. Hamilton, OH: Composers Autograph Publications, 1973.

Instrumentation: Voice (Baritone), Flute, Clarinet, Baritone Horn, Percussion.

The vocal line is always accompanied by non-tuned percussion or unaccompanied. It is rather recitative-like in short interrupted sections. Included are some glissandi and indications for irregular slide from one note to another. Meter changes are not frequent except in one section which includes such signatures as 3 1/2 / 4. At the end the composer gives instructions to repeat several extracted sections of the piece. One section is to be repeated with four different instruments in four different tempi.

093. COLGRASS, Michael. New People. New York: MCA, 1970.

1. Baby's eyes are chocolates
2. One day my shadow said to me
3. New People talk computer
4. Earth is the theatre
5. Skyscrapers are trees of the city
6. Startings compose
7. Goodnight Day

Text: Michael Colgrass.
Instrumentation: Mezzo-soprano, Viola, Piano.
Commissioned by the Lincoln Center Chamber Music Society.

The mezzo must have a strong low range; some long phrases lie below the staff. At one point, where the composer gives specific rhythm but only pitch direction, he also gives the following footnote: "Sing any convenient pitches. Strive for an atonal effect. Be a computer person." He also requires some special effects, such as hysterical whisper, laughter, whispering with a double tongue effect (ta-ka-ta-ka), etc. Irregular subdivisions of the beats and irregular placement of small value rests within those subdivisions contribute to the complexity of the ensemble. The tempo changes frequently.

094. CONSOLI, Marc-Antonio, Equinox I. New York: American Composers Alliance, n.d.

Text: Watanabe Wuika, translated by Geoffrey Bowans and Anthony Thwaite.
Instrumentation: Mezzo-soprano, Flute, Cello, Celesta, Piano, Percussion (3).
Composed: 1967.

The angular vocal line includes wide intervals but does not exploit the extremes of the range. Grace notes and multiple grace notes are prominent. Vocal pitches do not easily relate to the instrumental parts; occasional doublings occur, but more often the relationships are half or whole steps. The meter changes frequently, nearly every bar. Tempo changes occur fairly often, especially toward the end. On the printed page the staff lines have been removed from the score in any part when an extended period of silence appears.

095. CONSOLI, Marc-Antonio. *Equinox II*. New York: American Composers Alliance, n.d.

Text: Shoushi, Bownas, Thwaite, tr.
Instrumentation: Soprano, Flute, Clarinet, Violin, Cello, Piano, Percussion, Vibraphone, Celesta.

Score not available for review.

096. CONSOLI, Marc-Antonio. *Isonic*. New York: American Composers Alliance, n.d.

Instrumentation: Soprano, Flute, Piano, (2), Percussion (2).

Score not available for review.

097. CONSOLI, Marc-Antonio. *Tre Canzoni*. New York: American Composers Allinace, n.d.

Instrumentation: Soprano, Flute, Cello.

Score not available for review.

098. CONSOLI, Marc-Antonio. *Vuci Siculani*. Newton Centre, MA: Margun Music, n.d.

Instrumentation: Mezzo-Soprano, Flute, (Recorder), Clarinet, Guitar, String Quartet.
Duration: 21 Minutes.

Score not available for review.

099. CORY, Eleanor, *Aria Viva*. New York: American Composers Alliance, 1977.

Text: David Ignatow, "Marriage Song" from *Rescue the Dead*.
Instrumentation: Tenor, Flute, Oboe, English Horn, Bassoon, Guitar.

The vocal line, mostly angular with some chromatic alterations, lies mostly in the treble staff but makes excursions above, once to c'. Pitches relate to the instrumental parts with some doubling of isolated pitches. The pitch reference is obscured, however by the density of the texture. Various irregular subdivisions of the beats often occur simultaneously. The superimpositions of other nonsimilar rhythmic figures further complicate the ensemble.

100. CORY, Eleanor. Walking. New York: American Composers Alliance, n.d.

Text: Rukeyser.
Instrumentation: Soprano, Clarinet, Tenor Saxophone, Bassoon, Trumpet, Piano, Percussion, Violin, Viola, Cello, Bass.

Score not available for review.

101. COWELL, Henry. Sonatina. New York: Composers Facsimile Edition, 1962.

Instrumentation: Baritone, Violin, Piano.
Composed: 1944.
Dedication: to Sidney.

The baritone sings a vocalise on "ah" throughout this piece. His pitches relate closely to the instrumental parts. The tempo and meter remain constant. Rhythmic figures are simple with a prominent ostinato pattern in the piano.

102. COWELL, Henry. Toccanta. New York: Boosey & Hawkes, 1960.

I. Allegro quasi Andante
II. Interlude - Larghetto
III. Moderato pomposo ma vivo
IV. Interlude - Andante con moto
V. Allegro

Instrumentation: Soprano, Flute, Cello, Piano.

The following notes appear at the bottom of the first page: "The soprano is to be like a Vocalise, to blend instrumentally rather than to be a solo always. The vocal 'ah' may be used or at the wish of the singer, other vowels may be chosen." The vocal line moves mostly in steps and small leaps. The orchestral version, Symphonic Set, prepared by the composer is available on rental from the publisher.

103. COWELL, Henry. Vocalise. New York: C.F. Peters, 1964.

Instrumentation: Voice, Flute, Piano.
Duration: 8 Minutes

The piano part consists of a single line, all the notes falling between B and b. The following instruction appears: "Press the piano strings next to the bridge, dampening their tone throughout the whole work." Vocal pitches relate closely to the instrumental parts. In two sections the vocal line is designated 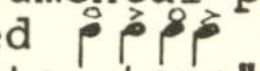 simile, with the following instructions: "Do not stop tone" and "o indicates an unaccented tone. The singer should stress the accents heavily by sudden thrusts of the diaphragm."

104. CRANE, Joella Wallach. Cords. New York: American Composers Alliance, n.d.

Instrumentation: Soprano, Contrabass (2).
Dedication: Bertram Turetzky.

The following notes appear: "The words sung by the soprano are various terms for the string bass in English (bass viol, contrabass viol), German (Kontrabass), and Italian (violone, contrabasso, basso). "Chords can be considered a 'mild' theatre piece, an ode to the string bass. Included are a few dramatic suggestions. More may be added by the performers." The vocal line moves frequently in large leaps. The soprano can relate entrance pitches to the contrabass by various intervals, but little doubling occurs either at vocal entrances or in the middle of phrases.

105. CROUNCE, Lydia. A Slumber did my Spirit Seal. Cape Vincent, NY: Worden Publications, 1969.

Text: William Wordsworth.
Instrumentation: Voice, Flute.

The voice moves mostly by steps and small leaps within a small range (f# - f#'). This is mostly a dialog between the voice and the flute, but, when they sound together, some doubling occurs. The tempo and meter remain constant and rhythmic figures are simple.

106. CRUMB, George. Ancient Voices of Children. New York: C.F. Peters, 1970.

I. El niño busca su vos.
(The little boy was looking for his voice.)
Dances of the Ancient Earth
II. Me He perdido muchas veces pos el mar
(I have lost myself in the sea many times)
III. ¿De dónde vienes, amor, mi niño?
(From were do you come, my love, my child?)
(Dance of the Sacred Life-Cycle)
IV. Todas las tardes en Granada, todas las tardes se muere un niño (Each afternoon in Granada, a child dies each afternoon)
Ghost Dance
V. Se ha llenado de luces
(My heart of silk is filled with lights)

Text: Federico García Lorca.
Instrumentation: Soprano, Boy Soprano, Oboe, Mandoline, Harp, Electric Piano, Percussion (3).
Duration: 27 Minutes.
Commissioned by the Elizabeth Sprague Coolidge Foundation.

The composer states, "The two purely instrumental movements - 'Dances of the Ancient Earth' and Ghost DAnce' - are dance interludes rather than commentaries on the texts. These two pieces, together with the third song, subtitled 'Dance of the Sacred Life-Cycle,' can be performed by a dancer." Crumb describes the vocal style of the cycle as ranging from "Virtuosic to the intimately lyrical." The following are a few special instructions to the soprano: "nasal sound - like muted trumpets," "expell breath violently, like sneeze," "whisper through a speaking tube." At some points she sings into the piano with the damper pedal depressed to produce sympathetic vibrations. Phonetic syllables often replace the text. The boy soprano sings from offstage in number I and barely offstage in number III. In the last piece he comes on stage and sings into the piano. Several of the performers play additional instruments: mandoline (antique cymbals, musical saw, bottle neck), soprano (glockenspiel), oboe (harmonica), piano (toy piano). The stage positioning chart incorporates a conductor.

107. CRUMB, George. Lux Aeterna. New York: C.F. Peters, 1972.

Instrumentation: Soprano, Bass Flute (Soprano Recorder), Sitar, Percussion (2).
For the Children of the Night.
Commissioned by the Philadelphia Composers' Forum.

Instructions state that "all performers...should wear black masks and, if possible, black robes. A single burning candle should be positioned at stage center." The piece is interrupted several times by a refrain, "Masked Dance: Elegy for a Dead Prince," which is purely instrumental. A solo dancer, if desired, may perform during these sections, in a "symbolic and ritualistic rather than expressionistic" manner. Vocal pitch reference is generally remote. Few doublings occur and entrance pitches are not obvious in the previous instrumental material. The vocal line covers a wide range and includes large intervals. Multiple grace notes appear in all parts. The text is Latin, but some of the vocal line is set on phonetic syllables. A footnote states: "The symbol ⟶ means: modulate very gradually from one vowel sound to the next. The modulation in vocal color should occupy the entire value of the note."

108. CRUMB, George. Madrigals: Book I. New York: C.F. Peters, 1971.

I. Verte desnuda es recordar la tierra
(To see you naked is to remember the earth)
II. No piensam en la lluvia, y se han dormido
(They do not think of rain, and they've fallen asleep)
III. Los muertos llevan alas de musgo
(The dead wear mossy wings)

Text: Based on fragments from Frederico Garcia Lorca.
Instrumentation: Soprano, Vibraphone, Contrabass.
Duration: ca. 9 Minutes.
Composed: 1965.

109. CRUMB, George. Madrigals: Book II. New York: C.F. Peters, 1971.

I. Bebe el agua tranquila de la canción añeja
(Drink the tranquil water of the antique song)
II. La Muerte entra y sale de la taberna
(Death goes in and out of the tavern)
III. Caballito negro ¿Donde llevas to jinte muerto?
(Little black horse, where are you taking your dead rider?)

Text: Based on fragments from Frederico García Lorca.
Instrumentation: Soprano, Alto Flute (doubling Flute in C and piccolo), Percussion.
Duration: 6 1/2 Minutes.
Composed: 1965.

110. CRUMB, George. Madrigals: Book III. New York: C.F. Peters, 1971.

I. La noche canta desnuda sobre los puentes de marzo
(Night sings naked above the bridges of March)
II. Quiero dormir el sueño de las manzanas
(I want to sleep the sleep of apples)
III. Nana, niño, nana, del caballo grande que no quiso el agua (Lullagy, child, lullaby of the proud horse who would not drink water)

Text: Based on fragments from Frederico García Lorca.
Instrumentation: Soprano, Harp, Percussion.
Duration: ca. 7 1/2 Minutes.
Composed: 1969.

111. CRUMB, George. Madrigals: Book IV. New York: C.F. Peters, 1971.

I. ¿Por qué nací entre espejos? (Why was I born surrounded by mirrors?)
II. To cuerpo, con la sombra violeta de mis manos, era un arcángel de frío (Through my hands' violet shadow, your body was an archangel, cold)
III. ¡La muerte me está mirando desde las torres de Cordoba! (Death is watching me from the towers of Cordoba!)

Text: Based on fragments from Frederico García Lorca.
Instrumentation: Soprano, Flute (double Piccolo & Alto Flute), Harp, Contrabass, Percussion.
Duration: 9 Minutes.
Composed: 1969.

Madrigals may be performed as a cycle or each book may be performed separately. The performance notes describe the positioning of performers for either option. Other prefatory notes explain notational symbols. Pitch reference is often remote to the disjunct and angular vocal line. Complex rhythmic patterns, including many grace notes and borrowed rhythms, are prominent. Some of the specific instructions to the singer follow: hushed voice, whispered, exuberant, hum, half sung (not exact pitches given), "white tone" (non-vib.). The instrumentalists participate vocally, usually speaking. Special effects required of the flute are flutter tonguing, partials, and speaking while fingering given pitches. The meter changes constantly and the tempo fluctuates frequently.

112. CRUMB, George. Night Music I. Nelville, NY: Belwin Mills, 1967.

Notturno I: Giocoso, estatico
Notturno II: "Piccola Serenata" - grazioso
Notturno III: La Luna Asoma (Lorca): lirico, fantastico
Notturno IV: Vivace, molto ritmico
Notturno V: Gacela de la Terrible Presencia (Lorca): Oscuro, quasi senza movimento; grave e drammatico; molto tranquillo
Notturno VI: "Barcarola" - Delicato e tenero
Notturno VII: Giocoso, estatico

Text: Federico García Lorca.
Instrumentation: Soprano, Keyboard (Piano, Celesta), Percussion (2).
Composed: 1963.

The suggested stage arrangement diagram includes a conductor who also plays in one segment. Crumb gives extensive general instructions and specific instructions for each performer. In a note the composer states, "The pitches given in the soprano part are more or less approximate and merely suggest the melodic contour. The singer should 'realize' her part by improvisation. The rhythmic values can be followed more closely.... The vocal effect should resemble 'Sprechstimme'...." Indications for various degrees of improvisation appear frequently in all parts. Dynamic extremes are common. When specific, the vocal pitches relate clearly to the piano. In number III the instruments each have eight segments printed in a circle, to be played either clockwise or counterclockwise. The instructions state, "Spacing of segments should be improvised. Ideally, one full turn of the circle will be made." The soprano's finger cymbal strokes, which divide the song into four equal segments, provide time frame references to the instrumentalists.

113. CRUMB, George. Night of Four Moons. New York: C.F. Peters, 1971.

i. La luna está muerta, muerta...
(The moon is dead, dead...)
ii. Cuando sale la luna...
(When the moon rises...)
iii. Otro Adám oscuro está soñando...
(Another obscure Adam dreams...)
iv. ¡Huje luna, luna, luna!...
(Run away moon, moon, moon!...)

Text: Based on fragments from Federico García Lorca.
Instrumentation: Alto, Alto Flute (Piccolo), Banjo, Electric Cello, Percussion.
Composed during the Apollo 11 flight, July 16-24, 1969.
Dedication: The Philadelphia Chamber Players.

Much of the piece is notated in rhythmic proportion, but some parts, especially the silences, are indicated in seconds. Except for silences indicated in seconds, 3/♪ is the most common meter in number i, and 7/♪ remains constant throughout number iii. No meter appears in number ii, but in some places stemless noteheads become the unit with tempo markings, e.g., ●● = 100. Tempo changes are frequent. The singer plays several percussion instruments. Her pitches, incuding quarter tones, are remotely related to the instrumental parts. The flutist uses a technique called "speak-flute" in the first movement. Many special instrumental effects appear in number ii. The fourth movement requires contrasting vocal timbre, inflection and gesture. The alto, flutist, percussionist and banjo player move to an offstage position for the Epilogue music which is identified as follows:

Electric Cello = "Musica Munda"
Offstage ensemble = "Musica Humana"

114. CRUMB, George. Songs Drones, and Refrains of Death. New York: C.F. Peters, 1971.

I. La Guitarra (The Guitar)
II. Casida de las Palomas Oscuras (Casida of the Dark Doves)
III. Canción de Jinete, 1860 (Song of the Rider, 1860)
IV. Casida del Ferido por el Agua (Casida of the Boy Wounded by the Water)

Text: A cycle of Poems by Federico García Lorca.
Instrumentation: Baritone, Electric Guitar, Electric Contrabass, Electric Piano (and Electric Harpsichord), Percussion (2).

All instrumentalists must speak and whisper in syllables indicated by the International Phonetic Alphabet. The baritone and pianist use speaking tubes. The guitar and contrabass players and the baritone also play a variety of percussion instruments. A conductor is required. In several sections the baritone has a continuous line while the instruments perform "Circle Music." The drones are carried out as long pedal points on the electric contrabass. Crumb employs many non-traditional uses of the voice and instruments.

115. CUCINOTTA, Robert. Beasts. New York: Lang Percussion, 1977.

Text: Richard Wilbur.
Instrumentation: Voice, Guitar, Percussion (2).

The vocal line, which is notated in the bass clef, includes some spoken parts. The guitar or tuned percussion sometimes doubles the vocal pitches, but more often the pitch reference is more difficult. The rhythmic configurations of the vocal part are moderately complex. Non-similar subdivisions of beats are superimposed frequently. Grace notes and multiple grace notes are common, and meter changes occur frequently.

116. CUMMING. Richard. As Dew in April. New York: Boosey and Hawkes, 1968.

Text: Anonymous 14th century English.
Instrumentation: High Voice, Oboe (or Violin or Clarinet), Piano.
Composed: 1960.
Dedication: Adele Addison and Norman Berger.

The vocal line moves mostly by steps and small skips. Pitches are usually doubled in the piano chords. This short piece makes no demands on the extremes of the vocal range.

117. CUSTER, Arthur. Cartagena Songs. New York: Composers Facsimile Edition, 1964.

I. The Emporium of Mr. Pedro Guillen
II. The Studio of Don Vicente Ros
III. Molinete

Text: Gerson Markowitt.
Instrumentation: Bass/Baritone, Oboe, French Horn, Piano,
Duration: ca. 5 Minutes.

The somewhat angular vocal line includes no large leaps. Pitches relate easily to the instrumental parts. Range: FF - e#. The oboe and horn often function as a unit, moving in the same or similar patterns.

118. DAILEY, Don. The Shell. New York: Seesaw, n.d.

Instrumentation: Soprano, Guitar, Percussion.

Score not available for review.

119. DAVIS, Sharon. Though Men Call Us Free. Los Angeles: Western International Music, 1976.

Text: Oscar Wilde, from "The Young King."
Instrumentation: (Dramatic) Soprano, Clarinet, Piano.

Vocal pitches relate clearly to the instrumental parts, with frequent doublings. A vocalise section on "ah" is quite angular; some is set in Sprechstimme; other sections move in steps and small leaps. The tempo and meter remain fairly constant.

120. DE BOHUN, Lyle. Songs of Estrangement. Washington, D.C.: Arsis Press, 1975.

I. Snow has lain
II. Flowers Fall
III. Death has Risen
IV. Love is a-Boining

Instrumentation: Soprano, String Quartet.

Vocal pitches relate easily to those of the string quartet. The lyric vocal line falls within a modest range. The meter changes frequently, but all parts have similar rhythmic patterns. This work is published with a score and four string parts, each including the vocal line.

121. DE JONG, Conrad. hist whist. New York: G. Schirmer, 1971.

Text: e e cummings, from his volume Poems.
Instrumentation: Voice, Flute, Viola, Percussion.

The composer has organized this piece in seconds, with each bar representing five seconds. Each performer should have access to a stopwatch; however, the following caution appears: "Do not overly labor the exactness." Performers should arrive simultaneously at cue points. A full page of definitions of symbols explains the extensive use of non-traditional notation. All performers speak "hist whist," etc. Following are some of the special vocal effects: glissando, ttttt (of little) spoken with a "studdering" effect. There is much dissonance and the singer's pitch cues often relate to the instruments at an interval of a major 7th or minor 9th.

122. DEL TREDICI, David. I Hear an Army. New York: Boosey & Hawkes, 1974.

Text: James Joyce, XXXCI from "Chamber Music."
Instrumentation: Soprano, String Quartet.
Commissioned by the Fromm Music Foundation for the Tanglewood Music Festival, 1964.
Duration: ca. 13 Minutes.
Dedication: Phyllis Bryn-Julson.

The meter changes frequently, often in every measure, and the rhythm is complicated by ties and small-value rests. Del Tredici sometimes outlines the main line in the string parts "when it does not seem obvious in relation to the surrounding texture." The angular vocal line moves mostly in large leaps. Special requirements include glissandi, "vocal sound like a string harmonic," "vocal tremolo," some grace notes at a large leap and Sprechstimme. Range: G - d''.

123. DEL TREDICI, David. Night Conjure-Verse. New York: Boosey & Hawkes, 1978.

I. Simples
II. A Memory of the Players in a Mirror at Midnight

Text: James Joyce, from "Poems Penyeach."
Instrumentation: Soprano, Mezzo-Soprano, (or Counter-Tenor), Piccolo (Flute II), Flute I, Oboe, Clarinet I (Bb, A), Bass Clarinet (Clarinet II in Bb), Bassoon, French Horn, String Quartet.
Composed: 1965, at the MacDowell Colony.
Dedication: Leon Kirchner.

Meter changes occur frequently, often in every bar. The ensemble is further complicated by the juxtaposition of non-similar rhythmic figures, including many rests. The singers' pitches relate directly to the instrumental parts, but fall in the middle of much dissonance. Both vocal lines are angular. Glissandi are common.

124. DERR, Elwood. I Never Saw Another Butterfly. n.d.: Dorn Productions, 1977.

Prologue: Terezín (Theresienstadt) (Hanuš Hachenburg)
The Butterfly (Pavel Friedmann)
The Old Man (Koleba, N.B.)
Fear (Eva Picková)
The Garden (Franta Bass, N.B.)

Instrumentation: Soprano, Alto Saxophone, Piano.
Composed: 1966.
Dedication: Michelle, Melita, Don.
To the Everlasting memory of the children who suffered and made these poems.

The composer gives specific instructions inlcuding many explanatory footnotes. He considers the piece a "Chamber cantata for three performers... not a work for soprano with two accompanying instruments." The movement of the vocal line is sometimes stepwise and sometimes quite angular. Often pitch reference is remote. Little doubling of the voice part occurs, but the relationship of a second is more common. The piece includes some spoken and some recitative-like parts. Tempo and meter changes occur frequently. Extremes in dynamics are common. Many grace notes and trills (various kinds of trills) appear in the instrumental parts.

125. DIAMOND, David. The Mad Maid's Song. New York: Southern Music Publishing, 1960.

Text: Robert Herrick.
Instrumentation: Soprano, Flute, Harpsichord (or Piano).
Composed: 1937; Revised: 1953.
Dedication: Marc Blitzstein.

The lyric vocal line moves mostly by steps, small leaps and some octave leaps. This piece makes no demands on the extremes of the vocal range. The flute uses some flutter tongue. Rhythmic figures are fairly homogeneous.

126. DIAMOND, David. Vocalises. New York: Southern Music Publishing, 1966.

Instrumentation: Soprano, Viola.
Composed: 1935; Revised: 1956.
Duration: 3 Minutes, 25 Seconds.
Dedication: Virgil Thomson.

The vocal line moves mostly by steps and small leaps. The viola frequently doubles the voice part, but second relationships are prominent also. The vocal range encompasses B - b'. Some tempo and meter changes appear.

127. DI DOMENICA, Robert. Four Short Songs. Newton Centre, MA: Margun Music, n.d.

Instrumentation: Soprano, Flute, Clarinet, Violin, Viola, Cello, Piano.
Duration: 9 Minutes.

Score not available for review.

128. DIEMENTE, Edward. Forms of Flight and Fancy. n.p.: Smith Publications, 1975.

Flight to Cleveland
Sarah Plays
Hearts Win
Cloudwalk

Text: Edward Diemente
Instrumentation: Soprano, Trumpet (2), French Horn, Trombone, Tuba.

The tempo and meter remain fairly constant except for small sections of shifting meter, but some dynamic extremes are required. The soprano line, which is usually angular, lies mostly on the staff. Pitches relate clearly to the instrumental parts with frequent doublings of isolated pitches. Vocal entrance pitches are usually played by an instrument immediately before the entrance. The trumpet players move around the stage and off stage for the various pieces. All instrumentalists sing-speak at the same time as playing, and also play assorted percussion instruments.

129. DIEMENTE, Edward. 3 - 31 - '70. New York: Seesaw, n.d.

Instrumentation: Voice, Trumpet, Trombone, Saxophone, Guitar, Contrabass, Percussion (5).

Score not available for review.

130. DIEMER, Emma Lou. Four Chinese Love Poems. New York: Seesaw Music, 1976.

I. People Hide Their Love (Wu-ti, 6th century A.D.)
II. Wind and Rain (from The Book of Songs, 800-600 B.C.)
III. By the Willows (from The Book of Songs)
IV. The Mulberry of the Lowland (from The Book of Songs)

Instrumentation: Voice, Harp (or Piano).
Composed: 1965.
Duration: 8 Minutes.
Dedication: Sylvia Meyer.

The vocal line moves mostly by steps and small leaps within a moderate range. Much doubling of the vocal line occurs. Melodic figures fall within the chordal structure of the harp part.

131. DIEMER, Emma Lou. Four Poems by Alice Meynell. New York: Carl Fischer, 1977.

I. Chimes
II. Renouncement
III. The Roaring Frost
IV. The Fold

Instrumentation: Soprano(Tenor), Flute, Harpsichord, Harp, Cello.
Duration: 15 Minutes.
Commissioned by Mu Phi Epsilon for their Diamond Jubilee Convention in Kansas City, Missouri, August, 1977.

The vocal line moves mostly by steps and small leaps with frequent doubling of pitches. Meter changes are sometimes frequent, but no complex rhythmic figures appear. The large score and performance materials are available on rental. This is also published in a piano-vocal score.

132. DINERSTEIN, Norman. Four Settings for Soprano and String Quartet. New York: Boosey & Hawkes, 1972.

I. Dying
II. The Bustle in a House
III. Apparently with no Surprise
IV. I Died for Beauty

Text: Emily Dickinson.
Composed: 1961.
Duration: ca. 13 Minutes.

The singer finds pitch references among much dissonance. Some sections move mostly by steps and small leaps, while other sections are quite angular. The range is G - bb'. The meter changes frequently in every movement.

Diverse rhythmic figures occur in the various parts simultaneously.

133. DONOVAN, Richard. Five Elizabethan Lyrics. New York: American Composers Alliance, 1957.

1. How Fie on Love! (James Shirley)
2. Fly Hence, Shadows! (John Ford)
3. The Rose (Thomas Howell)
4. Weep Eyes, Break Heart! (Thomas Middleton)
5. Farra Diddle Dino (Anonymous)

Instrumentation: Soprano, String Quartet.
Duration: ca. 9 Minutes.

The vocal line moves mostly by steps and small leaps within a moderate range. Entrance pitches relate to the instruments by unisons or consonant intervals. Some meter changes occur, but the score includes no complex rhythmic figures. This piece is published with a simplifed piano accompaniment for practice.

134. DREW, James. Aria. Bryn Mawr, PA: Theodore Presser, 1975.

Instrumentation: Soprano (2), Vibraphone.

The following introductory note best explains this piece: "After completing all musical segments (3 for the sopranos and 4 for the vibraphonist), each performer may choose different segments (in any order) for a period of four minutes (to be timed by the vibraphonist). By a prearranged signal the vibraphonist will indicate when the time is up. Precisely at that time, regardless of where the performers are, they all begin once more at the beginning and go through the 3 segments in order. After both sopranos have completed their segments they signal the vibraphonist who then repeats the last segment. The work is then concluded." The texts consist of a variety of words in different languages. Specific periods of silence (2-5 minutes) occur between the segments of the various parts. Aria is published with three parts but no score.

135. DRUCKMAN, Jacob. Animus II. New York: MCA, 1973.

Instrumentation: Soprano (Mezzo), Percussion (2), Tape.
Duration: Ca. 19 Minutes.

The following note is quoted from the score: "Animus II is a concert-theatrical work for one female singer and two male percussion players. Its subject matter is the sensuality of ensemble playing amplified to the point of eroticism." The performers move about the stage and hall, as well as singing and playing. The singer also plays several percussion instruments. Besides notes of exact pitch, approximate pitch, breathy chest tones, and voiced inhaling, the composer asks for special effects (choke, lingual trill) and special interpretations (surprised, embarassed, sensually). He uses IPA symbols instead of words. Vocal pitches relate, sometimes remotely, to the tape or marimba. New symbols and complex pitch patterns predominate. The entire piece is measured in seconds. Performance requires forty-seven or forty-nine percussion instruments. Large score, tape and other materials are available on rental.

136. DRUCKMAN, Jacob. Animus IV. New York: Boosey & Hawkes, 1978.

Instrumentation: Tenor, Violin, Piano (also Electric Piano with "wa" pedal), Electric Organ, Trombone, Percussion (2),Tape.
Commissioned by IRCAM (Institute de Recherche et Coordination Acoustique/Musique).
First performed by IRCAM, September 29, 1977, Centre George Pompidou, Salle Polyvalente, Paris. Composer was conducting.

The tape is not continuous; the score gives 3", 4", or 5" leader cues for tape entrances. Though mostly measured, even when the tape is playing, some segments of the piece are indicated in seconds. In many places the tape doubles or is similar to the instrumental and vocal parts. The content of the vocal line appears alternately in French, German and phonetic syllables. Vocal pitches relate to the instrumental parts and to the tape. In addition to singing an angular line, the tenor speaks and whispers. Grace notes are common. The score is printed in a manuscript. Performance requires a conductor. A quote from Liszt's "Die drei Zigeuner" appears in the voice and piano, in the violin, and then the greater part of the song appears later in the tape.

137. DRUCKMAN, Jacob. Dark upon the Harp. Bryn Mawr, PA: Theodore Presser, 1963.

Psalm XXII 12-17, 20 Allegro
Psalm LVII 4-9 Lento
Psalm XVIII 4-9 Affrettando
Psalm XXX 12, 13 Poco scherzando
Psalm CXXXIII Adagio
Psalm XVI 6-8 Moderato

Instrumentation: Mezzo-Soprano, Trumpet (2), French Horn, Trombone, Tuba, Percussion (2).
Duration: ca. 18 Minutes.

The vocal line is fairly angular, but usually relates clearly to the instrumental parts. Some superimposition of non-similar rhythmic patterns occur. More often the instrumentalists play similar patterns in contrast to the singer. Some dynamic extremes are required. The instrumental materials and vocal score are available on rental.

138. EVERHARD, Dennis. Parody. Newton Centre, MA: Margun Music, n.d.

Instrumentation: Voice, Flute (Piccolo), Clarinet (Bass Clarinet), Trombone, Percussion (3), Piano (Celesta), Violin, Cello.

Score not available for review.

139. ECKERT, Michael. Sea-Changes. New York: American Composers Alliance, n.d.

Text: Hart Crane.
Instrumentation: Mezzo-Soprano, Flute (2), Clarinet (2), French Horn, Trumpet, Harp, Celesta (Piano, Violin), Viola, Cello.

Score not available for review.

140. EDWARDS, George. The Captive. New York: American Composers Allinace, n.d.

Text: Proust.
Instrumentation: Soprano, Flute, Oboe, Clarinet, Bass Clarinet, Vibraphone, Harpsichord, Violin (2), Viola (2), Cello, Double Bass.

Score not available for review.

141. EDWARDS, George. Three Hopkins Songs (1972-9'). Hillsdale, NY: Mobart Music, n.d.

Instrumentation: Soprano (2), Piano (2).

Meter and tempo changes occur within each piece. The superimposition of non-similar irregular subdivisions of beats is common. E.g.

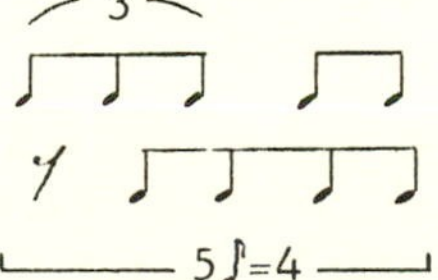

The first soprano part lies generally quite high, but jumps below the staff frequently. The second soprano part encompasses a more moderate range, but also includes large intervals. Both parts are angular and pitch reference is remote at best.

142. EDWARDS, George. *Veined Variety*. Hillsdale, NY: Bolke-Bomart, 1980.

Text: G.M. Hopkins.
Instrumentation: Soprano, Flute (Piccolo), Clarinet (Bass Clarinet), Violin, Cello.
Duration: 14 Minutes.

Score not available for review. The publisher has indicated that it is available in blue print edition, only.

143. EHLE, Robert. *Algorhythms*. New York: Carl Fischer, 1972.

i. Topography
ii. Illusion
iii. Precision
iv. Architecture

Texts: by the composer.
Instrumentation: Soprano, Prepared Piano, Clarinet, Double Bass.

The composer calls this "An Electronic Song Cycle." A microphone for the singer and one attached to each of the instruments modify the sound electronically. Someone, usually the pianist, controls the electronics. The score calls for adjustments in each microphone level as well as control of the tape reverberation. The soprano sings throughout, except for spoken words, indicated _/ or ‾\ , on ends of phrases. The vocal line is angular and pitch references are often remote; however, it is not rhythmically complex.

144. EVETT, Robert. *Billy in the Darbies*. New York: American Composers Alliance, n.d.

Text: Melville.
Instrumentation: Baritone, Clarinet, Strng Quartet.

Score not available for review.

145. FARBERMAN. Harold. *Evolution*. New York: Broude Brothers, 1966.

Instrumentation: Soprano, Percussion (7), French Horn.
Duration: ca. 17 Minutes.

Evolution is chiefly a piece for percussion. The soprano and horn appear only in the second of the three movements. Instead of a text, Farberman gives the soprano syllables, Mm, Na, Loo, etc. When the soprano and horn perform together, her pitch references are clear. In one section only non-pitched instrumental sounds and an occasional vibraphone chord accompany her. The meter remains constant throughout. The tempo changes frequently in the middle section and otherwise remains constant.

146. FARBERMAN, Harold. *Greek Scene*. New York: Broude Brothers, 1956.

Prologue
Part 1 (Clytemnestra)
Part 2 (Electra)
Part 3 (Clytemnestra)

Instrumentation: Voice, Piano, Percussion.

The meter and tempo change frequently, but no complex rhythmic patterns appear. The lyric vocal line moves mostly in steps and small leaps. Pitches at entrances are usually clear, but often at the interval of a minor second with the piano. The singer also speaks and shouts.

147. FARBERMAN, Harold. *New York Times, Aug. 30, 1964*. New York: General Music Publishing, 1965.

1. Southampton, England - "The Blue Whale"
2. Newport Beach, Calif.
Washington D.C.
Newport Beach, Calif.
Washington D.C.
Washington D.C. — "Politics"
3. Houston, Texas - "Science"
4. Birmingham, Alabama - "Civil Rights"

Instrumentation: Mezzo-Soprano, Piano, Percussion.
Duration: ca. 9 1/2 Minutes.
Written especially for Corinne Curry.

The composer states, "The piece should have a completely free quality when there are no bar lines. In those sections the vocal line will shape the movement and structure of the work." Some parts are measured and some are not. The vocal line includes many wide intervals and pitch cues are often obscured by clusters, range or timbre. This work incorporates Sprechstimme and playing inside the piano.

148. FELCIANO, Richard. Glossolalia. Cincinnati: World Library Publications, 1967.

Text: Psalm 150.
Instrumentation: Tenor (or Dramatic Tenor), Organ, Percussion, Electronic Tape.

The text, set in Latin, "is exploited for its phonetic qualities as well as its literal meaning and the effect of glossolalia (speaking with tongues) is often the result." Consonants are used in repeated rhythmic patterns or sustained, e.g., sss. The generally angular vocal line contains large intervals, but chromatic movement as well. Glissandi, multiple grace notes and indications for such vocal effects as "white tone" and "electronically" appear. Extremes in dynamics are required. Pitch reference is sometimes remote. Doubling of pitches does occur occasionally, however. The electronic tape and a separate part for the percussionist are available from the publisher.

149. FELDMAN, Morton. For Franz Kline. New York: C.F. Peters, 1962.

Instrumentation: Soprano, Violin, Cello, French Horn, Chimes, Piano.

The following note appears in the score: "The first sound with all instruments simultaneously. The duration of each sound is chosen by the performer. All beats are slow. All sounds should be played with a minimum of attack. Grace notes should not be played too quickly. Numbers between sounds indicate silent beats. Dynamics are very low." The score consists of a series of pitches (note heads) and rests (numbers with fermatas over them). Simultaneity is indicated only at the beginning. The vocal line has specific pitches throughout but no text. Pitch references are extremely difficult because the piece is non-metric and notes have non-specific lengths in all parts.

150. FELDMAN, Morton. Four Songs to e e cummings. New York: C.F. Peters, 1962.

1. ! black against white sky?
2. air, becomes (a) new (Live) now;
3. sitting in a tree
4. moan (is) ing the she of the sea

Instrumentation: Soprano, Cello, Piano.

The vocal part consists almost entirely of large intervals, many larger than an octave. Short value-notes among groups of rests are common. Rests often occur in the middle of a word. Consonants (even unvoiced consonants) are separated from the rest of the word and given separate pitches. Range: G - d''. The tempo and meter remain constant through all four songs. Pitch references and cues are remote at best. In number 3 a section for solo voice is indicated "whisper," but specific pitches are given.

151. FELDMAN, Morton. *I met heine on the rue fürstenberg*. New York: Universal Edition, 1973.

Instrumentation: Voice, Flute, Clarinet, Percussion, Piano, Violin, Viola.

The vocal part consists of isolated small groups of notes, mostly of medium to long values. Pitches easily relate to the instrumental parts, though the instrumentation is sparse. Meter changes occur in almost every measure. Feldman uses no text and gives no indication of syllables or types of sounds expected from the singer. Most of the piece appears in standard notation. However, other notation used in this piece is not common to most singers and is not explained in the score.

152. FELDMAN, Morton. *Intervals*. New York: C.F. Peters, 1962.

Instrumentaion: Bass-Baritone, Cello, Trombone, Vibraphone, Percussion.

Intervals begins with a composer's note which is the same as *For Franz Kline* ("The first sound.... Dynamics are very low.") and the two pieces indeed look very similar. The bass-baritone participates in only the first three of the four movements. In the first movement the entire vocal part lies on one note, F#.

153. FELDMAN, Morton. *Journey to the End of the Night*. New York: C.F. Peters, 1963.

1. Travel is a good thing
2. (instrumental)
3. Your going to die soldier boy
4. Good, admirable Molly

Text: based on the novel by Céline.
Instrumentation: Soprano, Flute, Clarinet, Bass Clarinet, Bassoon.
Composed: 1947.

In contrast to some of his later works, Feldman indicates specific rhythmic values and coordinates the ensemble by bar lines and tempo. The meter changes frequently, but the tempo remains constant throughout each piece. The singer's pitches clearly relate to the instrumental parts, but occur among much dissonance. Great demands are placed on the upper part of the range. Range: d - c#''.

154. FELDMAN, Morton. The O'Hara Songs. New York: C.F. Peters, 1963.

Text: Poem of Frank O'Hara.
Instrumentation: Bass-Baritone, Violin, Viola, Cello, Chimes, Piano.

All three songs are based on the same text. The first and last use the entire text while the second song repeats the first line of the text. The score includes the following instructions from the composer: "The first and last song begin with voice and given instruments sounding simultaneously. The duration of each sound thereafter is chosen by the singer and instrumentalists within ● = M 66-84. Numbers between sounds indicate silent beats. Broken lines are used to indicate sustaining sounds. All sounds should be played with a minimum of attack. Dynamics are very low." Exact pitches are given and the length of each is indicated by the number of notes (●---●---●---●) connected on the same pitch. Except for the beginnings of numbers 1 and 3 no ensemble coordination occurs. Each performer executes his part within the tempo limitations without regard for other parts and each finishes at a different time.

155. FELDMAN, Morton. RABBI AKIBA. New York: C.F. Peters, 1963.

Instrumentation: Soprano, Flute, English Horn, French Horn, Trumpet, Trombone, Tuba, Percussion, Piano-Celesta, Cello, Double Bass.

Some bars appear with meter signatures and tempo markings. Other bars contain sequences of sounds connected by dotted lines, in which each sound begins when the preceeding sound starts to fade. All sounds should occur with a minimum of attack and dynamics should be low throughout. In the first section the soprano's pitches fit into sequence with the other instruments. In number II a soprano solo is interrupted by pitch clusters in the instruments.

156. FELDMAN, Mortn. Vertical Thoughts III. New York: C.F. Peters, 1963.

Text: "Life is a passing shadow."
Instrumentation: Soprano, Flute (Piccolo), Trumpet, Trombone, Tuba, Piano-Celesta, Percussion (2), Violin, Viola, Cello.

Most of the work consists of sequences of single pitches, each played by a different instrument from the previous. Each pitch begins with a minimum attack as the previous pitch is fading. Five notes (one for each word), evenly spaced throughout the piece, are always accompanied by tuba and percussion. The pitch for the soprano, d#', and instruments repeat identically for each word. The d#' always relates easily to the previous sustained note. The entire piece is free and unmeasured except for the five measures in which the words occur. These are all 3/2, but each with a different metronomic marking. No specific dynamic markings appear in the score, but instructions indicate that the level should be very low throughout. Grace notes are to be played slowly.

157. FELDMAN, Morton. Vertical Thoughts V. New York: C.F. Peters, 1963.

Text: "Life is a passing shadow."
Instrumentation: Soprano, Violin, Tuba, Percussion, Celesta.

The entire piece consists of the soprano, violin, tuba and celesta performing a whole note (at 𝅗𝅥 = 48) for each of the five words. A percussion solo occurs between each of the words. The piece is extremely quiet and short, only three pages in length.

158. FENNELLY, Brian. Songs with improvisations. New York: American Composers Allinace, n.d.

Text: e e cummings.
Instrumentation: Medium Voice, Clarinet, Piano.

Score not available for review.

159. FERGUSON, Edwin Earle. Two Spanish Songs. New York: Associatated Music Publishers, 1967.

1. Luna Que Reluces
   (Moon with thy Loveliness Beaming)
2. Quiero Dormir y No Puedo
   ('Tis love that keeps me from sleeping)

Text: from the Cancioneros. English version by the composer.
Instrumentation: Medium Voice, Piano (Four Hands).
Duration: ca. 4 Minutes.
Dedication: Gail and Karen.

The vocal line moves mostly by steps and small leaps. Entrance pitches usually appear in the preceding piano part and much doubling occurs throughout. The fairly simple rhythmic structure includes few tempo changes and a constant meter. (This reviewer saw only #1)

160. FERRITTO, John. Oggi: A Setting for Soprano, Clarinet, Piano, Op. 9. New York: American Composers Alliance, 1974.

Text: Unidentified and some phonetic syllables.
Composed: 1969.
Dedication: Neva.

The vocal line, encompassing a range of Bb - c'', is angular and rhythmicallly disjunct (with lots of rests). It includes specific interpretive, or acting instructions as well as the following: some spoken, glissandi, grace notes, "moan with mouth closed," "shouted to players," "yelled." Some tempo and meter changes occur throughout. The superimposition of irregular subdivisions of beats (e.g., 6 against 5) are common. Small value rests are interspersed among these irregular subdivisions.

161. FERRITTO, John. Quattro Madrigali. New York: American Composers Alliance, n.d.

Instrumentaion: Baritone, Flute, Clarinet.

Score not available for review.

162. FINE, Vivian. The Confession. Shaftsbury, VT: Catamount Facsimile Edition, n.d.

Text: from Phaedra by Racine.
Instrumentation: Voice, Flute (Alto Flute), Violin, Viola, Cello, Piano.
Composed: 1963.

The piece requires speaking as well as singing and some vocal passages lie quite low. Pitches are doubled occasionally but not regularly. Tempo and meter changes occur frequently, the meter sometimes in every bar. The text is set in French.

163. FINE, Vivian. The Great Wall of China. New York: New Music Edition, 1948.

I. I can still remember quite well
II. But instead how vainly does he wear out his strength
III. Long-dead emperors are set on the throne
IV. One can perhaps safely discuss it now.

Text: based on excerpts from The Great Wall of China by Franz Kafka.
Instrumentation: Voice, Flute, Cello, Piano.

Number I is an unbarred duet for flute and soprano. In mumber III, the meter changes constantly. Number IV contains a segment of recitative. Singer's pitch cues are clear; instruments sometimes double the vocal line. The singing is occasionally interrupted by spoken passages.

164. FLANAGAN, William. Good-Bye, My Fancy. New York: Peer International, 1964.

Text: Walt Whitman.
Instrumentation: Soprano, Flute, Guitar.
Composed: 1957.
Dedication: Ned Rorem.

The composer states that "This composition may be, if necessary, for piano and voice by playing the guitar part an octave below the written pitch and the flute part at the written pitch." Vocal pitches relate closely to the instrumental parts. The meter changes frequently, but few other rhythmic complexities appear.

165. FLANAGAN, William. The Weeping Pleiads. New York: Peer International, n.d.

Instrumentation: Baritone, Flute, Clarinet, Violin, Cello, Piano.

Score not available for review. The publisher'sw catalog indicates that materials are available on rental.

166. FOSS, Lukas. Thirteen Ways of Looking at a Black-Bird. New York: Pembroke Music, 1979.

Text: Wallace Stevens.
Instrumentation: Soprano or Mezzo-soprano, Flute, Piano, Percussion.
Duration: ca. 17 Minutes.
Commissioned by WFMT Chicago.

The vocal line encompasses a fairly moderate range and includes some briefly repeated patterns and some speaking. Foss gives some specific tempo markings and indicates some sections as free and some in seconds. The instructions indicate that the percussionist plays "inside the piano on the strings," and also prescribes an "echo effect - two tape recorders (placed next to each other) for tape delay in #XIII. One records the live voice, while the other plays back three seconds later. (A backstage voice may be substituted for tape recorders.)"

167. FOSS, Lukas. Time Cycle. Boston: Carl Fischer, 1960.

I. We're Late (W.H. Auden)
II. When the Bells Justle (A.E. Houseman)
III. Sechzehnter Januar (Franz Kafka)
IV. O Mensch, gib Acht (Friedrich Nietzsche)

Instrumentation: Soprano, Clarinet, Cello, Percussion, Piano/Celesta.
Duration: ca. 22 Minutes.
Dedication: Adele Addison.
Commissioned by Ford Foundation's Humanities and Arts Program.
New York: Music Critics Circle Award, 1961.

Prominent intervals in the vocal line are 7ths and 9ths. Vocal pitch patterns often relate to figures in the instrumental parts. Sometimes the parts are disjunct melodically and rhythmicallly. Ensemble problems include irregular placement of rests and meter changes (in some places every measure). Foss gives extensive dynamic indications and specific instructions about how the instruments should be played. Time Cycle was originally composed for soprano solo with full orchestra. Full score and parts are available on rental.

168. FOX, Fred. Time Excursions. New York: Seesaw Music, 1977.

Text: Conrad Aiken, from Preludes from Memnon.
William Shakespeare, from King Henry IV, Part I.
Two anonymous pieces.
Instrumentation: Soprano, Reciter, Flute, Clarinet, Violin, Viola, Cello, Piano, Percussion (2).
Duration: 17 Minutes.
Composed under a grant from the National Endowment for the Arts.

Microphones and speakers are suggested for the soprano and reciter. In addition to singing, the soprano speaks and whispers into the mike. The reciter is required to sing on a few occasions, but no specific pitches are given. A rather lengthy section which is to be sung in vocalise style is marked "blend instrumentally (select and alternate vowels)." This vocalised section lies in the moderate range. In a section which is sung with text the vocal line is angular and often lies quite high. The pitch reference is strained at best with little doubling even of isolated pitches. Each performer plays a set of wind chimes. The first poem is recited and accompanied only by the various wind chimes and the Indian Bell. The seating arrangement diagram specifies a conductor. Some tempo and meter changes occur.

169. FRANCO, Johan. Ariel's Four Songs. New York: American Composers Alliance, n.d.

Text: from Shakespeare's The Tempest.
Instrumentation: High Voice, Guitar (or Marimba).

Score not available for review.

170. FRANCO, Johan. Little Lamb. New York: American Composers Alliance, 1977.

Text: William Blake.
Instrumentation: Voice, Guitar.
Dedication: Patrice and Tim Olbrych.

The vocal line moves mostly by steps and small leaps within a small rage (d - f'). Usually a consonant reationship exists between the voice and guitar. Some meter changes occur. The tempo remains constant.

171. FRANCO, Johan. The Lord Cometh. New York: American Composers Alliance, 1963.

Text: from The Master Key by Christina.
Instrumentation: Soprano (or Tenor), Clarinet, Bass Clarinet, English Horn.

The vocal part moves mostly by steps and small leaps and encompasses a moderate range (d - g'). Little doubling, even of isolated pitches, occurs. In this short piece of only 24 bars, the tempo is constant, but a few meter changes occur.

172. FRANCO, Johan. The Song of Life. New York: American Composers Alliance, n.d.

Text: Christina.
Instrumentation: Soprano (or Tenor), Clarinet, English Horn, Bass Clarinet.

Score not available for review.

173. FRANCO, Johan. Songs of the Spirit. New York: American Composers Alliance, 1960.

I. The eye of mine eye....
II. Oh, sing, beloved....
III. Oh, Joy of Joys....

IV. Come, Beloved....
V. Lo, The Glory....

Text: Excerpts from The Master Key by Christina.
Instrumentation: Soprano (or Tenor), Woodwind Quintet.

The vocal part moves mostly by steps and small leaps. Entrance pitches relate to the instrumental parts by unisons or consonant intervals. Doubling is common throughout. The piece ends with pianissimo humming in the upper range. Dynamic markings are quite specific. Few meter changes occur.

174. FRANCO, Johan. Sonnet. New York: Composers Facsimile Edition, 1952.

Sonnet 43 (XVIII)
Sonnet 152 (LXXI)

Text: Francis Bacon; Shakespeare.
Instrumentation: Voice, String Quartet.
Composed: 1945.
Dedication: #2 to Lucille Dresskell.

The tempo remains constant, some meter changes occur. The strings frequently double the vocal pitches, sometimes entire phrases. The vocal line includes much chromatic movement.

175. FRANCO, Johan. The Tempest, Incidental Music. New York: American Composers Alliance, n.d.

Text: Shakespeare.
Instrumentation: Soprano, Harpsichord, Celesta, Marimba, Percussion, Electronic Montages.

Score not available for review.

176. FRANCO, Johan. Two Duets for Voice and Flute. New York: American Composers Alliance, 1973.

I. La flute invisible
II. Vocalise

Text: Victor Hugo.
Instrumentation: Baritone (or Mezzo-Soprano), Flute (Flute in G).
Dedication: Ruth and Ralph.

The vocal line moves mostly in steps and small leaps. The flute frequently doubles the vocal pitch but some relationships of half and whole tones occur also. Few meter changes occur. The tempo is constant within each piece. The text is set in French.

177. GABER, Harley. *Voce II*. Cincinnati: Apogee Press, 1967.

I. Macenarngala (Issa)
II. Otto (Buson)
III. Akai Botan (Buson)
IV. Seshi (Bashō)
V. Naru ano Michi Nite (Bashō)
VI. Basho no Michi (Bashō)
VII. Yoru no Inazuma (Bashō)

Text: Issa, Buson & Basho. Japanese texts. No English given in the score.
Instrumentaion: Female Voice, Alto Flute, Percussion.

The composer gives extensive general instructions and specific instructions to each performer. The following is an excerpt: "The vocal part should be thought of as being very 'light,' 'clear,' and 'agile.' Louder passages should be sung in a more 'dramatic' manner without going outside the general stylistic framework." The vocal part requires some singing, some tones which are voiced but breathy and some unvoiced sounds. Pitch reference and cues are remote and the vocal line is angular. Coordination of the ensemble may be a problem. The tempo markings vary from MM=40 to MM=60, and each space, indicated , is equal to one pulsation of the metronome.

The number of notes in each unit is irregular. The piece also includes some lengthy bits of silence.

178. GABURO, Kenneth. *Cantilena 4*. n.p.: Lingua Press, 1975.

Instrumentation: Soprano, Trombone.
Duration: 8 Minutes.
Dedication: Candace and Jon English.

In the performance notes the composer explains his division of the soprano part into four registral segments (c-f, f#-b, c'-f', f#'-b'), and gives specific instructions for the types of sounds and other special considerations within each. Vocal instructions include the following: "unvoiced flutter," "trill," "hum/whistle," "micro-glissandi," "play/sing," "hand muting." The vocal line is mainly disjunct with some chant-like and some sustained sections. Most vocal pitches are notated exactly and do relate to the trombone part. The trombone part is also divided into four registral segments and includes many vocal sounds as well. Each part switches back and forth between two staves (four in all). The text is interspersed with phonetic symbols, using one staff for the text and the other for the phonetic symbols.

179. GABURO, Kenneth, *Two*. Bryn Mawr, PA: Theodore Presser, 1971.

Text: Virginia Hommel.
Instrumentation: Mezzo-Soprano, Alto Flute, Double Bass.

The composer's note states, "A voice is required which is capable of making perceptual distinctions between the several vocal qualities (e.g. normale, falsetto sotto voce, breathy) as designated in the score." The movement of the piece is sometimes indicated in seconds, sometimes metered and sometimes mixed. One of the most complex phrases contains a measure of eight seconds followed by a bar of 5/16 at ♩♪ = 160, then a measure of two seconds followed by another bar of 5/16 at ♩♪ = 160, a measure of seven seconds, etc.

Other parts of the piece are mostly metered but with constantly changing signatures. Special performance problems include constant changes in dynamics and rests between most syllables of the text. Vocal pitches clearly relate to the instrumental parts but are obscured by the complexity of ensemble coordination.

180. GIDEON, Miriam. *The Adorable Mouse*. n.p.: Joshua, 1973.

Text: A folk tale based on La Fontaine.
Instrumentation: Voice, Flute, Clarinet, Bassoon, French Horn, Timpani, Harpsichord.

Much of the text is spoken, and some is sung but unaccompanied. When the vocal line is accompanied, the pitches relate clearly to the instrumental parts, with some doublings, third relationships, etc. The range is narrow. *The Adorable Mouse* is published with a score and five parts.

181. GIDEON, Miriam. *The Condemned Playground*. Hillsdale, Mobart Music, n.d.

I. Pyrrha (Horace: Ode I, Book V. English translation by John Milton)
II. Hiroshima (Gary Spokes, Japanese translation by Saloka Akiya)
III. The litanies of Satan (Baudelaire. English translation by Edna St. Vincent Millay)

Instrumentation: Soprano, Tenor, Flute, Bassoon, String Quartet.
Composed: 1963.

Generally the tenor's line lies above the soprano's. The voices often fall into 1/2 tone relationships with each other, and much of the linear movement is chromatic. Sometimes the instruments double the vocal pitches. The string quartet generally functions as a unit, with similar figures. The flute and bassoon are sometimes integrated with the quartet and sometimes function as a separate unit. The meter changes frequently. This piece is published in score form. Parts are available on rental.

182. GIDEON, Miriam. The Hound of Heaven. New York: Columbia University Press, 1975.

Text: Francis Thompson.
Instrumentation: Voice, Oboe, String Trio.

Tempo and meter changes occur frequently, but there are no complex rhythmic figures. Instrumental parts frequently double the singer's pitches. The vocal part generally lies low. Range: c# - f'.

183. GIDEON, Miriam. Little Ivory Figures. New York: American Composers Alliance, 1959.

Text: Amy Lowell.
Instrumentation: Voice, Guitar.

Specific pitches appear for some single phrases, but directional lines, with no rhythmic indications, guide most of the vocal part (text). The guitar part is notated in specific pitches throughout.

184. GIDEON, Miriam. Nocturnes. New York: American Composers Alliance, 1978.

1. Prelude
2. To the Moon (Percy Bysshe Shelly)
3. High Tide (Jean Starr Untermeyer)
4. Interlude
5. Witchery (Frank Dempster Sherman)

Instrumentation: High Voice, Flute, Oboe, Violin, Cello, Vibraphone.

The vocal line moves mostly by steps, small leaps and chromaticism. Pitches relate closely to the instrumental parts with doublings of isolated pitches and some complete phrases. The moderate range lies mostly on the treble staff.

185. GIDEON, Miriam. _Questions on Nature_. Hillsdale, NY: Mobart Music Publications, 1978.

I. How the Earth Moves
II. Why the planets
III. Whence the winds arise
IV. Whether the Stars Fall
V. Whether Beasts have Souls
VI. Why we Hear Echoes
VII. Why Joy is the cause of Weeping

Text: Propounded by Adelard of Bath, early 12th century.
Instrumentation: Voice, Oboe, Piano, Glockenspiel, Tam-tam.
Composed: 1964.

Chromatic intervals predominate in the vocal part. Pitches sometimes relate quite remotely to the instrumental parts. The meter changes frequently and includes a wide variety of signatures. This work is published in manuscript which is difficult to read.

186. GIDEON, Miriam. _Rhymes from the Hill_. Hillsdale, NY: Mobart Music, 1978.

Bundeslied
Wiegenlied
Zwei Uhren: 1
Zwei Uhren: 2
Der Seufzer

Text: Christian Morgenstern, from the _Galgenlieder_ (Gallows Songs).
Instrumentation: Voice, Clarinet, Cello, Marimba.
Composed: 1968.

The vocal line contains much chromatic movement but no large leaps. The pitches relate to the instrumental parts, but seldom at a unison, third or other easily accessible interval. Isolated pitches which are doubled are found imbedded in the harmonic structure. The text is set in German. The tempo is fairly constant within each movement. In some areas the meter changes frequently. This piece is published in score. Parts are available on rental.

187. GIDEON, Miriam. _The Seasons of Time_. Hastings-on-Hudson, NY: Joshua, 1971.

Now it is Spring
The wild geese returning
Can it be there is no moon?
Gossips grow like weeds
Each season more lovey
In the leafy treetops

A passing shower
I have always known
To what shall I compare this world
Yonder in the plum tree

Text: Ten short pieces, based on the Tanka Poetry of Ancient Japan.
Instrumentation: High Voice, Flute, Cello, Piano (Celesta).

Vocal pitches relate closely to the instrumental parts. Some meter changes and many tempo changes occur throughout the work. The vocal range is moderate. This is also published in a version for voice and piano.

188. GIDEON, Miriam. Sonnets from Fatal Interview. New York: American Composers Alliance, n.d.

Text: Millay.
Instrumentation: High Voice, Violin, Viola, Cello.

Score not available for review.

189. GIDEON, Miriam. Sonnets from Shakespeare. New York: Composers Facsimile Edition, 1959.

Sonnet VIII: Music to Hear
Sonnet XIX: Devouring Time
Sonnet XXXIII: Full many a glorious morning
Sonnet LXXII: No longer mourn for me
Sonnet CXXIII: No, Time thou shalt not boast

Instrumentation: Voice, Trumpet, String Quartet.

The vocal line moves mostly by small intervals within a moderate range. Entrance pitches relate closely to the instrumental parts and frequent doubling of the vocal part occurs throughout. The first song begins and ends with solo voice. In some sections the meter chages in nearly every bar.

190. GODFREY, Daniel S. Two Wedding Airs. New York: American Composers Alliance, n.d.

Instrumentation: Soprano, Alto Recorder.

Score not available for review.

191. GRATZ, Reed. Earthbound. n.p.: Andewa Music, 1974.

Morning Thought
Aries
Time Sky
A Child's Spring
Once we
Sea Day

Instrumentation: Soprano, Electric Piano, Flute, Double Bass, Percussion.

Many small repeated sections appear in each song. Also, each song ends with an indication to go back to a particular place and perform to "fine." The vocal pitches relate easily to the harmonic content, and are often doubled by an instrument. Sections of improvisation happen in the instrumental parts. The manuscript score is difficult to read.

192. GRUNDMAN, Claire. Zoo Illogical. New York: Boosey & Hawkes, 1974.

Instrumentation: Voice, Flute, Clarinet, Bass Clarinet, Bassoon, Trumpet, Trombone, Percussion, Optional Piano.

All parts frequently move in similar rhythmic patterns which consist mostly of half, quarter and eighth notes. Ostinato patterns occur often in the instrumental parts. The lyric vocal part is often doubled by the instruments. The range is limited: c - d'.

193. HAINES, Edmund. Four Loves. Newton Centre, MA: Margun Music, n.d.

Instrumentation: Soprano, Flute, Oboe, Violin, Viola, Cello, Amplified Harpsichord, Piano.
Composed: 1974.
Duration: 13 1/2 Minutes.

Score not available for review.

194. HAMPTON, Calvin. Labyrinth. New York: McAffe Music, 1967.

Text: Michael Abrew.
Instrumentation: Soprano, Saxophone Quartet.

Labyrinth is published with five parts but no score. The voice participates in the second of two movements. Vocal cues appear in the sax parts and a variety of sax cues appear in the voice part. Vocal pitches relate closely to the sax parts, and are often doubled by the soprano sax.

Much of the vocal line lies quite high: B - e''. The meter changes frequently but the tempo remains fairly constant. Many dynamic variations and extremes are indicated.

195. HARDIN, Louis Thomas. Moondog on the Streets of New York. New York: Hollis Music, 1953.

Suite:
1. Avenue of the Americas (51st Street)
2. 2 West 46th Street (solo in 5/8 time)
3. Lullaby for Samisen (2 West 46th Street)
4. Fog on the Hudson (425 West 57th Street)
5. Utsu
6. On and off the Beat (study in 5/4 rhythm)
7. Chant (for Uni Utsu, Voice in 1/2 time)
8. From One to Nine (Nine quarter beats in Snake Time)

Instrumentation: Voice Percussion.

Only numbers 3 and 7 contain parts for voice. Number 3 requires humming and number 7 provides no text or other indication for the type of vocal sounds. The rest of the suite is scored for percussion alone.

196. HARRIS, Roy. Abraham Lincoln Walks at Midnight. New York: Associated Music Publishers, 1955.

Text: Vachel Lindsay, from Collected Poems.
Instrumentation: Mezzo-Soprano, Violin, Cello, Piano.

Harris calls this a Cantata of Lamentation. The tempo and meter change occasionally, but no complex rhythmic patterns appear. Vocal pitches closey relate to the instrumental parts. The vocal line lies mostly on the staff.

197. HARRISON, Lou. Air. New York: Peer International, 1966.

Text: William Morris (from the opera Rapunzel)
Instrumentation: Voice, Flute, String Trio, Harp, Piano.
Composed: 1954.

Recitative-like sections which begin and end the piece are unaccompanied or accompanied by sustained harp chords. In the lyric central section the violin doubles the voice part throughout. The piano moves mainly in continuous eighth notes, and the other instruments mostly in quarter and half notes.

198. HARRISON, Lou. Alma Redemptoris Mater. New York: Peer International, 1962.

Instrumentation: Baritone, Violin, Tack Piano, Trombone.

No bar lines appear in this short (3 pages) piece. All parts are angular but rhytmically simple, moving solely in quarter notes and pairs of eighths. The piano part consists of a single treble clef line, and the violin doubles the baritone throughout.

199. HARTLEY, Walter. A Psalm Cycle. n.p.: Tenuto Publications, 1970.

1. Andante molto
2. Allegro
3. Adagio
4. Andante con moto
5. Allegro con brio

Instrumentaion: Medium High Voice, Flute, Piano.
Commissioned by and dedicated to Carolyn Reyer.
Duration: ca. 13 1/2 Minutes.

The vocal line moves mostly by steps and small leaps and includes much chromaticism. Vocal entrance pitches usually relate by unison or consonant interval to the previous instrumental material. Frequent doublings of vocal pitches occur. The tempo and meter are constant within each movement.

200. HARTWAY, James. "Three ways of Looking at a Blackbird." ASUC Journal of Music Scores, Vol.3 (1974): 5-22.

I. Among twenty snowy mountains
II. I was of three minds
III. The Blackbird whirled in the autumn wind

Text: Wallace Stevens.
Instrumentation: Soprano, Flute, Piano (Prepared), Percussion.

The sound is sparse. Fragments in the various instruments are spacially separated on the page: a staff is used only for notes, not rests. The vocal line is angular and at one place a whisper is required. No demands are made on the extremes of the range. Vocal pitches relate remotely to the instrumental parts; no doubling occurs. A metronomic marking appears at the beginning of the song, but rests are indicated in seconds. Complete silences occur frequently.

201. HAUBIEL, Charles. A Threnody for Love. Los Angeles: Composer's Press, 1966.

Text: Frederika Blanker.
Instrumentation: Contralto, Flute, Clarinet, Violin, Cello, Piano.

Score not available for review.

202. HAUFRECHT, Herbert. Let's Play Maccabees, Children's Songs. New York: American Composers Alliance, n.d.

Text: Heidi Mayer.
Instrumentation: Medium Voice, Oboe, Clarinet, Harp, Percussion.

Score not available for review.

203. HEILNER, Irwin. Democracy. New York: American Composers Alliance, n.d.

Text: Langston Hughs.
Instrumentation: Voice, Guitar.

The vocal line moves in steps and small leaps within a small range (c - e'). Pitches clearly fit into the chord structures. The score gives a single vocal line with chord symbols for guitar.

204. HEILNER, Irwin. Every Day is Friday to a Seal. New York: American Composers Alliance, n.d.

Text: Claire Berger.
Instrumentaion: Medium Voice, Guitar (or Banjo or Ukelele).

Score not available for review.

205. HEILNER, Irwin. The Gift of Fire. New York: American Composers Alliance, n.d.

Text: Lisel Mueller.
Instrumentation: Voice, Guitar.

Score not available for review.

206. HEILNER, Irwin. _Henry at the Grating_. New York: American Composers Alliance, n.d.

Text: Aaron Kramer.
Instrumentation: Voice, Guitar.

Score not available for review.

207. HEILNER, Irwin. _Letter from the Draft Board_. New York: American Composers Alliance, n.d.

Text: Aaron Kramer.
Instrumentation: Voice, Guitar.

Score not available for review.

208. HEILNER, Irwin. _Peace is a Lovely Word_. New York: American Composers Alliance, n.d.

Text: D. Berger.
Instrumentation: Medium Voice, Guitar.

Score not available for review.

209. HEILNER, Irwin. _Rock-'n'-Roll Session_. New York: Anerican Composers Alliance, n.d.

Instrumentation: Voice, Guitar.

Score not available for review.

210. HEILNER, Irwin. _Stevenson_. New York: American Composers Alliance, n.d.

Text: C. Berger.
Instrumentation: Medium Voice, Guitar.

Score not available for review.

211. HEILNER, Irwin. _What Were They Like_? New York: American Composers Alliance, n.d.

Text: Denise Levertove.
Instrumentation: Medium Voice, Guitar.

Score not available for review.

212. HEILNER, Irwin. The Wild Anemone. New York: American Composers Alliance, n.d.

Text: James Laughlin.
Instrumentation: Voice, Guitar.

Vocal entrance pitches appear in the immediately previous guitar part, and some doublings of pitches occur throughout. The range is fairly low and narrow: B - e'. The meter and tempo remain fairly constant.

213. HELLERMANN, William. Poem for soprano and Four Instruments. New York: American Composers Alliance, n.d.

Text: W. Owens.
Instrumentaion: Soprano, Flute, Bass Clarinet, Trombone, Cello.

Score not available for review.

214. HENRY, Otto. The Sons of Martha. n.p.: Media Press, 1972.

Text: Rudyard Kipling.
Instrumentation: Soprano, Percussion (4).
Dedication: Charlene DeShaw.

The vocal line moves mostly in steps and small leaps. Pitches relate clearly to the mallet instruments, with frequent doublings. The meter remains fairly constant in this short piece, but some tempo fluctuations occur.

215. HIBBARD, William. Ménage. N.P.: Lingua Press, 1977.

Instrumentation: Soprano, Trumpet, Violin.
Duration: ca. 8 1/2 Minutes.
Commissioned by the Society for Commissioning New Music, Baton Rouge, LA.

The meter changes infrequently and the tempo remains constant throughout, but extremes in dynamic contrasts are required. The composer specifically indicates that timbrel considerations are most important. Instead of a text, IPA symbols determine the shapes of the vocal sounds. The trumpet and voice function as a group and the violin separately. Vocal pitches relate closely to the instrumental pitches and extend to c#''. The score does not specify a conductor, but the notes indicate that the composer conducted the first performance.

216. HILLER, Lejaren. An Avalanche. Bryn Mawr, PA: Theodore Presser, 1967.

I. Getting Ready for it
II. The Avalanche
III. Cleaning up the mess

Text: Frank Parman.
Instrumentation: Pitchman (Speaker), Prima Donna (Singer), Player Piano, Percussion, Prerecorded Playback.
Performers: Pitchman, Prima Donna, Percussionist, Stage Hand, Audio Technician, Costumiere.

All musical content occurs in number II. The materials are organized by seconds. Numbers I and III are theater events. The Pitchman performs the role of an actor. The Prima Donna's duties consist of singing the following:

1. Battle Hymn of the Republic
2. Santa Lucia
3. I Love You Truly
4. Hallelujah Chorus
5. Varkyrie's Song
6. La donna e mobile
7. Home on the Range
8. Toreador Song
9. Possum Hound
10. Tit-Willow

The composer provides specific instructions concerning the style of singing for each and the costume changes that take place between each. One or more maids assist her.

217. HOSKINS, William. Romance, Who Loves to Nod and Sing. New York: American Composers Alliance, n.d.

Text: Poe.
Instrumentation: Mezzo-Soprano, Viola, Piano.

Score not available for review.

218. HOVHANESS, Alan. Canticle. New York: C.F. Peters, 1954.

1. Pastoral
2. Song "Over Autumn Lake"
3. Song "Thick Fog on River"
4. Song "Melancholy Rain"

Text: Alan Hovhaness.
Instrumentation: Soprano, Oboe, Xylophone, Celesta, Harp, String Quartet, Double Bass.
Duration: 9 Minutes.

The vocal pitches clearly relate to the instrumental parts. In numbers 2 and 4 the first violin doubles the vocal part almost entirely. Overall the rhythm is quite simple, e.g. the vocal part includes only dotted half, half and quarter notes.

219. HOVHANESS, Alan. Hercules, Op.56, No.4. New York: C.F. Peters. 1966.

Text: Alan Hovhaness.
Instrumentaion: Soprano, violin.

The vocal part covers a moderate range and includes a few large intervals but mostly stepwise movement. Doublings or third relationships between the parts are frequent. Frequently the voice moves in sustained notes while the violinist plays faster figures. Repetitions of figures, parts of figures or similar figures are common. The meter changes frequently in some sections, but remains constant in the last section. Some parts are unmeasured.

220. HOVHANESS, Alan. O Lady Moon, Op. 139. New York: Edward B. Marks, 1964.

Text: Lafcadio Hearn from A Japanese Miscellany.
Instrumentation: Voice, Clarinet, Piano.

The tempo and meter remain constant throughout and no complex rhythmic patterns appear. The vocal part moves mostly in steps, and the pitches relate closely to the instrumental parts. A short melismatic duet occurs between the voice and clarinet. The range is moderate for a high voice.

221. HOVHANESS, Alan. Saturn, Op. 243. New York: C.F. Peters, 1971.

1. Prelude
2. Titan, Moon of Saturn
3. Orb Mysterious
4. Saturn, Celestial Globe
5. O Lost Note
6. My Hymn
7. Giant Globe
8. Vision
9. On Wings of a Soundless Note
10. What is Universe?
11. Intermezzo
12. Harp of Saturn

Text: Alan Hovhaness.
Instrumentation: Soprano, Carinet, Piano.
Duration: 25 Minutes.
Dedication: Long Island Chamber Ensemble.

The soprano line lies primarily between a and a'. Pitches relate easily to the instrumental parts and rhythmic patterns are simple. The soprano often sings sustained tones while the clarinetist plays a more interesting melody. At the beginning of several movements the clarinet has a free, unaccompanied section, which in numbers 6 and 8 becomes a free dialogue between soprano and clarinet. In number 12 the harp-like chords of the piano alternate with a voice and clarinet duet of parallel fourths and fifths to create a final etherial effect.

222. HOVANNISSIAN, Harpik der. Plea. Tampa, FL: Hovan Music Publishing, 1968.

Text: Dorothy Meister.
Instrumentation: Soprano, Flute.

The vocal line moves mostly by steps and small leaps. Entrance pitches appear in the previous instrumental material, and much doubling occurs throughout. Some meter changes appear, but the quarter note is always constant. Rhythmic figures are simple.

223. HUGGLER, John. Bittere Nüsse. New York: C.F. Peters, 1976.

Text: Paul Celan.
Instrumentation: Soprano, Flute, Clarinet (and Bass Clarinet), Violin, Viola, Cello.

Score not available for review.

224. HUGGLER, John. For Coloratura, Clarinet, Viola, Cello. Op. 20. New York: American Composers Alliance, n.d.

Text: Yeats.

Score not available for review.

225. IMBRE, Andrew. Tell me where is fancy bred. Delaware Water Gap, PA: Shawnee Press, n.d.

Text: Shakespeare, Merchant of Venice, Act III, Scene 2.
Instrumentation: Soprano, Clarinet, Guitar.

Vocal entrance pitches relate clearly to previous instrumental material. Little doubling occurs, however, and the voice often relates to the instruments by a half tone. The range is moderate. A few grace notes appear, but no complex rhythmic figures. The tempo and meter remain constant.

226. IVES, Charles E. Sunrise. Edited by J. Kirkpatrick. New York: C.F. Peters, 1977.

Text: Charles Edward Ives.
Instrumentation: Voice, Violin, Piano.
Composed: 1926.

Mr. Kirkpatrick gives several pages of discussion and comparison of sources. "This edition has the approval of the Charles Ives Society, Inc. wich is furthering and supporting the preparation of critical editions, both new and revised, of the works of Ives." The vocal line moves mostly by steps and small intervals; much is chromatic movement. The pitches relate clearly to the instrumental parts. Sunrise encompasses a moderate mezzo-soprano range: B - e'. Some meter chages and a few tempo changes occur. The quarter note is the unit except for two 6/8 bars.

227. IVES, Charles. Vote for Names. New York: Peer International, 1968.

Text: Charles Edward Ives.
Instrumentation: Voice, Piano (3).
Composed: 1912.

Of three pages the first is spoken and the others sung with some glissando and a "tremble." Few pitches are doubled, but Piano II plays the same chord (E, G, B, d, f#, a#, eb') continuously from beginning to end. The general tempo marking is "freely;" a secific indication to the singer is "free - singing words without bar lines: without reference to piano (no meter)." The vocal part is written with no bar lines while the pianos are in 9/16.

228. IVEY, Jean Eichelberger. Solstice New York: Carl Fischer, 1978.

At half-past night
There is the desert night
We have marked every day

Text: by the Composer.
Instrumentation: Soprano, Flute (Piccolo), Percussion, Piano.
Duration: ca. 15 Minutes.
Commissioned by Sigma Alpha Iota.

The composer notes "the score has been laid out so that each player can perform from the full score, rather than from a separate part, to facilitate coordination with the voice. Each player should have his own copy of the score." The vocal part includes some wide intervals, but remains within a moderate range. Entrance pitches usually relate to an instrumental part by a unison or a consonant interval. Frequently doublings of isolated pitches occur. The tempo and meter remain fairly constant within each piece. In one short section the percussion and voice move in an uneven accelerando, but end together at a specified point in the voice as the flute begins.

229. IVEY, Jean Eichelberger. _Terminus_. New York: Carl Fischer, 1972.

It is time
Fancy departs
As the bird
Time, it is time

Text: Ralph Waldo Emerson (abridged and adapted)
Andrew Marvel (fragments).
Instrumentation: Mezzo-Soprano, Two Channel Tape.
Duration: 9 Minutes, 45 Seconds.

The composer suggests that a stopwatch be used for practice, but states that it is "not necessary to syncronize with precise events on tape throughout." Quarter note always equals 60. Few tape cues exist, and those are mostly words rather than pitch cues. _Terminus_ requires some singing in chest tone, but generally does not exploit either extreme of the range.

230. IVEY, Jean Eichelberger. _Three Songs of Night_. New York: Carl Fischer, 1973.

1. The Astronomer (Walt Whitman)
2. I dreamed of Sappho (Richard Hovey)
3. Heraclitus (Callimachus, translated by William Cory)

Instrumentation: Soprano, Alto Flute, Clarinet, Viola, Cello, Piano, Tape.
Duration: ca. 15 Minutes.

The following appears in the performance notes at the beginning: "The tape does not play continuously but is turned on and off as indicated.... Although close synchronization with specific events on the tape is not called for...careful attention must be paid to _metronome markings_ and _note durations_ throughout all sections where the tape and the live performers play together." The pitches of the vocal line relate closely to the instrumental parts, often with doublings of isolated pitches. In some sections the meter changes frequently. Performance materials including tape are available on rental.

231. JAMES, Thomas S. <u>Four Poems of Michael Fried</u>. Hillsdale, New York: Boelke-Bomart, 1975.

1. Falling Asleep
2. (no title, instrumental)
3. Your Voice
4. The Black Snag...
5. (no title, instrumental)
6. The Flash of Lightning

Instrumentation: Soprano, Flute, Clarinet, Bass Clarinet, Violin, Viola, Cello.
Duration: ca. 6 Minutes.

Sparse scoring predominates. Isolated small value notes occur on various small subdivisions of the beats. All instrumental parts contain large leaps and isolated short notes which generate a continuous pattern when viewed in combination with short notes in other parts. The voice part is usually more connected but contains rhythmic figures modified by ties and dots, e.g.

The composer specifes some extremes and fast changes in dynamics. Tempo and meter remain fairly constant throughout each piece. The angular vocal part contains rare doublings by the instruments. Entrances often relate to the instruments by a half or whole step but displaced by an octave or two.

232. JENKINS, Joseph Willcox. <u>Three Carols from the Quiet Wars</u>. Ann Arbor, MI: University Microfilms, 1968.

Preface
Carol of a Bride
Carol of a Father
Carol of a Nun
Epilogue

Text: Samuel Hazo, from <u>The Quiet Wars</u>.
Instrumentation: Mezzo-Soprano, String Quartet, Piano.
Composed: 1964.
Dedication: "to Margaret, my beloved wife."

Vocal entrance pitches often appear in the instrumental parts. Some doublings of phrases or partial phrases occur. The vocal line lies generally low within a moderate range. Tempo and meter shift some within each movement. Sometimes the meter changes frequently. The composer lists the difficulty as "college: difficult - moderately difficult.

233. JENNI, Donald. Get Hence Foule Griefe. New York: American Composers Alliance, n.d.

Text: Sir Philip Sidney.
Instrumentation: Tenor, Harp.

Score not available for review.

234. JOHNSTON, Ben. Five Fragments Northampton, MA: Smith Publications, 1975.

Text: Thoreau, from Walden.
Instrumentation: Medium Voice, Oboe, Cello, Bassoon.

The score includes a description of Ben Johnston's microtonal music pitch notation and usage and pages of adjusted fingerings for oboe and bassoon. All instruments play in microtones. The piece is divided into several sections with voice and one instrument in most. The first is an unmetered section for unaccompanied voice, and the last is for full ensemble. Doublings of pitches occur infrequently in the angular vocal line. Pitch references are remote, with the added problems of microtones. Range: Fx+ - g#'.

235. JOHNSTON, Ben. A Sea Dirge Northampton, MA: Smith Publications, 1974.

Text: Shakespeare.
Instrumentation: Mezzo-Soprano, Flute, Violin, Oboe.

Specific instructions describe "pitch notation and usage" (discussion of use of just intonation). The extensive notes before the piece also include specific instructions and diagrams for fingering adjustments necessary for the flute and oboe players. The vocal pitches directly relate to the instrumental parts. Range: d#+ - g+'.

236. JOHNSTON, Ben. Three Chinese Lyrics. New York: Independent Music Publishers, 1955.

The jewel stairs' grievance
Taking leave of a friend
Lament of the frontier guard

Text: Ezra Pound.
Instrumentation: Soprano, Violin (2).

Score not available for review.

237. KAM, Dennis. Nocturnes. Hamilton, OH: Composers Autograph Publications, n.d.

Instrumentation: Female Voice, Flute, Violin, Guitar.

Score not available for review.

238. KARLINS, M. William. Four Inventions and a Fugue. York: York: American Composers Alliance, n.d.

Text: James Joyce, from Chamber Music.
Instrumentation: Alto, Bassoon, Piano.
Composed: 1962.
Dedication: Maurice Pachman.

Instructions state that "the voice may be omitted and an optional movement used instead." If used, the voice participates in "Invention #4, only. The tempo and meter change fairly frequently. Little doubling of the voice occurs, but consonant intervals are prominent.

239. KARLINS, M. William. Quartet. New York: American Composers Alliance, n.d.

Text: James Joyce.
Instrumentation: Soprano, String Quartet.

Score not available for review.

240. KARLINS, M. William. Songs for Soprano. New York: American Composers Allinace, n.d.

Text: William Blake.
Instrumentation: Soprano, Alto Flute, Cello.

The vocal line is sometimes angular, but includes short sections of repeated notes. Little doubling of pitches occurs; the relationship of a half tone between voice and instruments is common. The soprano part extends to c#''. The tempo and meter change fairly frequently.

241. KARLINS. M. William. Three Songs. Champaign, IL: Media Press, 1971.

1. Once
2. Chimes
3. Oak Trees

Text: Martha K. Graham.
Instrumentaion: Soprano, Flute, Piano.
Dedication: Martha and Marcha Graham.
Duration: ca. 4 Minutes, 30 Seconds.

The angular vocal line includes some Sprechstimme. Though large intervals are common, the piece does not exploit the extremes of the vocal range. Entrance pitches are sometimes sounded in the immediately previous instrumental material. The tempo and meter change fairly frequently.

242. KARLINS, William. Three Songs from 16th and 17th Century Poems. New York: American Composers Alliance, n.d.

I. Blame not my Lute (Sir Thomas Wyatt)
II. Golden Slumbers kiss your eyes (Thomas Dekker)
III. To the virgins to make much of time (Robert Herrick)

Instrumentation: Soprano, Flute, Violin (Viola), Cello.
Dedication: for The Lydian Chamber Ensemble.
Composed: 1961.

The voice moves mostly in steps, small leaps and triadic figures. Entrance pitches relate clearly to prevoius instrumental material; doubling is frequent. The vocal part remains mostly within the five lines of the treble staff, but extends from A to ab'. Few tempo and meter changes occur within each of the three pieces.

243. KAUDER, Hugo. Song from "Dierdre." New York: Seesaw Music, 1974.

Text: W.B. Yeats.
Instrumentation: Voice, Flute, Harp.

The entire piece is unmetered with no tempo markings. The vocal line generally lies within a moderately low range, A - c', and moves mostly by steps and small leaps. Vocal pitches clearly relate to the instrumental parts; much doubling occurs.

244. KAUDER, Hugo. Two Songs. New York: Seesaw Music, 1074,

Aleel's Song (from The Countess Cathleen).
Who Goes with Fergus?

Text: W.B. Yeats.
Instrumentation: Voice, Horn in F, Harp.

The vocal line moves mostly by steps and small skips within a small range (c - d'). Entrance pitches relate to the horn by unison or small interval. There are no tempo or meter indications, also no complex rhythmic figures.

245. KAVANAUGH, Patrick. *Jubal*. New York: Carl Fischer, 1978.

Text: The *Bible* (taken from 32 different passages from the *Bible*, using three separate translations, and assembled by the composer).
Instrumentation: Self-accompanied Soprano (or Tenor) (Accompanying instruments needed: Violin, Harpsichord, Piano, Harp, Percussion).

Throughout the piece the singer moves about the stage among the instruments in a prescribed manner playing them at the appropriate times. Most of the time she/he performs the vocal and instrumental parts simultaneously. To indicate approximation of pitches, the composer uses curved, straight and directional lines, and . Occasionally he indicates specific pitches.

246. KIM, Earl. *Earthlight*. Hillsdale, NY: Mobart Music, 1978.

Text: Samuel Beckett, from *Cascando*, *Endgame*, *Malone Dies*, *Play*, *Waiting for Godot*, *Watt*, *Words and Music*, and *The Unnamable*.
Instrumentation: High Soprano, Violin con sordini, Piano, Lights.
Composed: 1973.
For the Serge Koussevitzky Music Foundation in the Library of Congress and dedicated to the memory of Serge and Natalie Koussevitzky.

Performance notes state that a lighting cue sheet is available on request. Other performance notes, in this printed edition, are brief. No clef indications appear. The piano part is sometimes written on one staff and sometimes on two. If it is assumed that the soprano line is written in the treble clef, she must have a very high range: to a''. Assuming that the violin part is written in the same clef, some doubling and third relationships occur. The vocal part also includes some spoken and some unaccompanied parts. The violinist needs a variety of mutes. A diagram specifies the placement of performers at sixteen feet apart in an equilateral triangle.

247. KOLB, Barbara. *Chanson Bas*. New York: Carl Fischer, 1972.

1. Le Cantonnier
2. La Femme del'ouvrier
3. Le Marchand d'ail et d'oignons
4. Le Vitrier
5. Le Crieur d'imprimés
6. Instrumental Ensemble
7. La Marchande d'habits

Text: Stéphane Mallarmé.
Instrumentaion: Lyric Soprano, Harp, Percussion (2).
Composed: 1966.
Duration: ca. 6 Minutes, 30 Seconds.

Vocal pitch reference is remote at best; little doubling occurs. Groups of grace notes in angular relationship and a vocal tremolo require special consideration. Tuned percussion parts as well as the voice, must contend with approximate pitches. In some songs the meter changes frequently. In many places Kolb requires very specific dynamic shadings, including having the voice fade to ppp or niente several times. Performance parts for harp and percussion are available for sale through the Carl Fischer rental department.

248. KOLB, Barbara. Songs Before an Adieu. New York: Boosey and Hawkes, 1979.

1. The Sentences (Robert Pinsky)
2. now i lay (e e cummings)
3. Cantata (Howard Stern)
4. Gluttonous Smoke (Vasko Popa)
5. L'Adieu (Guillaume Appollinaire)

Instrumentation: Soprano, Flute (Alto Flute), Guitar.
Duration: ca. 18 Minutes.
Commissioned by WFMT, Chicago.
Dedication: Rosalind Rees and David Starobin.

The composer provides program notes and gives special performance notes for two of the pieces. Some parts are metered, some indicated in seconds, and some free. In #3 the ensemble is not coordinated exactly, but performers are to arrive at specific points together. Occasionally the instruments double vocal pitches, but half tone, and sometimes whole tone, relationships are more frequent. The guitarist becomes the speaker in #4.

249. KUPPFERMAN, Meyer. The Conceptual Wheel. Hastings-on-Hudson: General Music Publishing, 1978.

I. Psalm IV
II. Some Old Men
III. Coiffure

Text: Michael Benedikt.
Instrumentation: Soprano, Clarinet, Piano.

In numbers I and II the movement of the vocal line is somewhat angular, but with few large leaps. In number III the vocal line moves mostly in steps and small leaps. It lies on and above the treble staff - up to b'. The pitches relate to the instrumental parts, but with little doubling.

The vocal part includes much syncopation. Some meter changes occur in all movements.

250. LANG, Morris. Three Puerto Rican Songs. New York: Lang Percussion, 1975.

I. Morning
II. Cielo Marinero (Afternoon)
III. Evening

Instrumentation: Soprano, Percussion (5).
Dedication: Pepe and Margo LaO.

The composer states, "The soprano may start the songs on any pitch that is comfortable. The relationship between the notes must be as written." The vocal line moves mostly in steps and small leaps. In number I, in addition to singing, the soprano reads poetry while the percussionists repeat a two-bar vamp. The following instructions appear for number III: "Each instrument continues its pattern at its own tempo throughout the whole song.... After the voice finishes the whole ensemble fades to nothing." The tempo remains constant throughout the other two songs. The meter is constant in number II, but changes frequently in number I.

251. LEICHTLING, Alan. Psalm 37, Op. 39. New York: Seesaw Music, 1969.

I. 1. Fret not
2. Trust
3. Commit thyself
4. Resign thyself
5. The Lord Knoweth
II. 6. The wicked
7. The wicked borroweth
8. I have seen
9. The wicked watcheth
10. For the wicked
III. 11. And yet
12. It is
13. Wait
14. Mark the man
15. I have been

Instrumentation: Mezzo-Soprano, Harp, Piano (Celesta), Percussion (4), Violin (2), Viola, Cello.
Duration: ca. 15-16 Minutes.
Dedication: Anita Terzian.

The vocal part is angular, but the intervals are not especially large and some repeated notes appear. Except for a few short low sections, the range is moderate. The instruments double the vocal line infrequently. Numbers 9 and

14 are set for unaccompanied voice. The meter changes frequently and tempo fluctuations are common. Introductory notes state that the piece is built on two 12 tone rows.

252. LEICHTLING, Alan. Rubáiyát Fragments, Op. 55. New York: Seesaw Music, 1971.

1. Prelude a tre
2. Quatrain VIII
3. Quatrain X
4. Quatrain XIX
5. Quatrain XX
6. Interlude a tre
7. Quatrain XXVII
8. Quatrain XXIX
9. Quatrain XXXII
10. Quatrain XVIII
11. Postlude a tre

Text: Derived from Edward Fitzgerald's translation of The Rubáiyát of Omar Khayyám.
Instrumentation: Baritone, Clarinet, French Horn, Piano.
Duration: ca. 13 1/2 Minutes.
Dedication: John and Helen Derminaro, John Moses and Bob Benton.

The vocal line is somewhat angular, but does not contain large intervals and does not exploit the extremes of the range. Pitch reference is remote, with few doublings by the instruments. Many of the pieces are scored for less than the full ensemble: duets and trios. This is based principally, but not strictly on four 12 tone rows.

253. LEICHTLING, Alan. Three Songs by Emily Dickinson. New York: Seesaw Music, n.d.

Instrumentation: Baritone, Cello.

Score not available for review.

254. LEICHTLING, Alan. Trial and Death of Socrates. New York: Seesaw Music, n.d.

Instrumentation: Male Voice, Clarinet, Flute, Harp.

Score not available for review.

255. LEICHTLING, Alan. Two Proverbs, Op. 43. New York: Seesaw Music, 1969.

I. Proverbs 2:19-20
II. Proverbs 1:7-9

Instrumentation: Mezzo-Soprano, Piccolo Clarinet in Eb, Clarinet in A, Bass Clarinet.
Duration: ca. 5 Minutes, 30 Seconds.
Dedication: Anita Terzian.

Though the vocal range is mostly moderate, one extended low passage does appear. Entrance pitches usually relate to the previous instrumental material by a small interval, but little doubling occurs. The meter changes in almost every bar.

256. LERDAHL, Fred. Eros: Variations for Mezzo-Soprano and Chamber Ensemble. Hillsdale, N.Y.: Mobart Music Publications, 1978.

Text: Ezra Pound, "Coitus" from Lustra, 1915.
Instrumentation: Mezzo-Soprano, Alto Flute, Viola, Electric Guitar, Electric Bass Guitar, Harp, Electric Piano, Percussion (2).
Duration: ca. 23 Minutes.
Commissioned by the Koussevitzky Music Foundation.
In 21 Movements.

The poem is used in its entirety in numbers I, IV, and XII. Numbers X and XVI are purely instrumental. All other movements use fragments of the poem, the words of the poem in rearranged order, or repetitions of several words. The angular vocal part lies very low and approaches upper notes by large leaps. Often the scoring indicates a duet between the alto flute and the voice accompanied by the other instruments. The meter remains constant within each movement. Grace notes and rhythmic irregularities are prominent.

257. LERDAHL, Fred. Wake. Hillsdale, N.Y.: Mobart Music, n.d.

Text: Arranged from Book I, Chapter 8 of Finnegan's Wake.
Instrumentation: Soprano, Violin, Viola, Cello, Harp, Percussion (3).
Composed: 1967-68.

Although occassional doublings occur, the relationship between the voice and instruments is mostly dissonant. Half or whole tones are most frequent. The angular vocal line encompasses a wide range (G - c''). Some tempo and meter changes occur. All parts contain complex rhythmic figures which are interspersed with small value rests.

258. LESSARD, John. _Five Poems by Robert Herrick_. New York: American Composers Alliance, 1957.

I. Sappho
II. To the Virgins to Make Much of Time
III. Jack and Jill
IV. To Diamene
V. A Psalme of Hymne to the Graces

Instrumentation: Voice, Violin, Piano.
Dedication: Mrs. Justine Ward.

The vocal line includes mostly small intervals, especially chromatic movement. Entrance pitches usually appear in the previous instrumental material and doubling is frequent. The range is moderate, but fairly low (Bb - e'). The tempo and meter are fairly constant throughout each piece.

259. LEVI, Paul Alan. _The Truth_. New York: American Composers Alliance, n.d.

Instrumentation: Soprano, Flute, Clarinet, Bassoon, Harpsichord, Piano, Solo Cello, Violin (3), Viola, Cello (2).
Composed: 1975.

Vocal entrance pitches generally relate to the previous instrumental material by a small interval or the same note. Some doubling of pitches occurs, but a half tone relationship is just as common. The vocal range is mostly moderate but requires leger line b flat on the top. The meter changes frequently. The seating plan specifies a conductor.

260. LEWIS, Peter Tod. _Song_. New York: American Composers Alliance, 1968.

Instrumentation: Voice, String Trio.
Composed: 1961.

The angular vocal line contains wide leaps and covers a wide range (B - d''). Pitch references are remote at best; few doublings occur. The strings sometimes move in similar rhythms, but diverse rhythmic figures are more common.

261. LOMON, Ruth _Five Songs after Poems by William Blake_. Washington D.C.: Arsis Press, 1980.

1. The Sunflower
2. The Fly
3. The Sick Rose
4. The Clod and the Pebble
5. Injunction

Text: William Blake. The first four are complete poems from _Songs of Experience_ and the fifth is taken from Blake's _Satiric Verses and Epigrams_.
Instrumentation: Contralto, Viola.

The angular vocal part contains many half tone relationships with the viola and many chromatic alterations. Entrance pitches usually do not relate by a consonant interval. The vocal range includes G# - e'. The tempo and meter remain constant within each piece except for a few meter changes. The first two pieces begin with solo voice.

262. LOMBARDO, Robert. _Frosted Window: Variations on White_. New York: American Composers Alliance, n.d.

Text: Kathleen Lombardo.
Instrumentation: Soprano, Bassoon, Viola, Percussion.
Composed: 1975.
Dedication: The composer's daughter Andreana, and his favorite Bassoonist, Joe Urbinato.

The angular vocal line contains wide intervals but does not exploit the extremes of the range. Entrance pitches sometimes relate to the previous instrumental material by a small or consonant interval. More often, however, this relationship is remote. Doubling is not frequent. The score specifies some humming and spoken parts. Some meter changes and frequent tempo changes occur.

263. LORA, Antonio. _At Sunset Time_. New York: American Composers Alliance, n.d.

Text: P.L. Dunbar.
Instrumentation: Mezzo-Soprano, String Quartet.

Score not available for review.

264. LUENING, Otto. _The Soundless Song_. New York: Composers Facsimile Edition, 1954.

Grave, e molto rubato
Moonlight
String Quartet
The Silent Voice
Flute and Clarinette
The Soundless Song

Instrumentation: Soprano, String Quartet, Flute, Clarinet, Piano.

The singer participates in numbers 2, 4, and 6. In numbers 2 and 4 the meter changes frequently, nearly every bar. The vocal part lies mostly within the confines of the treble staff. Pitches often relate by a whole tone to at least one of the piano notes, but very little doubling occurs. Number 6 begins with recitative accompanied by piano. Later the full ensemble joins and the flute doubles the voice.

265. LUENING, Otto. Suite for Soprano and Flute. New York: Galaxy Music Corp., 197-.

Text: Phonetic syllables.
Instrumentation: Soprano, Flute.
Composed: 1936-37.

The vocal line covers a wide range (G - c'') and is generally lyric. It contains much chromatic movement, glissandi and trills. The tempo and meter remain fairly constant within each piece and rhythmic figures are not complex. A note states that "this composition may be performed by any other instrument with the proper range."

266. LYBBERT, Donald. Leopardi Canti. New York: American Composers Alliance, 1959.

I. L'infinito
II. Il passero solitario
III. Il tramonto della luna

Instrumentation: Soprano, Flute, Viola, Bass Clarinet.
Duration: 15 Minutes.

Though the vocal part lies mostly within a moderate range, some small sections lie fairly high and some large intervals are present. Little doubling of vocal pitches occurs: half-tone relationships are most common. Meter changes occur frequently. The sound is tossed back and forth between instruments with many small-value notes and rests.

267. LYBBERT, Donald. Lines for The Fallen. New York: C.F. Peters, 1969.

Text: Adapted from William Blake and the "Mass for the Dead."
Instrumentation: Soprano, Piano (2).
Duration: 8 Minutes.
Dedication: Phyllis Bryn-Julson.

Piano II must be tuned a quarter-tone lower than piano I. The soprano tunes to piano I. Specific symbols indicate raising or lowering a pitch by a quarter tone. This piece does make demands on the extremes of the range (G - e'') The following appears in the introductory material: "The note values and rests are only relatively proportional. Their length will be determined by the performer's interpretation." Non-traditional dynamic indications are used.

268. McBRIDE, Robert. Commentary. New York: American Composers Alliance, n.d.

Instrumentation: Tenor, Trumpet (2), Trombone (2), Piano, Contrabass, Drums, Synthesizer.

Score not available for review.

269. McBRIDE, Robert. Nonsense Syllables. New York: American Composers Alliance, n.d.

Instrumentation: Soprano, Flute.

Score not available for review.

270. McBRIDE, Robert. Vocalise. New York: American Composers Alliance, n.d.

Instrumentation: Soprano, Flute, Piano.

Score not available for review.

271. McBRIDE, Robert. Vocalise No. 3 On Nonsense Syllables. New York: American Composers Alliance, n.d.

Instrumentation: Tenor, Piano, Double Bass, Drums.

Score not available for review.

272. McNIEL, Jan Pfschner. Three Preludes To The Aureate Earth. New York: Carl Fischer, 1975.

I. Furiously (One Thing Is Certain)
II. Languidly ('Tis All a Chequer-Board)
III. Lyrically (The Aureate Earth)

Text: From the Rubáiyát of Omar Khayyám, translation by Edward Fitzgerald. Last two lines by the composer.
Instrumentation: Soprano, Six unspecified instruments.
Duration: I. ca. 5 Minutes; II. ca. 5 1/2 Minutes; III. ca. 6 Minutes.

Each movement is designed with 21 - 24 boxes, called fields, which contain material to be performed or directional information. The composer gives the following instructions: "Begin in any field (cell) and proceed to any adjacent field. Proceed in a predominantly vertical or horizontal direction. Once reaching a field of silence (indicated by an arrow) direction may be continued or changed in the direction of the arrow." Three Preludes is published with a score and six parts. According to the stage placement diagram each instrument faces a different direction. The instructions specifically indicate who begins a movement, who ends it and how the soprano's movement around the stage coordinates the ensemble. Materials for the soprano contain a wide variety: sung, spoken, whispered, hum, wide trill, slow trill, etc.

273. MAMLOCK, Ursula. Five Songs. New York: Composers Facsimile Edition, 1973.

I. In a sustained mood
II. Majestic
III. Very airy
IV. In a melancholy mood
V. Still with Utmost simplicity

Text: Rabindranath Tagaree, "Aphorisms" from Stray Birds.
Instrumentation: Soprano, Flute, Cello.
Composed: 1963.
Dedication: To the memory of John F. Kennedy.

The angular vocal line includes large intervals, and pitches most often relate to the instruments by 1/2 tones. Little doubling, even of isolated pitches, occurs. Some short sections are unaccompanied. Irregular subdivisions of beats and other diverse rhythmic figures are superimposed. Many grace notes and groups of grace notes (to be played as fast as possible) appear in the instrumental parts.

274. MATTHEWS, William. Paysage. New York: American Composers Alliance, 1980.

Text: Charles Baudelair.
Instrumentation: Soprano, Flute, Clarinet, Cello, Piano, Percussion.

Text is set in French with English translation. Score not available for review.

275. MAYER, William. Barbara -- what have you done? New York: Carl Fischer, 1968.

Text: Susan Otto.
Instrumentation: Soprano (2), Piano.
Dedication: Ray Lev.

Both voices lie within a moderate range. The piano often doubles vocal phrases or parts of phrases. There are few changes in tempo and meter, and no complex rhythmic figures. This may also be performed by women's chorus (SS).

276. MAYER, William, Eight Miniatures. Bryn Mawr, PA: Theodore Presser, 1978.

1. Outrageous Love (W.M.)
2. Deeply Down (Elizabeth Aleinikoff)
3. Land of Dead Dreams (Alfred Noyes)
4. Fireworks: Syllables and Sounds (W.M.)
5. Prophetic Soul (Dorothy Parker)
6. Isn't There some Mistake? (W.M.)
7. "...for no man" (W.M.)
8. Résumé (Dorothy Parker)

Instrumentation: Soprano, Flute (Piccolo), Trumpet in C, Violin, Cello, Percussion, Piano, Harmonium (or Melodica).
Duration: ca. 6 Minutes.
First Performed: 1968.
Commissioned by the Contemporary Music Society.
Dedication: Catherine Rowe.

Most of the vocal line is doubled in turn by the various instruments. Some parts are spoken, half sung or whispered. Interpretive suggestions include "morosely" and "overly caressed." The tempo remains fairly constant within each movement, but some meter changes occur. The score specifies a conductor.

277. MAYER, William. Two News Items. Bryn Mawr, PA: Theodore Presser, 1978.

News Item No. 1: "Hastily Formed Contemporary Music Ensemble Reveals Origins"
News Item 2: "Distraught Soprano Undergoes Unfortunate Transformation"

Text: William Mayer.
Instrumentation: Soprano, Flute (Piccolo), Trumpet in C, Violin, Cello, Percussion, Piano.
Duration: ca. 4 Minutes.
Dedication: Jack Kreiselman.

The angular vocal line contains many rests. Doubling of pitches is frequent; a single instrument may double a whole phrase or various instruments may alternate in the doubling. In addition to singing the soprano also must speak and do some acting. The second piece lies mostly at the top of the treble staff. The following note appears:

> "Despite numerous jazz sounds from ensemble (along with hymns and orientalisms), the singer remains imperturbably 'avant.' She must exaggerate (rhapsodic gestures and expressions, over-enunciation) to a point of preciosity, except for those few lapses when she reverts to a coarse jazz style."

The score implies the use of a conductor. Some tempo and meter changes occur.

278. MELBY, John. Due Canti di Leopardi. New York: American Composers Alliance, 1974.

1. L'infinito
2. A sè stesso

Instrumentation: Soprano (or Tenor), French Horn, Piano.
Composed: #1 in 1974; #2 in 1966.
Duration: ca. 6 Minutes, 15 Seconds.

The fairly angular vocal line lies within a moderate range. Some doubling occurs, but the voice often relates to the instruments by a half tone. The piece includes irregular subdivisions of beats and superimpositions of non-similar rhythmic figures.

279. MELBY, John. The Men that Are Falling. New York: American Composers Alliance, n.d.

Text: Wallace Stevens.
Instrumentation: Soprano, Piano, Computer-synthesized tape.
Composed: 1978.
Duration: 10 Minutes, 50 Seconds.
Composed under the auspicies of a grant from the National Endowment for the Arts.
Dedication: Phyllis Bryn-Julson and Donald Sutherland.

The vocal part is angular and includes some Sprechstimme. Pitch reference is remote, but no demands are made on the extremes of the range. Irregular subdivisions of beats and the superimposition of non-similar rhythmic figures are frequent. Both performers must have a stopwatch. Performance instructions are noted throughout the piece.

280. MELBY, John. Two Stevens Songs. New York: American Composers Alliance, 1975.

1. A Postcard from the Volcano
2. Domination of Black

Text: Wallace Stevens.
Instrumentation: Soprano, Computer-Synthesized Tape.
Duration: 9 Minutes, 43 Seconds.
Dedication: Phyllis Bryn-Julson.

The angular vocal line encompasses a range of B - bb'. The composer states that "most of the music in the tape part is written out in the score." He warns, however, that "due to the richness of the harmonic spectra on some of the notes, the pitches of these notes may be either partially or almost totally obscured. In such cases, the composer has attempted to provide other notations...." The songs include some changing of tempo and meter and irregular subdivisions of beats. The tape is available from American Composers Alliance.

281. MELBY, John. Valedictory. New York: American Composers Alliance, 1973.

Text: L.E. Kramer.
Instrumentation: Soprano, Tape.
Duration: 16 Minutes, 11 Seconds.

Most pitches indicated on the tape reduction are well over an octave away from the vocal part. The vocal line encompasses a range of A - c'', but lies mostly within a moderate range. Some spoken parts and sprechstimme are required. The tape includes a pre-recorded speaking voice as well as computer-synthesized sounds. Meter changes and irregular subdivisions of beats occur frequently.

282. MESTRES-QUADRENY, Joseph Maria. Invecions Movils II. New York: Seesaw Music, 1973.

Instrumentation: Voice, Trumpet, Electric Guitar.
Composed: 1960-61.

Invecions Movils II may be performed simultaneously with Invecions Movils I (flute, clarinet, piano) and # III (string quartet) as a chamber ensemble. It is printed in a large score with each part on one page. The instructions specify that the piece should be repeated four times at four different (given) tempi with various arrangements of the instrumentation. The composer states the following:

"The scores are written in measures of six half-notes and subdivided by a line of points into two measures ...for easier reading.

"At each measure a choice has to be made between two possibilities offered.

"The different sizes of notes indicate their relative loudness."

283. MILLER, Edward Jay. Bashō Songs. New York: Music for Percussion, 1967.

Part One: Liberamente
Part Two: Fast and Light

Text: Matsuo Bashō, English translation by Harold G. Henderson.
Instrumentation: Soprano, Percussion (3).
Dedication: Phi Mu Alpha Sinfonia (Zeta Omega Chapter), 1961.

The first movement begins with an unmeasured duet for soprano and maraca. In the second movement the singer performs several lines with "mouth closed." Ensemble problems arise from frequent meter changes and irregular and unmatched subdivisions of beats. Pitch reference is not impossible, but is sometimes obscured by the density of sound and the rhythmic complexity. The range is fairly wide: Bb - b'. Each of the two parts contains three verses of haiku. The final verse is set in pentatonic.

284. MILLER, Edward. *Mists and Waters*. New York: American Composers Alliance, n.d.

Text: Denise Levertov.
Instrumentation: Soprano, Volin, Clarinet, Piano, Percussion.

Score not available for review.

285. MOLINEUX, Allen. *Chrystals*. Huntington, NY: HaMar Percussion Publicaions, 1975.

I. ♩ = 48
II. ♩ = 50
III. ♩ = 60
IV. ♩ = 48

Text: Kathleen Geminder.
Instrumentation: Mezzo-Soprano, Percussion (3).

The vocal line consists mainly of half steps and whole steps, leaps of 7ths and 9ths or octave displacements. Often the pitch reference is obscure: sometimes only the timpani plays and sometimes the percussionists play thick clusters. The singer performs a section of hand clapping and plays the maracas, but never at the same time as singing. The ensemble problems include changing meter (sometimes every measure), irregular accents and irregular subdivisions of beats simultaneously and/or consecutively. The entire work is measured except for a section in movement IV which is indicated "Approximately 20"." The stage layout diagram specifies a conductor.

286. MOLLICONE, Henry. *Kyrie Eleison*. New York: American Composers Alliance, n.d.

Instrumentation: Soprano, Trombone.

Score not available for review.

287. MOLLICONE, Henry. *Murali*. New York: American Composers Alliance, n.d.

Text: Michaelangelo.
Instrumentation: Mezzo-Soprano, Harp, French Horn, Percussion (2).

Score not available for review.

288. MOLLICONE, Henry. *Two Love Songs*. New York: American Composers Alliance, n.d.

Text: Constable, Patchen.
Instrumentation: Tenor, Viola.

Score not available for review.

289. MONOD, Jacques-Louis. *Chamber Aria*. Hillsdale, New York: Boelke-Bomart, 1973.

Text: Paul Eluard.
Instrumentation: Voice, Flute, Oboe, Clarinet, Bassoon, Trumpet, French Horn, Piano.
Duration: 5 Minutes.
Composed: 1950; Revised, 1972.
Dedication: Bethany Beardslee.

Instrumental parts sometimes double the soprano part, but relationships of a major or minor third occur more frequently. A wide vocal range exploits the extremities (especially the upper extreme): G# - c''. The meter and tempo change frequently. Irregular subdivisions are common: 2/4 ♩. ♩. (5), and 5/16 ♪♩♪ (3).

290. MONOD, Jacques-Loius. *Passacaille*. New York: New Music, 1952.

Text: René Char and Paul Eluard, set in French.
Instrumentation: Soprano, Flute, Oboe, Clarinet, Bassoon, Trumpet, French Horn, Piano.
Dedication: Bethany Beardslee.

The meter and tempo change constantly. Irregular subdivisions of beats, e.g., 2/4 ♩. ♩. (5), are prominant.

A conductor is not specified in the score. Much dissonance occurs, frequently with 1/2 tone relationships between the voice and other instruments. The vocal line is angular, very irregular and requires a wide range: G# - c''.

291. MOORE, Douglas. <u>The Ballad of William Sycamore</u>. New York: King's Crown Music Press, 1974.

Text: Stephen Vincent Benet.
Instrumentation: Bass, Flute, Trombone, Piano.

Few tempo and meter changes occur. The trombone player needs a waw mute and a cup mute. The insrtuments frequently double the pitches of the lyric vocal line. The range is modest: AA - d#.

292. MOORE, Dorothy R. <u>From the Dark Tower</u>. New York: American Composers Alliance, n.d.

Instrumentation: Mezzo-Soprano, Cello, Piano.

Score not available for review.

293. MOORE, Dorothy R. <u>Songs</u>. New York: American Composers Alliance, n.d.

Text: Rubáiyát.
Instrumentation: Mezzo-Soprano, Oboe.

Score not available for review.

294. MOORE, Dorothy R. <u>Weary Blues</u>. New York: American Composers Alliance, n.d.

Text: Langston Hughes.
Instrumentation: Baritone, Cello, Oboe.

Score not available for review.

295. MORTON, David. <u>Tears, Idle Tears</u>. Ross, CA: Harp Publications, 1974.

Text: Alfred Lord Tennyson.
Instrumentation: Soprano, Oboe, Harp.

The tempo remains fairly constant while some meter shifting occurs. The key signatures change several times. The vocal line moves mostly in steps and small leaps. Pitches are doubled in the harmonic structure of the instrumental parts. <u>Tears</u> is published with a score and two parts.

296. MORYL, Richard. Corridors. New York: American Composers Alliance, n.d.

Instrumentation: Medium Voice, Percussion.

Score not available for review.

297. MORYL, Richard. Das Lied. n.p.: Joshua, 1976.

In erwartung des Freundes (Mong-Kao-Jen)
(Awaiting the Friend)
Der Abschied des Freundes (Wang-Wei)
(The Farewell of a Friend)

Text: Hans Bethge, translated from Die Chinesische Flöte.
Instrumentation: Soprano, Oboe, Amplified Contrabass, Amplified Piano, Percussion (2).
Dedication: American Artists Series.

The vocal line moves mostly by steps and small leaps and lies within a moderate range. Entrance pitches generally relate to the piano by a consonant interval: thirds and unisons are common. At the soprano's first entrance a note "whispering, dark and mysteriously" appears with instructions to "become involved dramatically with the audience." Dramatic impact seems most important at all times. The composer states that the notation is "'proportional' and does not always suggest a pulse or metric system." He does not expect the performance to be precise. A conductor may be used. The oboe plays into the piano, producing sympathetic vibrations.

298. MORYL, Richard. De morte contoris. Hastings-on-Hudson, NY: Joshua, 1974.

1. kyrie
2. dies irae
3. the castle bell
4. virgin mary
5. requiem (libera me)
6. o my god
7. the wild rose

Text: Numbers 3, 4, 6 & 7 - James Joyce.
Instrumentation: Soprano, Mezzo-Soprano, Oboe, Electric Piano, (Celesta), Percussion (2), Harp.

The anguar vocal line includes many grace notes but does not exploit the extremes of the range. Pitches relate closely to the instrumental parts and some doublings occur. Moryl also requires humming inside the piano, whistling and some spoken parts with pitch direction. He gives the following instructions:

"The notation used for the most part is 'Proportional,' and does not always suggest a pulse or metric system. The conductor should observe as closely as possible the 'apparent' spatial relationships in each system.... The changes in dynamics should be observed closely, and an attempt should be made to make the performance as dramatic as possible."

The voices, piano, harp and oboe should all be amplified. A long list of extra equipment is required for each performer.

299. MOSS, Lawrence. Unseen Leaves. New York: Carl Fischer, 1976.

Text: Walt Whitman, "Goodbye My Fancy" and "Song of Myself."
Instrumentation: Soprano, Oboe, Tapes (2), Slide Projections, Lights.
Duration: ca. 15 Minutes.
Composed under the auspices of a grant from the National Endowment for the Arts.

The composer divides the piece into small sections which he calls measures. Each measure is delineated by seconds indicated collectively from the beginning of the piece. A conductor coordinates the lights, projections, tape and live performers. The soprano produces many vocal and non-vocal sounds. Her duties include singing, mime, Sprechstimme, speaking, and imitation of the tape. She and the oboist move about the stage and offstage.

300. MOURANT, Walter. Two Songs. New York: American Composers Alliance, n.d.

Text: William Blake.
Instrumentation: Voice, Harp.
Composed: 1977.

The vocal line moves mostly by steps and small leaps and lies entirely on the treble staff. Pitches relate closely to the harp part. The tempo and meter remain constant in each movement.

301. MYERS, Gordon. A Mini-Song Cycle for Soprano and Flute. Little Neck, NY: Eastline Music Corp., 1968.

1. Encounter (Peggy Reese)
2. All (Peggy Reese)
3. Spring (Adris B. McElveen)
4. Just My Luck (Marsha Trotti)

5. Love Walked By Me (Betty Fryga)
6. One Day I Met (Betty Fryga)

Instrumentation: Soprano, Flute.
Dedication: Written for and dedicated to Barbara Harris.

The vocal line moves mostly by steps and small leaps and often in third relationship with the flute. Entrance pitches usually appear in the previous instrumental material and some doublings occur throughout the piece. The tempo and meter are constant within each of these six short pieces, and rhythmic figures are simple.

302. MYROW, Fredric. Four Songs In Spring. New York: Mills Music, 1960.

I. Wenn ich in Deine Augen seh
II. Im wunderschönen Monat Mai
III. Das macht den Menschen glücklich
IV. Am Leuchtenden Sommermorgen

Text: Vier Lieder Im Frühling from poems by Heinrich Heine, set in German.
Instrumentation: Soprano, Flute, Viola, Cello, (2).
Also published in a version for Soprano and Piano.

A footnote states: "These songs will generally require a conductor, who, whether seated or standing, should remain as inconspicuous as possible." The tempo remains constant throughout each movement, and few meter changes occur. The composer specifies much dynamic shading. The vocal line moves mostly in steps and small leaps. Vocal pitches relate closely to the other parts, but often with much dissonance. The parts sometimes fall into clusters.

303. MYROW, Fredric. Songs From the Japanese. New York: Mills Music, 1963.

At Twilight I. In the Blue Sky
II. Solo
III. Preface
Haiku I. ...(leaves)...
II. ... (wind)...
III. ... (memory)...

Instrumentation: Soprano, Flute, Clarinet, Percussion, Piano (Celesta), Violin, Viola, Cello, Contrabass.

The angular vocal line encompasses a range of Bb - d'' and includes a sustained b'. Some doublings of pitches occur, but more often the voice relates to the instruments by a half or whole tone. The meter changes frequently, but the tempo remains fairly constant within each piece. Irregular subdivisions of beats and small-value notes tied across beats are common.

304. NELHYBEL, Vaclav. Concerto Spirituoso No. 1. Valley Forge, PA: J. Christopher Music, 1976.

Text: Martin Luther.
"Christ lag in Todesbanden."
Instrumentation: Voice, Flute (12), Amplified Harpsichord (or Electric Piano).
Duration: ca. 15 Minutes.

See next entry. This piece is very similar to Concerto Spirituoso No. 2.

305. NELHYBEL, Vaclav. Concerto Spirituoso No. 2. Valley Forge, PA: J. Christopher Music, 1976.

Text: Martin Luther.
"Christ lag in Todesbanden."
Instrumentation: Voice, Saxophones (12), Amplified Harpsichord (and/or Electric Piano).
Duration: 15 Minutes.

The voice appears only at the beginning and is notated in the bass clef. Nelhybel prefers a bass-baritone or a dark alto as a second choice. The composer states that "thematic material...comprises the modality of 11th century plainsong, tonality of Bach's 18th century harmonic counterpoint, and chromaticism, used in contemporary aleatory manner." This is a set of variations on B-A-C-H and "Christ lag in Todesbanden."

306. NELHYBEL, Vaclav. The House that Jack Built. Hastings-on-Hudson, NY: General Music Publishing, 1972.

Instrumentation: Baritone, Piccolo, Clarinet, French Horn, Bassoon, Percussion (Xylophone), Harp.
Also arranged for voice and piano.

This is a thirteen verse accumulative song. Each verse adds a bit of text and then goes backwards through the content of the previous verses. The instruments frequently double the voice part - sometimes an entire line, sometimes isolated notes. The accompanying instruments often appear in rhythmic unison including much syncopation. The meter and tempo remain constant.

307. NEUMANN, Richard. Sephardic Kiddush. New York: Transcontinental Music Publications, 1975.

Instrumentation: Voice, Flute.

The voice moves mostly by steps and small leaps within a small range (e - e'). Entrance pitches relate to the previous instrumental material by small intervals or the same notes. This piece is set mostly as a dialog between the voice and the flute, but, when the two sound together, some doublings occur.

308. NOWAK, Lionel. Five Songs. New York: American Composers Alliance, n.d.

Text: Nemerov.
Instrumentation: Mezzo-Soprano, Cello, Piano.

Score not available for review.

309. NOWAK, Lionel. Maiden's Song. New York: American Composers Alliance, n.d.

Text: Gerard Manley Hopkins, from St. Winefred's Well.
Instrumentation: Soprano, Clarinet, Violin, Piano.
Composed: 1970.

A half-tone relationship between the voice and other parts is common, and doubling, even of isolated pitches, is infrequent. The vocal line contains some large intervals but most are a fifth or smaller. The composer gives the following instruction for a spoken part: "a recitation. The performer choses speech-pitch and nuance; rhythm given."

310. NOWAK, Lionel. Summer is Away. New York: American Composers Alliance, n.d.

Introduction
1. Not seeing, still we know
2. Too few the Mornings be
3. A Wind that rose
4. There is a solitude of space
5. Meeting by Accident
6. Had I not seen the Sun
7. Wild Nights
8. More than the Grave is closed to me
9. There comes a Warning
Conclusion

Text: Emily Dickinson.
Instrumentation: Low Voice, Flute, Clarinet, Bassoon, Cello, Piano.
Composed: 1976.

Vocal entrance pitches often relate to the previous instrumental material by a unison or small interval, but sometimes distantly. Little doubling of pitches occurs; the relationship of a half tone is common. The piece contains some large intervals, but does not exploit the extremes of the range (except for six beats of G in number four).

311. OLIVE, Joseph. Mar-ri-ia-a. New York: American Composers Alliance, n.d.

Text: Joan Olive.
Instrumentation: Soprano, Flute (Piccolo), Clarinet (Bass Clarinet), French Horn, Violin, Cello, Percussion, Four Channel Tape.
Written with the help of a grant from the National Endowment for the Arts.

The soprano line lies fairly high (many b' and bb') and contains many glissandi. Some parts are sung, some spoken, some whispered and some require Sprechstimme. Pitch reference is often remote. The meter changes frequently, sometimes in every bar.

312. ORGAD, Ben-Zion. Leave Out My Name. New York: Mercury Music, 1953.

Text: R. Tagore.
Instrumentation: Mezzo-Soprano, Flute.

Score not available for review.

313. ORLAND, Henry. Love and Pity. New York: Seesaw Music, 1970.

Text: Cecil Day Lewis.
Instrumentation: Voice, Clarinet, Viola.

The vocal line sometimes moves by steps and sometimes by large leaps, but remains within a moderate range. It often relates to the instruments by a half tone or whole tone, but rarely by unison. Few meter changes occur and the tempo remains constant throughout each piece.

314. ORREGO-SALAS, Juan. Garden Songs, Op. 47. New York: Peer International, 1977.

Praeludium; Allegro
Canti I; Semplice
Canti II; Agitato
Canti III; Piacevole
Canti IV; Tempo di Valse
Canti V; Tranquillo
Postludium; Allegro

Text: Carmen (the composer's wife).
Instrumentation: Soprano, Flute, Viola, Harp.

A cadenza connects each song to the next. All are instrumental except the last in which the voice appears as a vocalise. The vocal pitches lie mostly on and above the treble staff and relate closely to the instrumental parts. The meter changes at the beginning of each song but remains constant within each.

315. PARRIS, Robert. Dreams. New York: American Composers Alliance, n.d.

Text: Parker, Bogan, Cather.
Instrumentation: Soprano, Flute, Clarinet, Oboe, Double Bass, Violin, Cello, Piano, Celesta, Percussion.

Score not available for review.

316. PASATIERI, Thomas. Far from Love. New York: Belwin-Mills, 1976.

Text: Emily Dickinson.
Instrumentation: Soprano, Clarinet, Violin, Cello, Piano.
Duration: 22 Minutes.
Commissioned by The David Ensemble, Warren Wilson, director.

Far from Love is set in many continuous sections with a new tempo in each. In most sections the meter remains constant; in a few some shifting occurs. Several cadenzas appear in the clarinet part. The lyric vocal lines move mostly by steps and small leaps. Pitches relate closely to the instrumental parts with much doubling, especially between the voice and piano.

317. PASATIERI, Thomas. Heloise and Abelard. New York: Belwin-Mills, 1973.

Text: Louis Phillips.
Instrumentation: Soprano, Baritone, Piano.
Commissioned by Evelyn Lear and Thomas Stewart and dedicated to them.

Some meter and tempo changes occur. The vocal parts move mostly by steps and small leaps. Pitches relate closely to the piano and to each other. Frequently the piano doubles entire phrases or partial phrases.

318. PASATIERI, Thomas. Rites de Passage. New York: Belwin-Mills, 1974.

Text: Louis Phillips.
Instrumentation: Voice, String Quartet.
Dedication: Elaine Bonazzi.

The vocal line contains mostly stepwise movement and small leaps. A general flow is maintained even in sections where large intervals appear. The vocal pitches clearly relate to the instrumental parts. The meter and tempo remain fairly constant. Rhythmic figures are generally quite simple; however, a short section near the middle may present problems in ensemble coordination. Rites de Passage is also available in an orchestal version and in an edition for voice and piano. String quartet or orchestral materials are available on rental.

319. PECK, Russel. Automobile. New York: Carl Fischer, 1977.

I. Straight (score notation): "STOPP"
II. Mobile (cards for each player): "Mobile"

Instrumentation: Soprano, Flute, Double Bass, Percussion.

Movement 1: The composer gives the following note to the soprano: "The first movement provides only one opportunity for soloistic projection. Otherwise the voice should participate 'as an instrument' on equal footing with the other players. Except for the solo... non vibrato: the quality should be very steady and clear. Intonation of sustained tones is crucial and should create where possible pure (breathless) consonant intervals with the other instruments." Most measures are metered, though a few are indicated in seconds. Some shifting of meter and tempo occurs. Irregular subdivisions of beats appear frequently, often including one or more small value rests on a beat. The vocal range is moderate (mostly on the treble staff), but the pitch references are remote. All players hum and the flutist also plays the woodblocks. Movement II: All players have cards which may be arranged in any order, except the "first" and "last" cards. At certain cues, "all players abandon their parts, perform the appropriate cue card, then resume their parts immediately, As if never interrupted". The singer gives the cue for the final card. "Players may have to abandon their unfinished parts to perform this card."

320. PENN, William. Three Songs on Three Teton Sioux Poems. New York: Seesaw Music, 1976.

In a Sacred Manner, No. 1
With the Wind
In a Sacred Manner, No. 2

Instrumentation: Soprano, Piano (2), Percussion (2).
Composed: 1968.

The score specifies a soprano, but many pitches lie below the treble staff. The range is G - g'. The vocal line is angular and pitch reference is remote at best. Some speaking and whispering are required. The tempo and meter remain fairly constant except in No. 1. However, the superimposition of non-similar subdivisions of beats is common. The pianist plays sometimes inside the piano. Percussionists use only cymbals and tom-toms.

321. PERERA, Ronald. Dove sta amore. Boston: E.C. Schirmer, 1973.

Text: Lawrence Feringhetti, from A Coney Island of the Mind.
Instrumentation: Voice, Tape.
Duration: 7 Minutes, 35 Seconds.
Dedication: Phyllis Bryn-Julson.

The angular vocal line, liberally interspersed with rests, sometimes shifts to Sprechstimme. Pitch references appear on the tape. This piece demands a wide range encompassing B - eb''. A preface note states, "...the composer intends the soloist to have considerable freedom within the given framework.... Each singer may make her own improvisations on the general contour of the notated voice part. "The tape part...is designed to provide the performer with all cues necessary for coordination. The principal cues are indicated by arrows. Each measure lasts 5"; each page lasts 40"." A stopwatch may be used.

322. PERERA, Ronald. Three Poems of Günter Grass. Boston: E.C. Schirmer, 1977.

I. Gleisdreieck (Spider Music)
II. Klappstühle (Waltz Fantasy)
III. Schlallos

Instrumentation: Mezzo-Soprano, Flute (doubling Piccolo, Alto Flute), Clarinet (doubling Alto Sax, Bass Clarinet), Piano, Violin, Viola, Stereo Tape.
Duration: I. ca. 9 Minutes; II. ca. 8 Minutes; III. ca. 5 Minutes.
Commissioned by the Goethe Institute of Boston for the Boston Musica Viva, Richard Pittman, conductor.

The stage arrangement diagram indicates the use of a conductor. The ensemble is coordinated in seconds or by exact metronome markings. In sections where the tape is not running the metronome markings are noted specifically and change frequently. The text is in German, but bits of it occur on the tape in translation. In addition to singing, the soprano part includes Sprechstimme and parts which are spoken, shouted and half whispered. An instrument often doubles an entire phrase of the angular vocal line. Except for a few brief spots the range is moderate. There is some use of prepared piano and the flute and clarinet are required to play into the piano. All performers speak. A section at the beginning explains the notational symbols used in the piece.

323. PERRY, Julia. <u>Stabat Mater</u>. New York: Southern Music Publishing, 1954.

I. Grave: Stabat Mater
II. Andantino: O quam trestis et afflicta
III. Allegro: Quis est homo
IV. Allegro: Propeccatis sue gentis
V. Moderato, ma non tropo: Eia Mater
VI. Andante: Sancta Mater
VII. Allegro molto: Fac me verum
VIII. Misterioso: Virgo virginum
IX. Presto: Fac me plagas vulnerari
X. Calmo: Fac me cruce

Text: Latin poem by Jacopone da Todi (XIII Century) Translation by the composer.
Instrumentation: Contralto, String Quartet (or String Orchestra).

The vocal line moves mostly by steps and small leaps. Instruments sometimes double the voice, but the relationship of a second is more prominent. Shifting of meter and tempo changes appear within many of the movements.

324. PICCOLO, Anthony. <u>Found in Machaut's Chamber</u>, Op. 3. Redono Beach, CA: Composers Autograph Publications, 1969.

Text: Kenneth Patchen.
Instrumentation: Tenor, Flute, Guitar, Cello.

In this short piece of only twenty-four bars, two tempo changes appear but the meter remains constant. The superimposing of non-similar rhythmic patterns and non-similar subdivisions of beats may create ensemble coordination problems.

Most of the vocal part lies on the treble staff, but the range encompasses nearly two octaves. Pitch references are clear.

325. PINKHAM, Daniel. <u>Eight Poems of Gerard Manley Hopkins</u>. Boston: Ione Press, 1970.

I. Jesus to cast one thought upon
II. Spring
III. Heaven-Haven (A nun takes the veil)
IV. Pied Beauty
V. Strike churl
VI. Spring and fall

VII. Christmas Day
VIII. Jesu that in Mary dwell

Instrumentation: Baritone (or Tenor-Baritone), Viola.
Duration: 15 Minutes.

The vocal line moves mostly by steps and small leaps. Pitches relate closely to the viola part, but half and whole tone relationships predominate. Though the vocal part encompasses F - f#' (printed in the treble clef), it lies mostly in the middle range. The meter changes frequently.

326. PINKHAM, Daniel. Letters from Saint Paul. Boston: Ione Press, 1971.

I. (Hebrews 12: 1 & 2)
II. (Romans 8: 35, 37, 38, 39)
III. (Clossians 3: 16)
IV. (I Thessalonians 5: 1-6)
V. (Philippians 4: 4-7)
VI. (Romans 13: 11 & 12)

Instrumentation: High Voice, Violin (5), Viola, Cello, Contrabass.
Dedication: Richard Conrad.

The vocal line moves mostly by steps and small leaps with few large intervals. Much doubling of pitches occurs throughout. Some tempo and meter changes appear within the various pieces. This was originally written for high voice and organ or piano, and is arranged for string octet or string orchestra. Parts are available from the publisher on a rental basis.

327. PINKHAM, Daniel. Man that is born of a woman. Boston: Ione Press, 1971.

Three untitled songs.
Text: Book of Common Prayer.
Instrumentaion: Mezzo-Soprano, Guitar.
Dedication: Miriam Boyer.

The pitches of the angular vocal line often relate to the guitar by a half tone, and lie mostly on the lower part of the treble staff. The meter changes frequently, often in every bar.

328. PINKHAM, Daniel. Now the Trumpet Summons Us Again. New York: C.F. Peters, 1970.

Text: from the Inaugural Address of John F. Kennedy.
Instrumentation: High Voice, Trumpet in C, Glockenspiel (or Celesta), Violin (5), Viola, Cello, Double Bass.
Also available in two other versions: For large orchestra, or for high voice and piano.

The work begins with an instrumental prelude and a break before the song begins. The glockenspiel is used only in the prelude and once near the end of the piece. Strings often play sustained chords while the voice performs in quasi recitative style. Vocal pitches relate closely to the instrumental parts. No complex rhythms appear and ensemble problems are minimal.

329. PINKHAM, Daniel. Safe in their Alabaster Chambers. Boston: Ione Press, 1974.

I. Safe in their Alabaster Chambers
II. There's a certain Slant of light
III. These are the days when Birds come back

Text: Emily Dickinson.
Instrumentation: Voice, Tape.
Duration: 9 1/2 Minutes.
Commissioned by Merimack College on the occasion of its 25th anniversary.

The score is published with the voice part and very few tape cues. Tape pitch references are not indicated in the score. Though the vocal line is somewhat angular, very wide leaps do not occur frequently. The vocal line lies mostly in the moderate range, but extends down to F#. Following is a note by the composer: "The sounds (of the tape) are intended to be affective. They set the mood and give occasional pitches. They are not, however, meant as accompaniment, but rather a non-synchronous theatrical adjunct like scenery or lighting enhancing the effect of the otherwise unaccompanied vocal line."

330. PINKHAM, Daniel. Two Motets. Boston: Ione Press, 1971.

I. Non vos relinquam orphanos (St. John XIV: 18 & 28) (I will not leave you comfortless)
II. Te lucis ante terminum (from the Latin hymn attributed to St. Ambrose, translated by John Mason Neal) (Before the ending of the day)

Instrumentation: Soprano (Tenor), Flute, Guitar.
Dedication: I. Jean Lunn; II. Julio Prol.

In number I the guitar doubles the voice throughout. The pitch references are not as easy in number II, but some doublings occur. The tempo and meter remain constant and there are no complex rhythmic figures.

331. PISK, Paul. Meadow-Saffrons, Op. 37a. New York: New Music Edition, 1956.

I. Very Slowly
II. More Fluently
III. Again Slowly

Text: by the composer, after oriental proverbs.
Instrumentation: Contralto, Clarinet in A, Bass Clarinet in A.

The meter and tempo remain constant throughout each section. Vocal pitches clearly relate to the instrumental parts, though with some dissonance. The modest range includes c# - f'.

332. PISK, Paul. The Waning Moon, Op. 23B. New York: American Composer Alliance, n.d.

Text: Dobo.
Instrumentation: Voice, Violin, Cello, Piano.

Score not available for review.

333. PLESKOW, Raoul. For Five Players and Baritone. New York: American Composers Alliance, 1969.

Text: Stefan Wolpe.
Instrumentation: Baritone, Flute, Clarinet, Violin, Cello, Piano.

Vocal entrance pitches relate closely to the previous instrumental material, and some doubling of pitches occurs. The baritone begins about half way through the piece with a spoken part; otherwise the vocal line is fairly angular. The text is largely in English, but partially in German. The tempo and meter change fairly frequently.

334. PLESKOW, Raoul. Motet and Madrigal. New York: American Composers Alliance, n.d.

Instrumentation: Tenor, Soprano, Flute, Clarinet, Violin, Cello, Piano.
Written on a grant by the National Endowment for the Arts.

The vocal line is sometimes angular and sometimes moves chromatically. Any doublings of pitches appear among thick textures. The range demands are not extensive for either singer. Some words are initiated by one singer and completed by the other. Consonants which are enclosed in brackets are not to be articulated, thus leaving some words incomplete.

335. PLESKOW, Raoul. On Three Old English Rhymes. New York: American Composers Alliance, n.d.

Instrumentation: Medium Voice, Flute, Clarinet, Cello, Piano.

Score not available for review.

336. PLESKOW, Raoul. On Two Ancient Texts. New York: American Composers Alliance, n.d.

Instrumentation: Soprano, Flute, Clarinet, Cello, Piano.

Score not available for review.

337. PLESKOW, Raoul. Three Songs. New York: American Composers Alliance, n.d.

Text: Ancient writings.
Instrumentation: Tenor (or High Baritone), Violin, Viola, Cello, Clarinet, Bass Clarinet, Piano.

Score not available for review.

338. PLOG, Anthony. Four Sierra Scenes. West Hollywood, CA: Brightstar Music Publications, 1976.

I. Mountains
II. Sunset
III. Temples
IV. Sunrise

Text: from John Muir's diary: "My First Summer in the Sierra."
Instrumentation: Soprano, Trumpet (2), French Horn, Trombone, Bass Trombone.

In the forward the composer states: "When performing the work, brass players should realize that dynamics are subjective -- the soprano must be heard at all times." The singer's pitches relate closley to the instrumental parts, with some doubling. The meter changes frequently, but the tempo remains constant throughout each movement and there are no complex rhythmic figures. A horn cadenza appears in number III.

339. PLOG, Anthony. Two Scenes. Nashville, TN: Brass Press, 1977.

Text: Daveda Lamont.
Instrumentation: Soprano, Trumpet, Organ.

Score not available for review.

340. POPE, Conrad. At that hour. Hillsdale, NY: Mobart Music, 1978.

Text: Adapted from III of Chamber Music by James Joyce.
Instrumentation: Mezzo-Soprano (or Contralto), Flute, Clarinet, Violin, Viola, Cello, Piano.
Duration: ca. 11 Minutes.

The angular vocal line begins after a long instrumental section. Many entrance pitches are doubled or appear in the immediately preceeding instrumental material. Some phrases are sung continuously and some are interrupted after a word or two by brief instrumental bits before continuing. The ensemble seems to function as four units: voice, woodwinds, strings, piano. Many different tempo sections appear and the rhythmic structure is complex. Irregular subdivisions of beats are superimposed and small-value rests interspersed.

341. POPE, Conrad. Rain. Hillsdale, NY: Mobart Music, n.d.

Text: James Joyce, from XXXII of Chamber Music.
Instrumentation: Contralto, Violin, Cello, Clarinet, Piano.
Composed: 1976.

The vocal line is angular. Many entrance pitches are doubled or appear in the immediately preceeding instrumental material. Frequent changes in meter and complex rhythmic figures (including irregular subdivisions of beats) are common. The score implies the use of a conductor. This piece is fairly short and the composer probably intends for it to be performed with other of his James Joyce songs.

342. POWELL, Mel. Settings. New York: G. Schirmer, 1979.

Instrumentation: Soprano, Chamber Ensemble.
Duration: 10 Minutes.

Score not available for review.

343. POWELL, Mel. Two Prayer Settings. New York: G. Schirmer, 1964.

Instrumentation: Tenor, Oboe, Violin, Viola, Cello.
Duration: ca. 5 Minutes.
Commissioned by the New York Chamber Soloists and first performed by them in 1964 at the Library of Congress.

Tempo changes occur continuously, especially in number two. Meter changes and compound meter arrangements, [1/4 & 3/8], [2/8 & 3/16], appear frequently. The vocal line is very angular. Pitch reference is remote; doublings are very rare. The superimposition of non-similar rhythmic figures is prominent. These also include various irregular subdivisions of the beats; e.g., not only 5, but also 5 or 6.

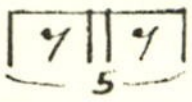

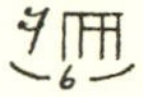

344. POWELL, Morgan. Faces. Northampton, MA: Smith Publications, 1977.

Instrumentation: Voice, Cello.

The vocal part includes some specific pitches and some non-specific. An instruction to the singer states "sing (ad lib,) on pitch (non-vibrato) parlando." End notes identify the symbols to be observed by the singer: e.g., "hand over mouth," "lowest sung pitch possible," etc. The singer also plays the crotale and glass wind chimes. Much of the score is indicated in seconds, but in some places a given unit and metronomic indications appear. The staff is removed where a part is silent. Quarter tones are used only in the cello part.

345. POWELL, Morgan. Three Poems of Paul Zelanske. Champaign, IL: Media Press, 1971.

Instrumentation: Soprano, Violin (2).

This piece requires a wide vocal range, F# - c''. Some doubling occurs, but seconds are more common. Entrance pitches often relate to the violins by a unison or a consonant interval. The three movements bear no titles, but the indication for number three reads "Swinging (with a jazz feel)."

346. PRESSER, William. A Hymne to God the Father. Bryn Mawr, PA: Tenuto Publications, n.d.

Text: John Donne.
Instrumentation: Voice, Viola (or Cello), Piano.
Duration: 7 Minutes.
Dedication: Clifton Ware.

Often the piano doubles the vocal line, but some dissonances appear. The range is moderate. The tempo and meter remain constant throughout. Rhythmic figures are simple.

347. PRESSER, Willaim. Songs of Death. Hattiesburg, MS: Tritone Press, n.d.

To Musique, To Becalme Fever
The Curse
Lay A Garland on My Hearse

Text: Robert Herrick.
Instrumentation: Mezzo-Soprano, String Quartet.
Duration: ca. 1 Minute.

The string quartet generally moves with the same or similar rhythmic figures. Tempo and meter remain constant throughout each movement. The lyric vocal line moves mostly by steps and small leaps. Instrumental parts usually double the vocal pitches. The songs encompass a two octave range (A - ab'). Songs of Death may be performed with a string orchestra. A piano reduction is also available.

348. PUSZTAI, Tibor. Requiem Profana. Newton Centre, MA: Margun Music, n.d.

Instrumentation: Mezzo-Soprano, Tenor, Oboe, Clarinet, Bassoon, French Horn, Trumpet, Trombone, Percussion, Harp, Piano (Electric Piano), Violin, Cello, Contrabass.
Duration: 13 Minutes.

Score not available for review.

349. RAN, Shulamit. O The Chimneys. New York: Carl Fischer, 1973.

I. A dead child speaks
II. Already embraced by the arm of heavenly solace
III. Fleeing
IV. Someone comes
V. Hell is naked (from Glowing Enigmas II)

Text: Poems of Nelly Sachs
Instrumentation: Mezzo-Soprano, Flute, Clarinet in A, Cello, Percussion, Piano with Tape.

In some sections the tempo and meter change frequently and the superimposition of non-similar rhythmic figures presents further complications. Other sections are rhythmically free. In one section the composer gives the following instruction: "Exact rhythmic coordination between instruments is not necessary unless otherwise indicated by broken lines. Cues for entrances and stops are marked with arrows." Some sections are designated "Improvise on given notes." Number I is purely instrumental. Others require mostly singing with some Sprechstimme and speaking. Occasionally the instruments double the vocal part. The doubling often appears in the middle of a chord or cluster.

350. RANDALL, J.K. "Improvisations on a poem by e e cummings." ASUC Journal of Music Scores, Vol. 3 (1974):41-65.

Instrumentation: Soprano (or Contralto), Clarinet in A, Alto Saxophone, Trumpet, Guitar, Piano.
Composed: 1961.
Reprinted by permission of the American Composers Alliance.

The angular vocal line contains many glissandi. Vocal range is F# - a' and doubling by any instrument is rare. The meter and tempo remain constant and rhythmic figures are simple. Improvisation is published in score form. Performance materials may be obtained from the American Composers Alliance.

351. REALE, Paul. Pange Lingua. New York: American Composers Alliance, n.d.

Text: Prijatel.
Instrumentation: Baritone, Oboe (2), Clarinet, Cello, French Horn (2).

Score not available for review.

352. REALE, Paul. The Traveler. New York: American Composers Alliance, n.d.

Text: Prijatel.
Instrumentation: Tenor, Flute, Piano.

Score not available for review.

353. REALE, Paul. Three Songs from the Chinese. New York: American Composers Allinace, n.d.

Text: Rexroth, tr.
Instrumentation: Mezzo-Soprano, Xylophone, Oboe (English Horn), Timpani.

Score not available for review.

354. RECK, David. *Night sounds (and Dream)*. Davis, CA: Composer/Performer Edition, 1967.

Text: e e cummings.
Instrumentation: Soprano, Percussion, Double Bass.
Commissioned by Ars Nova Consort.

Most of the piece is set with bits of material alternating with simultaneous silence in all parts. Toward the end of the piece the silences become less frequent. The text begins about two thirds of the way into the piece. Various parts are sung, half sung, whispered or spoken. The soprano plays some percussion, but usually not at the same time as performing the text. All three performers play percussion instruments and should be grouped in a cluster within reach of the appropriate instruments. Explanations of symbols for all parts appear on the first page. The composer indicates dynamics very specifically.

355. REIF, Paul. *The Artist*. New York: Seesaw Music, 1970.

Text: Kenneth Koch.
Instrumentation: Baritone, Alto, Flute, Clarinet, Bassoon, French Horn, Trumpet, Percussion, Violin.

Both singers function as narrator and singer with the sung bits being interspersed among the narration. Sometimes the vocal parts contain sequences of pitches which are to begin at any pitch level and are specific only in their relationship to each other. When pitches are notated exactly they relate closely to the instrumental parts. The instrumental parts include speaking as well as playing. Sometimes they follow cues of the narration. This work can be performed in either dramatic or concert form.

356. REIF, Paul. *Reverence for Life*. New York: Leslie Productions, 1960.

Instrumentation: Voice, String Quartet, Piano.
A tribute to Albert Schweitzer's 85th birthday.

Homogeneous rhythmic movement is common in the strings. No complex rhythmic patterns and few meter and tempo changes appear. Though the pitch references are clear, there is little doubling of the vocal part by the instruments. The vocal range encompasses CC - gb.

357. REYNOLDS, Roger. Again. New York: C.F. Peters, 1970.

Instrumentation: Soprano (2) Percussion (2) Contrabass (2), Flute (2), Trombone (2), Tape (Four Channel), Lights.
Duration: 22 Minutes.

The vocal parts are notated mostly in specific pitches, but with much "ad lib." They are set with phonetic sounds rather than a text. Performers and speakers (electronic) are arranged in a circle surrounding the audience. At points within the piece "performers move to new positions performing as they go." The format of the printed score changes with this repositioning. The entire piece is notated in seconds. The light cues and indications are specified in minutes. A conductor is mentioned.

358. REYNOLDS, Roger. Compass. New York: C.F. Peters, 1975.

Text: Jorge Luis Borges (Translated by Alistair Reid).
Instrumentation: Tenor, Bass, Cello, Contrabass (all amplified), Tape, Black and White Projections.

Following are some of the many effects required of the singers: "voiceless flutter," "multiphonic speech," "husky purr" and "glottal amplitude modulation." Letters of the words of the text are often divided in ways other than by syllable, e.g. day and night = da-ya-ndni-ght. Some figures without pitch appear for the instrumentalists as well as for the singers. Instrumental parts include vocal sounds. Live performance, taped sounds and black and white projections fade in and out "as sensitivity dictates."

359. RHODES, Phillip. Autumn Settings. New York: C.F. Peters, 1973.

1. autumn fragments
2. prophecy
3. remembrance/reality

Text: Patricia V. Schneider.
Instrumentation: Soprano, String Quartet.
Duration: ca. 11 Minutes.
Composed: 1969.
Comissioned by the Berkshire Music Center in cooperation with the Fromm Music Foundation and dedicated to Phyllis Bryn-Julson.

The tempo and meter change frequently. Many rests are placed irregularly on small subdivisions of beats, resulting in possible problems of ensemble coordination. The angular vocal part includes some indications for half spoken and whisper. The singer's pitch reference is usually quite remote, often appearing in clusters in the ensemble. Autumn Settings requires a singer to have a wide range, G - eb'', and much flexibility.

360. RIEGGER, Wallingford. Music for Voice and Flute, Op, 23. Long Island City, NY: Bomart Music, 1950.

Instrumentation: Voice, Flute (or Oboe).
Duration: 3 Minutes.

The vocal line requires a fairly high voice. Doublings of pitches or third relationsips between the parts are common. An oboe or flute may be substituted for the vocal part which is set on "ah" throughout. The tempo and meter are constant except for a slow introduction and a brief section at the end.

361. RILEY, Dennis. Cantata I, Op. 8. New York: C.F. Peters, 1978.

Text: Poems by D.H. Lawrence.
Instrumentation: Mezzo-Soprano, Piano, Vibraphone, Cello, Tenor Saxophone.
Composed: 1966.
Duration: ca. 7 Minutes.
Dedication: Susan Burge, and in memory of Luella Riley.

Little, if any, doubling of vocal pitches occurs. The relationship of a half tone is common. The meter changes frequently, sometimes in every bar. As an example, a sequence of 2/8, 3/16, 2/8, 5/8, 5/16, 3/8, etc. appears within a tempo of eithth note equals 126. The rhythmic configuration is generally complex. A conductor is indicated in the stage diagram. The staff is removed for each part when it is silent.

362. RILEY, Dennis. Five Songs on Japanese Haiku. New York: C.F. Peters, 1971.

i. Bashō: on the road to Nara
ii. Buson: the spring sea
iii. Bashō: the entrance of spring
iv. Shiki: letter and spirit
v. Hō-ō: in the meadow

Text: Haiku translated from the Japanese by Harold Stewart in A Net of Fireflies.
Instrumentation: Soprano, Clarinet in A, Violin, Cello.
Composed: 1963.
Dedication: Phyllis Bryn-Julson.

The vocal line is somewhat angular, but contains few large intervals and makes no demands on the extremes of the range. It includes some spoken parts and Sprechstimme, but mostly singing. Pitches often relate remotely to the instrumental parts. The tempo and meter vary within each miniature. Some diverse rhythmic figures are superimposed. The dynamics vary continuously from f-ppp.

363. ROCHBERG, George. Blake Songs. New York: Leeds Music, 1963.

1. Ah! Sunflower
2. Nurse's Song
3. The Fly
4. The Sick Rose

Text: William Blake.
Instrumentation: Voice, Flute, Clarinet, Bass Clarinet, Celesta, Harp, Violin, Viola, Cello.
Duration: 12 Minutes.

The tempo and meter change frequently with the following being the usual meter markings: 2/8 and 7/16. Various irregular subdivisions of beats are interspersed with small value rests. The very angular vocal part also includes Sprechstimme. Though the vocal pitches always relate to the instrumental parts, that relationship is sometimes less than obvious. The score does not specify a conductor. Instrumental parts are available on rental.

364. ROCHBERG. George. String Quartet No. 2 with Soprano. Bryn Mawr PA: Theodore Presser, 1971.

Text: Rainer Maria Rilke, from 9th Duino Elegy, translated by Harry Behn.
Duration: ca. 28 Minutes.
Dedication: Mrs. Herbert C. Morris.

The angular vocal line includes wide leaps, grace notes at a large leap and considerable use of the extremes of the range. Pitch reference is remote; doublings are very rare. All parts are rhythmically diverse and include many rests and irregular subdivisions of beats. The ensemble is complicated by the superimposition of these non-similar rhythmic figures. This is published in score form. All players are to use the full score for performance.

365. ROE, Betty. Hot Sun, Cool Fire. n.p.: Viola da Gamba Society, Supplementary Publication No. 68, 1968.

Text: George Peel (1599).
Instrumentation: High Voice, Treble Viols (2), Tenor Viol, Bass Viol.

The piece is rhythmically simple with few meter changes and no tempo changes. Many dynamic indications appear. The singer's pitches relate clearly to the instrumental parts, but with dissonance. The vocal range is modest: e - f#'.

366. ROOSEVET, J. Willard. An American Sampler. New York: American Composers Alliance, n.d.

Instrumentation: Soprano, French Horn, Piano.

Score not available for review.

367. ROOSEVELT, Willard. Four Songs for Soprano and Viola. New York: American Composers Alliance, 1975.

Autumn Song on Perry Street (Lloyd Frankenberg)
a paper rose (Lloyd Frankenberg)
crazy jay blue) (e e cummings)
spring! may (e e cummings)

The vocal range is moderate with few large intervals. Pitches usually relate fairly closely to the viola part. Doublings as well as half tone and whole tone relationships are common. Meter changes occur frequently. The tempo remains constant within each piece.

368. ROOSEVELT, Willard. Three Songe from Poe. New York: American Composers Alliance, n.d.

Eldorado
The conqueror Worm
To one in Paradise

Instrumentation: Soprano, Clarinet, Piano.

The vocal line moves mostly in small intervals, including many chromatic sections. Entrance pitches relate closely to the instrumental parts and some doublings occur. The tempo and meter are fairly constant except for meter changes in number three.

369. ROREM, Ned. Ariel. New York: Boosey & Hawkes, 1974.

I. Words
II. Poppies in July
III. The Hanging Man
IV. Poppies in October
V. Lady Lazarus

Text: Sylvia Plath.
Instrumentation: Soprano, Clarinet, Piano.
Duration: 20 Minutes.
Dedication: Phyllis Curtin.

A moderately angular vocal line includes many major sevenths and larger intervals. Pitches usually relate to the instrumental parts. Special considerations include a two octave glissando with a gasp and the following special indications: "half yelled," "shouted," "hysterical" and "parlando." Number V is not metered, but the eighth note remains invariable throughout. Irregular subdivisions of beats are common. Rorem asks for extreme dynamics, especially ffff.

370. ROREM, Ned. Four Dialogues. New York: Boosey & Hawkes, 1969.

The Subway
The Airport
The Apartment
In Spain and In New York

Text: Frank O'Hara.
Instrumentation: Voice (2), Piano (2).
Composed: 1954.
Duration: ca. 20 Minutes.

The composer states that this "...falls somewhere between concert cantata and staged opera," and that "...pianists...[should] ...consider themselves of equal importance to the singers; the music was created as a Quartet of Dialogues."

The fairly lyric vocal lines move mostly in steps and small leaps. The two parts are designated "man and woman" (probably tenor and soprano). Entrance pitches generally appear in the harmonic structure of the piano parts. The two voices are usually in a dialogue, but, when they sing together, they relate by a consonant interval.

371. ROREM, Ned. Last Poems of Wallace Stevens. New York: Boosey & Hawkes, 1974.

Not Ideas about the Thing but the Thing Itself
The River of Rivers in Connecticut
A Child Asleep in Its Own Life
The Planet on the Table
The Dove in Spring
Interlude
Of Mere Being
A Clear Day and No Memories.

Instrumentation: Voice, Cello, Piano
Duration: 24 Minutes.
Commissioned by the David Ensemble.

The vocal line is fairly angular, but very wide leaps are infrequent. Some repetitions of melodic figures or partial repetitions occur. Though the range encompasses two octaves, B - bb', the vocal part lies mostly on the treble staff. "Of Mere Being" is scored mostly for unaccompanied voice. The tempo and meter remain constant within each movement.

372. ROREM, Ned. Mourning Scene. New York: Henmar Press, 1963.

Text: II Samuel I:19-27.
Instrumentation: Voice, String Quartet.
Duration: 6 Minutes.
Composed: 1947.
Dedication: Lee Hoiby.

The vocal line moves mostly by steps and small leaps. Pitches relate clearly to the quartet and some doublings occur. The modest range lies mostly on the treble staff. Mourning Scene is published with a score and four string parts. The quartet functions rhythmically homogeneously in contrast to the vocal line.

373. ROREM, Ned. Serenade on Five English Poems. New York: Boosey & Hawkes, 1978.

Hold back thy hours, dark Night (John Fletcher)
Th'expense of spirit in a waste of shame (Shakespeare)
Flower in the crannied wall (Tennyson)
Peace (Gerard Manley Hopkins)
Never weather-beaten sail more willing bent to shore (Thomas Campian)

Instrumentation: Voice, Violin, Viola, Piano.
Duration: ca. 18 Minutes.
Commissioned by the Cuyahoga Valley Arts Ensemble.

The work begins with a lengthy solo for violin. The piano and viola each have a solo between the various poems, but the voice is always accompanied. The composer indicates that the music is to be continuous, with no pauses between sections. The lyric vocal line moves mostly by steps and small leaps. Pitches always relate directly to the instrumental ensemble. Though entire phrases are not doubled, frequent doublings of isolated pitches occur. The vocal part lies mostly on the treble staff. Serenade is published with full score and parts for violin and viola.

374. ROSEN, Jerome. Serenade. New York: American Composers Alliance, 1964.

I. Prelude
II. Improvisation I
III. Nocturne
IV. Improvisation II
V. Finale

Instrumentation: Soprano Voice, Alto Saxophone.
Dedication: Pat and Art Woodbury.

Serenade encompasses a vocal range of F - a'. It is a vocalise, with no text. Numbers 1, 3 and 5 contain some wide interval grace notes. Pitch reference is often by half tone relationship. "Improvisation I" gives the performers source materials and instructions. "Improvisation II" is presented in a graphic, pictorial manner of totally non-traditional notation.

375. ROUSE, Christopher. Aphrodite Cantos. New York: American Composers Alliance, 1976.

Eight untitled pieces.
Texts: 1. Sappho
2. Attributed to Baeju Bavra
3. Yakamochi
4. Anonymous
5. Li Bai
6. Fionn
7. Georg Trakl
8. Walt Whitman
Instrumentation: Mezzo-Soprano, Clarinet in Eb, Percussion, Piano, Viola, Cello.
Duration: ca. 30 Minutes.
Written for Rosalind Rees.
Dedication: Bernadette Towey.

The vocal range is moderate. Entrance pitches relate closely to the instrumental parts with some doubling of single notes as well as some entire phrases. The meter changes frequently, sometimes in every bar. Some tempo changes occur. A conductor is required, and all performers play percussion instruments. The eight texts are set in eight different languages: Greek, Hindi, Japanese, Italian, Chinese, Gaelic, German and English.

376. ROUSE, Christopher. Ecstasis Mane Eburnei. New York: American Composers Alliance, n.d.

Text: Misura.
Instrumentation: Offstage Soprano, Alto Recorder (Celesta), Piano (Vibraslap), Viola (Percussion), Percussion (2).

Score not available for review.

377. ROUSE, Christopher. First Stratum of Empyrean. New York: American Composers Alliance, n.d.

Instrumentation: Soprano, Flute, Percussion (2), Piano, Violin (2), Viola, Cello.

Score not available for review.

378. ROUSE, Christopher. The Kiss. New York: American Composers Alliance, n.d.

Instrumentation: Baritone, Bass Clarinet, Harp, Piano, Celesta, Percussion.

Score not available for review.

379. ROUSE, Christopher. Nox Aeris Temporis. New York: American Composers Alliance, n.d.

Instrumentation: Offstage Soprano, Violin (3), Cello, Oboe, Piano (2), Percussion.

Score not available for review.

380. ROUSE, Christopher, Subjectives V. New York: American Composers Alliance, n.d.

Instrumentation: Contralto, Percussion.

Score not available for review.

381. ROVICS, Howard. Echo. New York: American Composers Alliance, n.d.

Text: Christina Rossetti.
Instrumentation: Voice, Flute, Piano.
Composed: 1965.

The angular vocal line lies generally high in some places, though the highest note is only bb'. The meter and tempo change frequently. Irregular subdivisions of beats and notes tied across beats are common.

382. ROVICS, Howard. *Haunted Object*. New York: American Composers Alliance, n.d.

Text: Johanna Pragh and Stefan Wolpe.
Instrumentation: Soprano, Male Narrator, Oboe, English Horn (Oboe), Hekelphone (English Horn), Bassoon, Tape.
Written under a composing-fellowship grant from the National Endowment for the Arts, 1974.

Haunted Objects begins with a long instrumental section before the voice enters. The score specifies a conductor. The angular vocal line encompasses a wide range, A -db'', and includes grace notes at a wide leap. Pitches relate closely to the instrumental parts, but little doubling occurs. The soprano part includes some speaking also.

383. ROVICS, Howard. *The Hunter*. New York: American Composers Alliance, n.d.

Text: Johanna Pragh.
Instrumentaion: Soprano, Viola.

Score not available for review.

384. RUSSELL, Armand. *Ballad with Epitaphs*. New York: Seesaw Music, 1973.

Text: "The Butcher's Boy," Traditional American or English Epitaphs: Kent, Arabella Young, Thorp, John Hill, Epitaph without Words.
Instrumentation: Voice (2), Percussion (2).

Since all percussion instruments are non-pitched, there is no pitch reference. Instructions state that the verses should be transposed to whatever pitch level suits the individual vocalists. The nine verses of the ballad, "The Butcher's Boy," are interrupted by five Epitaphs. "The epitaphs should be be performed separately from the ballad verses under the title 'Epitaphs.'" Notational symbols are explained at the beginning and also in many footnotes. The following appears: "Voice parts are shown graphically in all epitaphs so that the highest and lowest notes in the notated space...represent correspondingly highest and lowest pitches in singers range."

385. SACCO, P. Peter. *Three Psalms*. Daly City, CA: Astara Press, 1973.

I. How Long wilt Thou forget me, O Lord (Psalm 13)
II. The Sorrows of Death (Psalm 18)
III. Keep Not Thou Silence, O God (Psalm 83)

Instrumentation: Tenor (or Soprano), Trumpet (2), French Horn, Trombone, Tuba.
Composed: 1966.

The tenor line lies most often at an interval of a half or whole step with an instrument. Very little doubling occurs. Though the voice part is angular, the leaps are not especially large. Number I contains a section for solo voice. Three Psalms is published with a score and set of parts.

386. ST. JOHN, Kathleen. Her Drifting from Me These Days. n.p.: Experimental Arts Society, 1977.

Text: Harmohan Singh.
Instrumentation: High Baritone, Viola, Marimba, Tubular Bells, Percussion.
Duration: 6 Minutes, 10 Seconds.
Dedication: Harmohan Singh.

Vocal pitches sometimes relate by a unison, octave or consonant interval to the viola or marimba. Speaking and whispering are included as part of the vocal line. The shape of each note indicates its length in seconds. The score includes specific instructions for lighting, movement of the singer around and off stage, attire and other visual arrangements. Or, the piece may be performed in concert version without any special visual effects.

387. SAMUEL, Gerhard. The Relativity of Icarus. Melville, NJ: Belwin-Mills, 1974.

Text: Jack Larson.
Instrumentation: Singer-Speaker (Contralto or Young Bass-Baritone), Flute, Oboe, Clarinet, Violin, Viola, Cello, Piano, Percussion.

Some sections are measured and some are indicated in seconds. The score requires a conductor. The following note appears before the piece: "The singer should use a directional microphone for spoken and whispered passages only." Many specific performance instructions appear in footnotes throughout the piece. Though the vocal part is angular the pitch references are fairly clear. The singer also sings, speaks, and whispers. Some of the sung parts are unaccompanied or accompanied by one sustained note. The vocal part is notated in the bass clef. This is published in score form, and instrumental parts are available on rental.

388. SARGON, Simon. Patterns in Blue. New York: Boosey & Hawkes, 1976.

I. Cabaret Song (James Agee)
II. Snatch of Sliphorn Jazz (Carl Sandburg)
III. Lonesome Boy Blues (Kenneth Patchen)

Instrumentation: Medium Voice, Clarinet, Piano.
Dedication: Bonnie Glasgow.

The vocal line moves mostly by steps and small leaps and lies withim a range of A - eb'. Pitches relate closely to the instrumental parts with some doublings. Following is a quote from the composer: "...is a cycle of three mood pieces employing elements of the jazz idiom..." The tempo and meter remain fairly constant within each piece. This is published with a score and a part for clarinet.

389. SCHICKELE, Peter. The Lowest Trees Have Tops. Bryn Mawr, PA: Theodore Presser, n.d.

Instrumentation: Soprano, Flute, Viola, Harp.

Score not available for review.

390. SCHRAMM, Harold. Songs of Tāyumānavar. Bryn Mawr, PA: Theodore Presser, 1969.

Instrumentation: Soprano, Flute.
"Tāyumānavar, a Saivite Saint (a Saivite worships the god Shiva) lived in South India (Tamilnad) during the 16th and 17th century and was well known for his poetry."

Vocal entrance pitches relate to the flute by a unison or small interval. When specific pitches are indicated, mostly large intervals appear; when approximate pitches, smaller intervals. Many special effects are required. Performance notes give instructions for such things as slow glissandi, quarter tones, approximate pitch, spoken, monotone spoken. Some changes in tempo occur. About half of the piece is unmeasured.

391. SCHULLER, Gunther. Six Renaissance Lyrics. New York: Associated Music Publishers, 1979.

1. Sonnet 87 (William Shakespeare)
2. Noche Oscura (Juan de la Cruz)
3. Unter der Linden (Walter von der Vogelweide)
4. Sonnet 126 (Francesco Petrarca)
5. La Contunuation des Amours, No. 33 (Pierre de Ronsard)
6. O Notte, O Dolce Tempo (Michelangelo Buonerotti)

Instrumentation: Tenor, Flute, Oboe, Piano, Antique Cymbal, Violin, Viola, Cello, Double Bass.
Duration: 15 Minutes.
Composed: 1962.
Commissioned by the Fromm Foundation and first performed in 1962 at Tanglewood with the New York Chamber Soloists, A. Kouguell conducting.

The tenor line sometimes lies quite high for an extended segment. Some parts move in steps and small skips; other parts are quite angular. Instruments occasionally double isolated pitches in the vocal line, but more frequently the voice relates to the instruments by a half tone. The tempo remains fairly constant throughout each movement, but meter changes and irregularities occur in most. In number 3, 6/8 and 2/4 meters appear simultaneously. Number 6 begins with the following meter structure:

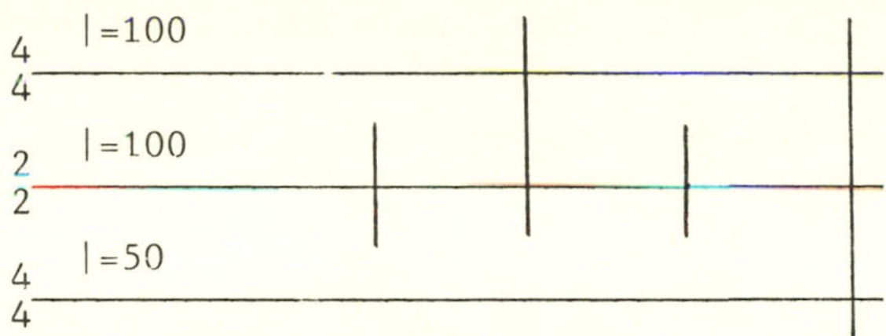

This is published in score form. Orchestral material is available from the publisher.

392. SCHUMAN, William. _In Sweet Music_. Bryn Mawr, PA: Merion Music, 1978.

Text: William Shakespeare, from _Henry VIII_.
Instrumentation: Voice, Flute, Viola, Harp.
Duration: ca. 25 Minutes.
Dedication: "To all my associates -- the artists, administrators, and patrons -- who made possible the realization of my dream for a permanent organization at Lincoln Center devoted to chamber music."

The singer is seated for most of the piece, humming and singing without text. Text appears only at the beginning and end. Though the range is generally moderate, an optional octave lower is indicated in one section of humming. The vocal line moves mostly by steps and small leaps. Pitches relate to the instrumental parts, but often within thick textures. Doublings are not frequent. Words are written under some of the flute part with the following instruction: "The words are given to enable the flutist to perform the melody with the clarity of a singer's projection. The following instructions appear for the singer: " The suggested sounds for singing the textless music reflect the composer's concept of the most appropriate phonetics for conveying the spirit of the music...."

393. SCHWANTNER, Joseph. _Shadows II, Consortium IV_. New York: American Composers Alliance, n.d.

Text: Rexroth.
Instrumentation: Baritone, Flute, Clarinet, Mandolin, Guitar, Violin, Viola, Cello, Bass Clarinet, Tape, (all doubling percussion).

Score not available for review.

394. SCHWANTNER, Joseph. _Wild Angels of the Open Hills_. New York: C.F. Peters, 1979.

I. Wild Angels of the Open Hills
II. Angels of the Shadowed Ancient Land
III. There
IV. Coming of Age
V. The Hawk Shapes the Wind.

Text: Ursula Le Guin.
Instrumentation: Soprano, Flute (Alto Flute), Harp.
Commissioned by the Jubal Trio and the Naumberg Foundation.

Vocal pitch reference is distant (few small or consonant intervals) with occasional doublings. The vocal range encompasses G - b'. Multiple grace notes and melismatic passages occur frequently. Complex rhythmic figures, including many short value notes and rests are common. Frequent dynamic changes include extremes. In the metered sections, the meter changes frequently. Tempo changes occur frequently, also. All performers play several percussion instruments as well.

395. SCHWARTZ, Elliott. _Septet: Five Instruments, Piano and Speaker/Singer_. New York: Carl Fischer, 1972.

Instrumentation: Voice, Piano and any five of the following:
Woodwind I - any treble woodwind instrument
Woodwind II - any other woodwind instrument
Brass - any brass instrument
Strings I - Violin (or Viola or Cello)
Strings II - any other bowed instrument
Percussion I
Percussion II
Duration: 12 Minutes.

Performance consists of eight pages (full score on each) which are performed in order three times for each movement. Each performer plays his own material only once during the movement and is silent during the other two performances of the page. It should be arbitrarily arranged ahead of time so that there will be several solos and several dense pages. The second movement consists of the same players, same parts, same procedure, but in a different sequence. The composer gives extensive notational information. All performers are required to treat their instruments in non-traditional ways as well as to speak, sing, whisper and move around. The vocal part is mostly indicated as non-specifically pitched sounds: hum, whisper, whistle, clap, snap, rub hands and wildly sweep and scrape piano strings. A few pitched notes appear on the staff with instructions to insert your own appropriate clef.

396. SEIGMEISTER, Elie. Songs of Experience. New York: Carl Fischer, 1978.

The Voice of the Bard
Earth's Answer
The Fly
The Garden of Love
The Thief and the angel
The Tyger

Text: William Blake.
Instrumentation: Voice, Viola, Piano.
Composed: Between 1966 and 1977.
Duration: ca. 15 Minutes.
Dedication: The Cantilena Chamber Players.

The vocal line is angular, but includes few large leaps. Though some doubling of isolated pitches occurs, the relationship of a second (most often a minor second) is more common. No demands are made on the upper extremes of the vocal range, but low F and F# appear several times. The meter changes frequently, sometimes in every bar. In most movements tempo changes occur often.

397. SEMEGEN, Daria. Lieder auf der Flucht. New York: American Composers Alliance, n.d.

Text: I. Bachmann.
Instrumentation: Soprano, Flute, Clarinet, French Horn, Piano, Percussion (2), Violin, Cello.

Score not available for review.

398. SEREBRIER, Jose. Erotica. New York: Peer International, 1972.

Instrumentation: Off-stage Soprano (or Trumpet), Flute, Oboe, Clarinet, French Horn, Bassoon.

The entire piece is written without bar lines. Some sections are organized in appproximate seconds, others with specific units and metronome markings. The stage arrangement diagram indicates a conductor. The off-stage vocal part is angular and sometimes unaccompanied. Pitches relate to the instruments, but within much dissonance. For example, in a duet between the voice and flute, half step relationships are prominent.

399. SEYFRIT, Michael. Winter's Warmth. New York: American Composers Alliance, n.d.

Text: J. Smith.
Instrumentation: Bass, Clarinet, Bassoon, Harp, Violin, Viola, Cello.

Score not available for review.

400. SHAPEY, Ralph. Incantations. New York: Composers Facsimile Edition, 1963.

Instrumentation: Soprano, Cello, Trumpet, Alto Sax, French Horn, Piano, Percussion (2).
Dedication: Bethany Beardslee.

Incantations is published in a very difficult to read score. Notational symbols are explained in notes at the bottom of the pages of the score. The stage arrangement diagram indicates a conductor. The angular vocal part includes very large leaps - leaps from one end of the range to the other. The pitch reference is remote at best. Few doublings, even of isolated pitches, occur. The tempo is constant but the meter shifts continuously through a wide variety: 1/4, 3/16, 4/4, 3/32, 1/8. Also the superimposition of non-similar rhythmic figures contributes to the ensemble problems.

401. SHAPEY, Ralph. Walking Upright. New York: American Composers Alliance, n.d.

1. what is a morning glory
2. shattering the wit rainbow
3. idly I snapped a tulip
4. I pricked my finger
5. laughter tipped the ashcloth of my soul
6. might and a warm mouth
7. o give me a stone colossus
8. walking upright

Text: Vera Klement.
Instrumentation: Female Voice, Violin.
Composed: 1958.

The eight short pieces are published in a difficult to read manuscript. The tempo is constant throughout each piece; however, each has a continuously changing meter or no meter at all. The angular vocal line encompasses a moderate range which lies mostly on the treble staff (often the bottom half of the staff). Pitch reference is remote at best. Very little doubling, even of isolated pitches, occurs.

402. SHIELDS, Alice. Wildcat Songs. New York: American Composers Alliance, n.d.

Instrumentation: Lyric Soprano, Piccolo.

Score not availale for review.

403. SHIFRIN, Seymour. A Renaissance Garland. Hillsdale, NY: Mobart Music, 1979.

I. Sonnet (Sir Thomas Wyatt)
II. Ballad (Anon)
III. An Excellent Sonnet of a Nimph (Sir Philip Sidney)
IV. Sonnet (William Sakespeare)

Instrumentation: Soprano, Tenor, Recorder, Lute, Percussion, Viol.
Dedication: Mir.

The recorder and viol players each need several instruments: 1. bass, tenor, alto and soprano recorders; 2. bass and tenor viols. Each of the four pieces requires a different instrument-voice combination. Both vocal lines are angular and contain frequent large leaps. Very little doubling, even of isolated pitches, occurs. The two voices often relate to each other by a half or whole tone.

404. SHIFRIN, Seymour. Satires of Circumstance. New York: C.F. Peters, 1971.

I. Waiting Both
II. The Convergence of the Twain
III. What's There to Tell?

Text: Thomas Hardy.
Instrumentation: Soprano, Flute (Piccolo), Clarinet, Violin, Cello, Double Bass, Piano.
Duration: ca. 16 1/2 Minutes.
Dedication: Paul Fromm.

Leaps larger than an octave are common in the angular vocal line. The large intervals move so quickly that little chance occurs to tune with the instruments. In addition, the instruments seldom double the voice part. In some places various irregular subdivisions of the beats occur simultaneously, sometimes spread across more than one beat. The inclusion of many small value rests further complicates the music. Grace notes are prominent.

405. SILSBEE, Ann. Scroll. New York: American Composers Alliance, n.d.

Text: Old Japanese Haiku by Bashō, Chora, Ringai.
Instrumentation: Soprano, Flute, (Alto Flute), Trumpet, Percussion, Violin, Contrabass, Piano.
Composed: 1977.

The vocal range includes C - c#'', but most of the piece lies within a moderate range. Little doubling of vocal pitches occurs. Special instructions for the soprano include "senza vibrato - bleak, heavy, monotonous," and "throat closed." Glissandi are common. Scroll requires some preparation of the piano and various kinds of sounds from the flute as well as the use of quarter tones. Rhythmic complexities include irregular subdivisions of beats and some short value notes tied over beats.

406. SIMONS, Netty. Songs for Wendy. Bryn Mawr, PA: Merion Music, 1977.

1. The Fly (William Blake)
2. A Centipede (Anon)
3. On the Grasshopper and Cricket (John Keats)
4. The Caterpillar (Christina Rossetti)
5. Was Worm (May Swenson)

Instrumentation: Voice, Viola.
Duration: ca. 9 Minutes.

The vocal line moves by small leaps, many repeated pitches and a few large leaps. Pitch reference is remote at best; few doublings, even of isolated notes, occur. The range is moderate: B - f#'. The composer gives a full page of performance instructions for numbers 1 and 5. In number 3, the only one with bar lines, the meter changes frequently. Number 4 is scored for unaccompanied voice.

407. SIMONS, Netty. Trialogue. New York: Composers Facsimile Edition, 1964.

Text: Dylan Thomas.
Instrumentation: Alto, Baritone, Viola.
Duration: 6 1/2 Minutes.

A low G appears frequently in the alto line, but Trialogue does not exploit the upper range of either voice. Vocal pitch reference is difficult, with very little doubling of either part. The meter changes frequently, but rhythmic figures are not complex.

408. SIMS, Ezra. Cantata 3. New York: American Composers Alliance, 1967.

Instrumentation: Mezzo-Soprano (Castanets, Tabla)
Commissioned by Cathy Berberian and to her dedicated.

The vocal line incudes large intervals, grace notes, quarter tones and some spoken parts. There are changes in tempo, but no bar lines. Some parts are notated on one line with only pitch direction; others are specifically notated, but with no pitch reference.

The composer states that

> "Cantata 3 is designed to be performed by one person - the arrangement in score is intended to make the structure of the work self evident. While the vocal part might be performed by more than one singer -.... The percussion part could more justifiably be entrusted to a second performer...."

409. SIMS, Ezra. Celebration of Dead Ladies. New York: American Composers Alliance, n.d.

1a. Ambling, lazy, offhand and inward
2a. Quick and cheerful
III. Smooth and faster
2b. As before
IV. Slow
2c. Yet again
1b. Ambling as before - but not quite so lazy

Text: F.R. Higgins, "Song For the Chatterbones," from Gap of Brightness.
Instrumentation: Voice, Alto Flute, Basset Clarinet in A, Viola, Cello, Percussion (2).
Composed: 1976.
Made possible in part by a grant from the National Endowment For the Arts.
Dedication: Aaron Copland.

The prefatory notes explain symbols and give instructions for the use of 1/6, 1/4, and 1/12 tone alterations of pitches. In the sections which include voice, the tempo and meter are constant and rhythmic figures are not complex. More rhythmic intricacies appear in the instrumental sections. The voice participates in only 2a, 2b, and 2c. Pitch relationsips between the voice and instruments involve microtonal alterations. The range is moderate and lies generally low.

410. SIMS, Ezra. Elegie. New York: American Composers Alliance, 1976.

I. ...oh aber gleich darüber
II. Nur die jungen Toten...
III. Aber dort, wo sie wohnen
IV. Und wir, die an steigendes Glück denken...

Text: Rainer Maria Rilke.
Instrumentation: Soprano, Flute, Clarinet in A, Violin, Viola, Cello.
Commissioned for Boston Musica Viva by the Goethe Institute of Boston.
Dedicated to the memory of Lois Ginades.

The vocal line lies fairly low for soprano except for number four which lies almost entirely above the treble staff and reaches to f''. An f'' is marked "pp and lunga possible." Some doubling of vocal pitches occurs. Sprechstimme, spoken parts and exact pitches are mixed intermittantly in the same phrases. Also, 1/4, 1/6 and 1/12 tone alterations are used. The meter changes frequently, nearly every bar: e.g. 11/12, 16/16, 7/8, 13/16, 17/16. In general the ensemble coordination is complex.

411. SIMS, Ezra. The Owl and the Pussycat. New York: American Composers Alliance, n.d.

Text: E. Lear.
Instrumentation: Basso, Harmonica, Electric Guitar.

Score not available for review.

412. SMIT, Leo. Four Motets. New York: Broude Brothers, 1960.

I. Wake up, my Love
II. O Katherine, Dearest
III. Venus, You and Your Son
IV. O Mother Tell Me how to Die

Text: Translated from the German by Sylvia Wright.
Instrumentation: Alternate instruments may be substituted for those indicated in the score.
Voice
Flute I (Alto Recorder)
Flute II (Tenor Recorder)
Violin (Bass Recorder or Flute in G)
Duration: 5 Minutes.

The vocal part encompases a modest range d - f#', with clear pitch references. The meter and tempo remain constant within each piece and all parts are rhythmically simple.

413. SOWERBY, Leo. God Mounts His Throne. Cincinnati, OH: World Library Publications, 1966.

Text: Psalms 46:6 and 67:18-19.
Instrumentation: Soprano, Baritone, Organ.
Commissioned by the Music Commission of the Diocese of Pittsburgh.

The vocal lines move mostly by steps and small leaps in octave relationship with each other. They are most often doubled by the organ. There are no demands on extremes of the range. The tempo and meter are constant and no complex rhythmic figures appear.

414. SOWERBY, Leo. Happy the Nation. Cincinnati, OH: World Library Publications, 1968.

Text: Psalms 32:12 & 6.
Instrumentation: Soprano, Baritone, Organ.

The vocal lines move mostly in steps and small leaps. The ranges are moderate and the organ often doubles the vocal pitches. The tempo is constant within each of the two sections, and the meter is constant throughout. No complex rhythmic figures occur.

415. STEARNS, Peter Pindar. Five Lyrics from "The Prophet." New York: American Composers Alliance, n.d.

Text: Kahlil Gibran.
Instrumentation: Soprano, Flute, Viola.
Composed: 1960.
Dedication: Carol Beran.

The somewhat angular vocal line contains few large leaps and lies within a moderate range. Most entrance pitches relate to the previous instrumental material by a small interval, but usually not by the same pitch. Specific metronomic markings appear for each piece, but measures are irregular and no meter indications are given. Syncopated rhythmic figures are common.

416. STEARNS, Peter Pindar. Three Love Songs. New York: American Composers Alliance, n.d.

I. I dare not ask a kiss (Harrick)
II. Yon rising Moon (Rubáiyát)
III. I have but to be by thee (Browning)

Instrumentation: Soprano, Clarinet, Bass Clarinet, Trumpet, Trombone, Harp, Violin, Viola, Cello.
Composed: 1959.

The rather angular vocal line lies mostly within a moderate range, but includes c''. The voice often relates to the instrumental parts by a half tone, major seventh or minor ninth. The tempo and meter remain constant within each piece.

417. STEARNS, Peter Pindar. Three Sacred Songs. New York: American Composers Alliance, n.d.

Text: The Bible.
Instrumentation: Soprano, Oboe, French Horn, Cello.
Composed: 1959.

Only a partial score was available for review. The vocal line is fairly angular. Little doubling of vocal pitches occurs, but half tone relationships are common. In the piece which was available for review, the tempo remains fairly constant. However, it includes irregular subdivisions of beats and small value notes tied across beats.

418. STEIN, Leon. String Quartet No. 5 - Ekloge. New York: American Composers Alliance, n.d.

Text: D. Thomas.
Instrumentation: Soprano, String Quartet.

Score not available for review.

419. STEINER, Gitta. Dream Dialogue 1974. New York: Seesaw Music, 1974.

Text: Gitta Steiner.
Instrumentation: Soprano, Percussion.

The angular vocal line includes wide leaps, multiple grace notes and wide leap grace notes. However, no demands are made on the extremes of the range. The following indications appear: "half spoken," "spoken," and "whispered." The piece is in two movements; the first indicated in seconds and the second in 6/8. The accompaniment consists of all non-pitched percussion, except for a vibraphone used in one small section. The relationship with the vibraphone is mostly dissonant.

420. STEINER, Gitta. Four Songs for Medium Voice and Vibraphone. New York: Seesaw Music, 1970.

I. Wild Wild Nights Wild Nights
II. Restless petals drop in the night
III. Long have I waited for your return
IV. Beneath the rain.

Text: Emily Dickinson.

The angular vocal line contains irregular rhythmic figures, multiple grace notes, gllissandi and indications such as "half spoken indefinite pitch." Pitch reference is remote. Little doubling occurs, but a half tone relationship is common. The four songs are mostly metered with some meter changes within each.

421. STEINER, Gitta. Interlude. New York: Seesaw Music, 1970.

In three untitled movements.
Instrumentation: Medium Voice, Vibraphone.

The angular vocal line contains many wide leaps. Dynamic changes are indicated frequently and explicitly. Steiner includes metronomic tempo markings, but no bar lines. Irregular subdivisions of beats are superimposed and interspersed with small value rests. Multiple grace notes appear in both parts.

422. STEINER, Gitta. New Poems. New York: Seesaw Music, 1974.

Five untitled songs.
Two texts by the composer
Two texts by Emily Dickinson
One text, unidentified
Instrumentation: Voice, Vibraphone.

The generally angular, but sometimes lyric, vocal line often relates to the vibraphone by a half step. Some glissandi and large leaps appear. The tempo and meter remain fairly constant within each movement.

423. STEINER, Gitta. Three Poems. New York: Seesaw Music, 1970.

In three untitled movements.
Text: Gitta Steiner.
Instrumentation: Voice, Percussion (2).
Duration: ca. 8 Minutes.

The following are explanatory notes from the composer:

"In proportional notation, the entrances of instruments are lined up according to visual relationships. By the spatial distribution, the performers can coordinate their own parts with those of others.

"Beams indicate the approximate durations of notes.

"Groups of grace notes figures are played as fast as possible. The varying difficulties in the execution of such passages results in a natural and spontaneous irregularity.

"Groups of free notes are proportional."

The singer contends with an angular vocal line and remote pitch references including much dissonance.

424. STEVENS, Halsey. Three Japanese Folksongs. New York: American Composers Alliance, n.d.

Instrumentation: Medium Voice, Violin, Cello, Piano.

Score not available for review.

425. STEVENS, Halsey. Two Shakespeare Songs. New York: American Composers Alliance, 1960.

Come Away Death (Twelfth Night)
Under the Greenwood Tree (As You Like It)

Instrumentation: Voice, Flute, Clarinet.
Duration: ca. 4 Minutes, 40 Seconds.
Dedication: Margery Mackay.

The vocal part moves mostly by steps and small leaps. Little doubling occurs, but the vocal pitches relate closely to the instrumental pitches. The tempo and meter remain fairly constant in each piece.

426. STEVENS, Halsey. When Icicles Hang by the Wall. New York: Composers Facsimile Edition, 1954.

Text: William Shakespeare, "Loves Labours Lost."
Instrumentation: Voice, Flute, Cello, Piano.
Composed: 1940, 1951.
Dedication: Joseph B. Holloway.

The lyric vocal line moves mostly in steps and small leaps. Instruments frequently double the vocal pitches.

The range is modest: c - f#'. The tempo remains constant, but some meter changes occur.

427. STEWART, Don. Wait. New York: Carl Fischer, 1979.

Text: Galway Kinnell.
Instrumentation: Soprano, Flute, Piano.

Vocal entrance pitches usually relate to the flute by a small interval (minor thirds or smaller) or unison, but sometimes with an octave displacement. Very little other doubling occurs, however. The vocal line includes some spoken parts and an occasional indication for "no vib," or "wide vib." The tempo and meter change frequently. Some superimpositions of irregular subdivisions of beats occur.

428. STEWART, Frank. The First Joy of Marriage. New York: Seesaw Music, 1976.

Text: translated excerpt from a late 15th century French manuscript called The Fifteen Joys of Marriage.
Instrumentation: Voice, Marimba (2).
Composed: 1970.

The printed vocal range includes A - ab'. However, the composer states the following: "Pitches are to be considered as being approximations. There may be places where the vocalist will need more of a spoken sound, rather than a sung sound." Some meter changes occur. Four and a half over four is a favorite diversion, but for only one bar at a time. Superimpositions of diverse subdivisions of beats are common.

429. STOCK, David. Scat. Newton Centre, MA: Margun Music, 1979.

Fast, Swinging
Slow, relaxed
Very fast

Instrumentation: Soprano, Flute, Bass Clarinet, Violin, Cello.
Duration: 9 Minutes.
Written for the Boston: Musica Viva, Richard Pittman, conductor.

Instead of a text Stock gives the singer such syllables as "ska-boo da-dih." Large intervals, many larger than an octave, predominate the vocal line. Occasional doublings by the instruments and some third relationships occur. Some bits and one large section are written for unaccompanied voice. A wide range is required: Ab - d''. The composer states, "The voice is treated instrumentally, as a slightly-more-than-equal partner to the instruments." A page of performance notes preceeds the piece, in which a conductor is indicated.

430. STOUT, Alan. An Allegory: Pride, Op. 73. New York: American Composers Alliance, n.d.

Text: L. Handy.
Instrumentation: Soprano, Clarinet, Percussion, Piano, Cello.

Score not available for review.

431. STOUT, Alan. Christmas Antiphon, Op. 37. New York: American Composers Alliance, n.d.

Instrumentation: Soprano (or Tenor), Cello, Organ, Tom-toms (4).

Score not available for review.

432. STOUT, Alan. Commentary of T'ung Jen, Op. 14. New York: American Composers Alliance, n.d.

Instrumentation: Soprano (or Tenor), Oboe, Piano, Small Drum.

Score not available for review.

433. STOUT, Alan. Die Engel. New York: Autograph Editions, 1970.

Text: R.M. Rilke (Das Buch der Bilder).
Instrumentation: Soprano, Trumpet (6), Trombone (3), Tuba, Piano, Cymbals, Violin (or Flute or Oboe).
Composed: 1957.
Duration: 5 Minutes, 45 Seconds.
Dedication: Richard Pittman.

Except for the angular opening phrase, the voice part moves mostly by steps and small leaps. The violin (or flute or oboe) usually doubles the vocal line which encompasses a range of B - e'', and in some parts lies generally quite high. The tempo is constant but the meter changes frequently. The vocal part contains simple rhythmic figures (mostly quarter and half notes or longer at quarter note = 100). Stage directions indicate the use of a conductor. Strings or multiple strings may be substituted for the brass.

434. STOUT, Alan. Landscape, Op. 36. New York: American Composers Alliance, n.d.

Text: Hsuch-Ton.
Instrumentation: Mezzo-Soprano, Flute, English Horn, Tam-Tam, Harp.

Score not available for review.

435. STOUT, Alan. Two Songs of Ariel, 1957. New York: American Composers Alliance, n.d.

Text: Shakespeare.
Instrumentation: Soprano, Oboe, Violin, Cello, Bass Clarinet, Celesta, Percussion (2), Harp.

Score not available for review.

436. STRAVINSKY, Igor. In Memoram Dylan Thomas. New York: Boosey & Hawkes, 1954.

Dirge-Canons: Prelude
Song: Do not go gentle...
Dirge-Canons: Postlude

Text: Dylan Thomas.
Instrumentation: Tenor, String Quartet, Trombones (4).
Duration: 6 Minutes.

The "Prelude" and "Postlude" are antiphonal canons between a quartet of trombones and the string quartet. "Song" is accompanied by the string quartet. Though the vocal line moves mostly in steps and small leaps, some large leaps occur. Much of the movement is chromatic. The strings frequently double isolated pitches in the vocal line. The vocal range is moderate.

437. STRAVINSKY, Igor. Three Songs from William Shakespeare. New York: Boosey & Hawkes, 1954.

I. Musick to heare
II. Full fadom five
III. When Daisies pied

Instrumentation: Mezzo-Soprano, Flute, Clarinet, Viola.
Dedicated to Evenings on the Roof (Los Angeles)

Except for frequent meter changes in number one, the tempo and meter remain constant throughout each piece. Regular duple subdivisions of beats prevail throughout. Vocal pitches relate to those of the instruments, but doublings, even of isolated pitches, occur infrequently. The vocal line is angular.

438. STUCKEY, Steven. Schneemusik. New York: American Composers Alliance, n.d.

Text: Celan and Goll.
Instrumentation: High Soprano, Piano (Percussion).

Score not available for review.

439. SWACK, Irwin. Psalm VIII: O Lord, Our Lord, How Excellent Is Thy Name. New York: Chaplet Music, 1967.

Instrumentation: Voice, Piano, Trumpet (or Clarinet).

The vocal range is moderate, f - gb', and the piano frequently doubles the vocal pitches. Meter changes occur often, but rhythmic figures are simple, mostly half notes, quarter notes and groups of eighth notes.

440. SYDEMAN, William. Four Japanese Songs. Boston: Ione Press, 1970.

In four movements.
Text: Translated form the Japanese by Kenneth Rexroth.
Instrumentation: Soprano, Violin (2).

Some meter and tempo changes appear in all movements. Rhythmic figures are simple, and ensemble coordination is not likely to be a problem. Vocal pitches relate clearly to the violin parts. Much doubling of isolated pitches occurs. This work is published with a score and two separate violin parts.

441. SYDEMAN, William. Encounters. New York: Okra Music, 1968.

Blue Guitar (Wallace Stevens)
Gertrude Stein Statement
(Procne)
Vase of Tears
Sons of Our Fathers, Mother and Child
Variations on a Chisel

The Defiance of Prometheus
Finale: Praise We Great Men

Instrumentation: Baritone, Violin, Cello, Piano.
Dedication: Jacques Lipchitz.

"The Defiance of Prometheus" is sung, but other parts are instrumental with rhythmically free spoken parts. The vocal line contains many chromatic alterations, and isolated pitches are doubled by the instruments. A wide range is required: EE - g.

442. SYDEMAN, William. Jabberwocky. Boston: Ione Press, 1970.

Text: Lewis Carroll.
Instrumentation: Soprano (or Tenor), Flute, Cello.

The fairly lyric vocal line moves mostly in steps and small leaps. Pitches relate clearly to the instrumental parts, but with some dissonance. Range is B - b'. Jabberwocky is one continuous piece. Some tempo and meter changes occur.

443. SYDEMAN, William. Malediction. New York: Okra Music, 1970.

Instrumentation: Tenor, String Quartet, Tape.
Duration: ca. 25 Minutes.

The players come on stage with their instruments still in the cases and pushing a black box. The players get ready, the audience gets quiet, then the tenor pops out of the box. He pops out and goes back into the box at various times throughout the perfromance. The tenor sings, speaks and whispers. Special indications include "a hooting quaver," "Italian opera!," "falsetto," etc. Some doubling of isolated pitches occurs, but more often the vocal line relates to an instrument by a 1/2 tone. Some parts of the piece are measured; some are organized by seconds.

444. SYDEMAN, William. Three Songs. Boston: Ione Press, 1970.

I. I heard a fly buzz when I died
II. I taste a liquor never brewed
III. Hope is a thing with feathers.

Text: Emily Dickinson.
Instrumentation: Soprano, Cello.
Composed: 1959.

The vocal line moves mostly by steps and small leaps, with only a few large leaps. Pitches relate closely to the cello part. The meter and tempo are fairly constant within each movement, and rhythmic figures are simple.

445. SYDEMAN, William. Three Songs of Elizabethan Texts. Boston: Ione Press, 1970.

I. A Modest Love (Sir Edward Dyer)
II. Elegy (Chidiock Tichborne)
III. The Fly (William Oldys)

Instrumentation: Soprano (or Tenor), Flute.

The vocal line lies mostly within the treble staff. Pitches relate easily to the flute, with occasional doublings. The meter changes frequently. Tempo fluctuations and irregular subdivisions of beats are common.

446. TANENBAUM, Elias. Images. New York: American Composers Alliance, n.d.

Instrumentation: Female Voice, Piano, Percussion, Tape.

Score not available for review.

447. TANENBAUM, Elias. Images III. New York: American Composers Alliance, n.d.

Text: "My Fellow Americans."
Instrumentation: Soprano, Tape.

Score not available for review.

448. TANENBAUM, Elias. Mirage and Incantation. New York: American Composers Alliance, n.d.

Instrumentation: Female Voice, Piano, Violin, Cello, Clarinet, Electronic Tape.

Score not available for review.

449. TANENBAUM, Elias. Peter Quince At the Clavier. New York: American Composers Alliance, 1959.

Text: Wallace Stevens.
Instrumentation: Soprano, Flute (Piccolo), Clarinet, Guitar, Viola, Bass Trombne.
Duration: 12 Minutes.

The vocal line is fairly angular. Some doublings of pitches occur, but dissonant relationships are more common. The meter changes frequently, often in every bar, but rhythmic figures are not complex.

450. TAUB, Bruce J. *"...of Things Past"*. New York: American Composers Alliance, n.d.

Text: Proust; Translated by Moncrieff.
Instrumentation: Soprano, Piano, Violin (2), Viola, Cello.

Score not available for review.

451. TAUB, Bruce J. *O Sweet Spontaneous Earth*. New York: American Composers Alliance, n.d.

Text: e e cummings.
Instrumentation: Soprano, Flute.

Score not available for review.

452. TAYLOR, Clifford. *Quattro Liriche from "Mattino Domenicale"*. New York: American Composers Alliance, n.d.

Text: Stevens.
Instrumentation: Medium Voice, Eb Alto Saxophone, Piano.

Score not available for review.

453. TAYLOR, Clifford. *Two Songs*, Op.5. New York: American Composers Alliance, n.d.

Text: Sandburg.
Instrumentation: Soprano (or Tenor), Clarinet, Piano.

Score not available for review.

454. THOMAS, Andrew. *Dirge in the Woods*. Newton Centre, MA: Margun Music, n.d.

Instrumentation: Soprano, Percussion, Harp.
Duration: 8 Minutes.

Score not available for review.

455. THOMSON, Virgil. _Five Phrases from the Song of Solomon_. New York: American Music Edition, 1953.

I. Thou that dwellest in the gardens
II. Return, O Shulamite!
III. O, my dove
IV. I am my beloved's
V. My night

Instrumentation: Soprano, Percussion.
Composed: 1926.
Dedication: Hildegard Watson.

The lyric vocal line moves mostly by steps and small leaps. Since only non-pitched percussion instruments are used, there are no pitch references. Number 2 is scored for unaccompanied voice. The meter changes frequently, but rhythmic figures are simple.

456. THOMSON, Virgil. _Four Songs to Poems of Thomas Campion_. New York: G. Ricordi, 1953.

1. Follow your Saint
2. There is a Garden in her Face
3. Rose check'd Laura, Come
4. Follow thy Fair Sun

Instrumentation: Mezzo-Soprano, Clarinet, Viola, Harp.
Also available in a version for piano and voice.

The meter changes occasionally, but no complex rhythmic figures appear. The tempo remains fairly constant throughout each movement. The vocal part relates directly to the instrumental parts, often with doublings. Moving mostly in steps and small leaps, the lyric vocal line frequently outlines chord patterns.

457. TRIMBLE, Lester. _Four Fragments From the Canterbury Tales_. New York: C.F. Peters, 1967.

I. Prologue: Molto vivace e leggiero
II. A Knight: Allegro quasi pesante
III. A yong Squier: Suave e leggiero
IV. The Wyf of Beside Bathe: Vivace

Text: Geoffrey Chaucer
Instrumentation: Soprano, Flute, Clarinet in A, Harpsichord.
Duration: 17 Minutes.

The score includes a "Guide to Pronunciation of Middle English." Trimble states, "Middle English is probably the better language. The great preponderance of vowels is open." Fast tempo, placement of rests, irregular rhythmic figures and changing meters may present ensemble problems in the final movement. Changing meters and balance between the four instruments demands special attention in all movements. The vocal line is somewhat angular, but pitches relate closely to the instrumental parts. The following appears in a cover note: "According to the composer, Four Fragments from the Canterbury Tales was conceived as a narrative monodrama, in which the individual sections add up to a formally balanced piece of chamber music."

458. TRIMBLE, Lester. Petit Concert. New York: C.F. Peters, 1969.

I. (no title)
II. Arioso
III. Intermezzo
IV. Arioso
V. Finale con Arioso

Texts: II. William Shakespeare, from The Merchant of Venice.
IV. & V. William Blake, from Songs of Experience.
Instrumentation: Medium Voice, Violin, Oboe, Harpsichord (Piano).
Duration: 12 Minutes.
Dedication: The New York Chamber Soloists.

The meter changes frequently in some sections, but the tempo remains constant throughout each movement. Triple subdivisions of the beat are used extensively in duple meter, but there are no superimposed complex rhythmic figures. The vocal pitches relate easily to the instrumental parts. Numbers I and III are instrumental only.

459. TUBB, Monte. Five Haiku for Soprano and String Quartet. Ann Arbor, MI: CMP Library Edition University Microfilms, c. 1968 by Monte Tubb.

Snow whispering down...
Into a cold night...
Oh, cuckoo...
He who climbs...
Even the soldiers...

Text: Anonymous Japanese.
Duration: ca. 9 Minutes.

This work was written for the Atlanta School System under the MENC Contemporary Music Project for creativity in Music Education. The composer describes the difficulty as "advanced high school - college: difficult." Each of the five sections is written in a constant 3/4 meter with some tempo changes. The vocal part relates closely to the string parts.

460. UDOW, Michael. Eight American Indian Children's Poems. New York: American Composers Alliance, n.d.

Uncertain Admission (Frances Brazil)
Direction (Alonzo Lopez)
Interlude
Battle Won Is Lost (Phil George)
A Silver Mist (Paricia Irving)
Loneliness (Loyal Shegonee)
I Go Forth (Alonzo Lopez)
Red Eagle (Janet Campbell)
That Lonesome Place (Calvin O'John)

Instrumentation: Soprano, Oboe (English Horn), Bassoon, Piano.
Dedication: Phil and Beth Kolker.

Some doubling of the vocal part occurs, but often concurrently by a half tone reationship with another instrument. Soprano includes c'' at the top. Number three is scored for unaccompanied voice; numbers five and six have an ostinato accompaniment; and number seven is a duet with soprano and bassoon doubling each other nearly all the way. Some meter changes occur, but the tempo is constant in each.

461. UDOW, Michael. Electric Silence. New York: Composes Alliance, n.d.

Text: Winfield T. Scott.
Instrumentation: Basso, Flute (Piccolo), Bass Clarinet, Bassoon, Trombone, Percussion (2), Piano, Violin, Cello.

Score not available for review.

462. UNG, Chinary. Mohori. New York: C.F. Peters, 1976.

Text: No text. IPA symbols indicate the shapes of the sounds.
Instrumentaion: Mezzo-Soprano, Flute, Oboe, Classical Guitar, Cello, Harp, Piano, Percussion (2).
For the Serge Koussevitzky Music Foundation in the Library of Congress, and dedicated to the memory of Serge and Natalie Koussevitzky.

The seating arrangement diagram specifies a conductor. Extensive instructions at the beginning give explanations of the non-traditional symbols. Ung uses symbols for the voice which are different from those that other composers are using for non-traditional techniques and sounds. Mohori requires a wide, esecially low range: E - a'. Several sections for solo voice appear. The vocal pitches relate closely to the instrumental parts, but rhythmically the piece is complex. Varieties of intricate rhythmic figures are superimposed.

463. UNG, Chinary. Tall Wind. New York: C.F. Peters, 1975.

(untitled - no text)
Sunset
Sonnet

Text: e e cummings, "stringing gold swarms" and "a wind has blown the rain away," from his volume Poems.
Instrumentation: Soprano, Flute, Oboe, Guitar, Cello.
Duration: ca. 6 Minutes.
Dedication: Frances Riley.
Composed: 1970.

A page of performance notes at the beginning explains various notational symbols and special effects required. The composer specifies a great deal of dynamic shading and quick dynamic changes. Dynamic extremes most often lie in the quiet area. Wide leaps appear in all parts. Grace notes are often a wide leap away from the note to which they are attached. Instruments double some isolated pitches in the vocal line, but more frequently the voice relates to the instruments by a 1/2 tone. In the first movement the composer asks the soprano to sing "ah" and to hum.

464. VAN NOSTRAND, Burr. Earth Manual - 1976. New York: American Composers Alliance. 1976.

I. California Travelogues
II. Song of the Trees (Chippewa)
III. Song of the Night (Papago)
IV. Dream Song (Chippewa)
V. Mide Chant (Ojibwa)
VI. Song of Failure (Sioux)

Instrumentation: Soprano, Flute (Piccolo), Clarinet (Bass Clarinet), Violin, Cello, Prepared Piano, Percussion.
Duraion: ca. 19 Minutes.
Commissioned by the National Endowment for the Arts

The vocal line includes numerous glissandi and multiple grace notes. Whispers and spoken parts and many other non-traditional requirements are interspersed. The vocal line encompasses G - c#'' and ends with a sustained chant-like section in the high range. The soprano also plays scullery chimes and wine glasses. Some of the piece is metered, some indicated in seconds. Extensive information at the beginning includes the following: abbreviations, notational symbols, quarter-tones and tone bending, preparations for the piano (baby grand). "Amplification is required for the Prepared Piano and for the Timpani in the sixth movement." The composer states

"any movement may be excerpted and played independently. Any given group of movements may be recorded and played independently. However, the theatrical scenario should be omitted when the piece is not played in its entirety."

465. VAN NOSTRAND, Burr. Lunar Possession Manual - 1973, a Winter Ceremonial. New York: American Composers Alliance, n.d.

Instrumentation: Soprano, Flute (Piccolo), Clarinet, Violin, Cello, Contrabass, Piano, Percussion, Optional Dancers.

Score not available for review.

466. VERRAL, John. The Rose of the World. New York: American Composers Alliance, n.d.

Text: Yeats.
Instrumentation: Soprano, Flute, Piano.

Score not available for review.

467. WARREN, Elinor Remick. Sonnets for Soprano and String Quartet. New York: Carl Fischer, 1974.

Text: Edna St. Vincent Millay, from "Fatal Interview"

The lyric vocal line moves mostly by steps and small leaps. The instruments double many pitches and even some complete phrases. Few meter and tempo changes occur. The work is published with a score and four string parts, each with vocal cues. It is also available for string orchestra (material on rental).

468. WEBER, Ben. Concert Aria after Solomon, Op. 29. New York: America Composers Alliance, 1953.

Instrumentation: Soprano, Flute, Oboe, Clarinet, French Horn, Bassoon, Violin, Cello, Piano.
Composed: 1949.

Most of the vocal line lies fairly high and moves generally in steps and small leaps with some chromaticism. Some doubling by the instruments occurs. Changes in tempo and meter are infrequent. This is also published in a version for soprano and piano (reduction).

469. WEBER, Ben. Four Songs, Op. 40. New York: New Music Edition, 1954.

An Immortality (Ezra Pound)
Animula Blandula Vagula (The Emperor Hadrian, translated by Charles Glenn Walls)
The Vine To the Goat (Euenus, translated from the Greek by L.R. Lind)
The Moon (Bhasa, translated from the Sanskrit by A. Berriedale Keith)

Instrumentation: Soprano (or Tenor), Cello.
Dedication: Bethany Beardslee.

The meter changes frequently except in number 1 where unequal bars appear with no meter signatures. The vocal line alternates between angular movement and movement by steps and small leaps. Pitches relate to the instrumental parts, but little doubling, even of isolated pitches, occurs. The moderate range lies mostly on the treble staff. The singer is also required to whistle.

470. WEBER, Ben. Three Songs, Op. 48. Hillsdale, NY: Boelke-Bomart, 1978.

Text: Dehmel, George, Rilke.
Instrumentation: Soprano (or Tenor), String Quartet.
Composed: 1958.
Duration: 13 Minutes.

Score not available for review. The publisher has indicated that it is available in blue print edition, only.

471. WEIGL, Karl. Five Songs. New York: John Markert, 1957.

1. Consolation (Ina Seidl)
2. Summer Afternoon (Vally Weigl)
3. Rain Song (Klaus Groth)
4. Ave Maria (Rud. List)
5. Invitation for Supper at Martinmas (Wunderhorn)

Text: English words by Ronald V. Smith.
Instrumentation: Soprano, String Quartet.

The lyric vocal line moves mostly by steps and small leaps. Pitches relate closely to the instrumental parts and doubling is common. A moderate range lies mostly on the treble staff. The ensemble generally moves in homogeneous rhythm.

472. WEIGL, Karl. _Three Songs_. New York: American Composers Alliance, n.d.

Text: L. Perera and V. Weigl, tr.
Instrumentation: Mezzo-Soprano, String Quartet.

Score not available for review.

473. WEIGL, Vally. _Along the Moving Darkness_. New York: American Composers Alliance, n.d.

Instrumentation: Medium High Voice, Flute (or Violin), Piano.

Score not available for review.

474. WEIGL, Vally. _Beyond Time_. New York: American Composers Alliance, n.d.

1. Remainder
2. The Hills Have Great Hearts
3. Happy Summer
4. Fill! Fill the Cup
5. Treasure

Text: Frederika Blankner, from _Secret Bread_.
Instrumentation: High Voice, Violin, Piano.

The voice moves mostly in steps, small leaps or triadic patterns within a moderate range. Entrance pitches relate closely to the previous instrumental material. The tempo and meter remain fairly constant within each piece.

475. WEIGL, Vally. _Birds in Springtime_. New York: American Composers Alliance, n.d.

Text: G.S. Bail.
Instrumentation: High (or Medium-High) Voice, Piano, Flute (or Clarinet).

Score not available for review.

476. WEIGL, Vally. _Brief Encounters_. New York: American Composers Alliance, 1977.

I. Lament
II. Intermezzo
III. Evocation
IV. Alla Dansa
V. Arioso

VI. Rondelette
VII. Old Time Divertemento

Instrumentation: Mezzo-Soprano (or Clarinet), Violin (or Oboe or English Horn), French Horn.

There seems to be confusion about the instrumentation of this piece. The composer gives the above instrumentation and indicates that this is for voice and instrumental duo or for an instrumental trio. In number VII, however, she specifies Trumpet (or Clarinet), French Horn and Bassoon. The voice part is set entirely on "ah" and does function as another instrumental part. It contains mostly scale-wise and triadic movement and encompasses a sizable range: G - db''. Much doubling occurs.

477. WEIGL, Vally. Cardinal in March. New York: American Composers Alliance, n.d.

Text: E.R. Weigl.
Instrumentation: High (or Medium) Voice, Piano, Flute (or Clarinet).

Score not available for review.

478. WEIGL, Vally. Challenge. New York: American Composers Alliance, n.d.

Text: Edith Segal.
Instrumentation: Mezzo-Soprano (or Baritone), Piano, Flute (ossia Clarinet or Violin obbligato).

Score not available for review.

479. WEIGL, Vally. Christ Child's Lullaby. New York: American Composers Alliance, n.d.

Instrumentation: Mezzo-Soprano, Flute (or Clarinet), Piano.

Score not available for review.

480. WEIGL, Vally. City Birds. New York: American Composers Alliance, 1957.

Text: Madeline Mason.
Instrumentation: Voice, Flute, Piano.

Vocal entrance pitches relate closely to the previous instrumental material, and much doubling occurs throughout. This lies within a moderate but generally middle/low range: A - f'. Some meter changes occur, but the tempo is constant and rhythmic figures are simple.

481. WEIGL, Vally. Dear Earth: A Quintet of Poems. New York: American Composers Alliance, n.d.

Text: F. Blankner.
Instrumentation: Medium High Voice, French Horn, Violin, Cello, Piano.

Score not available for review.

482. WEIGL, Vally. Do Not Awake Me. New York: American Composers Alliance, n.d.

Text: Marion Edey.
Instrumentation: Mezzo-Soprano, Violin, (or Flute or Clarinet), Piano.

Score not available for review.

483. WEIGL, Vally. The Drums of War. New York: American Composers Alliance, n.d.

Instrumentation: Medium Voice, Guitar.

Score not available for review.

484. WIEGL, Vally. Echos. New York: American Composers Alliance, 1958.

I. The Singing of the Earth
II. Winter Night
III. Lantern in the Snow
IV. The Angelus
V. Of Heaven and Earth

Text: Patricia Benton.
Instrumentation: Medium Voice (and/or French Horn), Violin, Piano.
Dedication: Joseph and Dixie Eger.

The vocal line moves mostly in steps, small leaps and triadic patterns. It lies generally low F - f'. The instruments frequently double the voice. Some meter changes occur, but the tempo is constant within each song. The composer provides two versions with an extra part for French Horn in the second version.

485. WEIGL, Vally. Five Songs of Remembrance. New York: American Composers Alliance, n.d.

Text: Dickinson.
Instrumentation: Contralto (or Mezzo-Soprano), String Quartet.
[or - Mezzo-Soprano, Flute (or Violin or Clarinet), Piano.]

Score not available for review.

486. WEIGL, Vally. Glimpse of Hope. New York: American Composers Alliance, n.d.

Text: R. List
Instrumentation: Mezzo-Soprano (or Baritone), Violin (or Flute), Piano.

Score not available for review.

487. WEIGL, Vally. The Huntsman. New York: American Composers Alliance, n.d.

Text: R.L. Stevenson.
Instrumentation: Medium Voice, Recorder, Piano.

Score not available for review.

488. WEIGL, Vally. I Saw two Birds. New York: American Composers Alliance, 1975.

Text: Edith Segal.
Instrumentation: Medium Voice, Clarinet, Bass Clarinet (or Bassoon).

Much doubling and many third relationships exist between the voice and instruments throughout. Vocal entrance pitches relate closely to the previous instrumental material. Some meter changes occur.

489. WEIGL, Vally. The Little Singers. New York: American Composers Alliance, n.d.

Text: E. Hammond.
Instrumentation: Medium Voice, Soprano Recorder (or Flute), Piano.

Score not available for review.

490. WEIGL, Vally. Long, Long Ago. New York: American Composers Alliance, n.d.

Text: A Christmas Carol.
Instrumentation: Medium Voice, Soprano Recorder (or Flute), Piano.

Score not available for review.

491. WEIGL, Vally. Lyrical Suite. New York: American Composers Alliance, n.d.

Text: F. Blankner.
Instrumentation: Mezzo-Soprano, Flute (or Clarinet), Cello Obbligato, Piano.

Score not available for review.

492. WEIGL, Vally. Nature Moods. New York: American Composers Alliance, 1974.

I. Whippoorwill
II. Winter Reverie
III. Afterthoughts
IV. Insect Orchestra
V. Gardener's Prayer

Text: Harry Woodbourne, from The Green Kingdom.
Instrumentation: High Voice, Clarinet (or Flute), Violin.
Dedication: Stanley Drucker.

The vocal entrance pitches relate closely to the previous instrumental material, and some doubling of pitches occurs. Nature Moods does not exploit the extremes of the vocal range. Each song includes some tempo and meter changes.

493. WEIGL, Vally. Nightfall in the Mountains. New York: American Composers Alliance, 1975.

Text: Vally Weigl.
Instrumentation: Voice, Viola (or Violin), Piano.

The vocal line moves mostly by steps, small leaps and triadic patterns within a range of G - f#'. Pitches are usually doubled by the instruments. This is set in both German and English.

494. WEIGL, Vally. Pippa's Song. New York: American Composers Alliance, n.d.

Text: R. Browning.
Instrumentation: Voice (1 or 2), Soprano Recorder, Piano.

Score not available for review.

495. WEIGL, Vally. Rabbles of Shattered Leaves. New York: American Composer Alliance, n.d.

Text: Carl Sandburg.
Instrumentation: Voice, Violin, Piano.

The text is short (only 11 bars for voice) and the range is moderate. Vocal entrance pitches relate closely to the previous instrumental material Some meter changes occur, but the tempo is constant.

496. WEIGL, Vally. Rain at Night. New York: American Composers Alliance, n.d.

Text: Hesse.
Instrumentation: Low Voice, Viola, Piano.

Score not available for review.

497. WEIGL, Vally. Requiem for Allison. New York: American Composers Alliance, 1971.

Text: Peter Davies.
Instrurmentation: Mezzo-Soprano (or Soprano), String Quartet.

Vocal entrance pitches relate closely to the previous instrumental material, and some doubling of pitches occurs. The range is moderate. Few meter and tempo changes appear.

498. WEIGL, Vally. The Rock-A-By Lady. New York: American Composers Alliance, n.d.

Text: Eugene Field.
Instrumentation: Medium Voice, Recorder, Piano.

Score not available for review.

499. WEIGL, Vally. The Salvation of the Dawn. New York: American Composers Alliance, n.d.

Text: Translated from the Sanskrit.
Instrumentation: Voice, Clarinet (or Violin), Piano (or Organ).

The vocal line lies fairly low, but within a moderate range. Entrance pitches relate closely to the instrumental parts and much doubling occurs throughout. The meter changes a few times, the tempo is constant and rhythmic figures are simple.

500. WEIGL, Vally. The Sea Moves Always. New York: American Composers Alliance, 1976.

Text: Carl Sandburg.
Instrumentation: Voice, Flute (or Clarinet or Violin), Piano.

The vocal line moves by steps, small leaps and triadic figures within a moderate range. Pitches are almost always doubled by an instrument.

501. WEIGL, Vally. Seal Lullaby. New York: American Composers Alliance, n.d.

Text: Kipling.
Instrumentation: Mezzo-Soprano, Piano, Recorder (or Oboe).

Score not available for review.

502. WEIGL, Vally. Seeking You. New York: American Composers Alliance, 1957.

Text: Harry Woodbourne.
Instrumentaion: Medium Low Voice, Violin (or Flute), Piano.

The vocal line moves mostly in steps and small leaps. Entrance pitches appear in the previous instrumental material and doubling is prominent throughout. Few tempo and meter changes occur.

503. WEIGL, Vally. Silver. New York: American Composers Alliance, n.d.

Text: de la Mare.
Instrumentation: Medium Voice, Recorder, Piano.

Score not available for review.

504. WEIGL, Vally. Songs for a Child. New York: American Composers Alliance, n.d.

Instrumentation: Voice (1 or 2), Recorder (or Flute), Piano.

Score not available for review.

505. WEIGL, Vally. Songs from "Native Island." New York: American Composers Alliance, n.d.

Text: Gerta Kennedy.
Instrumentation: Medium-Low Voice, Piano, Oboe, Clarinet (or Violin).

Score not available for review.

506 WEIGL, Vally, Songs from "No Boundary." New York: American Composers Alliance, n.d.

Text: Leonore Marsall.
Instrumentation: Medium Voice, Violin (or Viola), Piano.

Score not available for review.

507. WEIGL, Vally. Songs of Love and Leaving. New York: American Composers Alliance, n.d.

I. Loam [Medium Voice, Violin (or Clarinet), Piano]
II. Solo For Saturday Night Guitar [High Voice, Flute (or Violin or Viola), Piano]
III. Calls [Voice, Violin (or Viola), Piano]
IV. Valley Song [Medium Voice, Violin (or Viola), Piano], c. 1975.
V. At a Winslow [Medium High Voice, Violin (or Clarinet or Flute), Piano]
VI. Death Snips Proud Men by the Nose [Voice, Piano] c.1971; Composed, 1965.
VII. And This Will Be All? [Mezzo-Soprano, Violin (or Viola), Piano]
VIII. Stars, Songs, Faces [Medium High Voice, Violin (or Viola), Piano]
IX. On Langsyne Plantation [Medium High Voice, Violin (or Viola or Clarinet), Piano] c.1976.
X. Wind Horses [Medium Voice, Violin, Piano], c.1976.

Text: Carl Sandburg.

This appears to be a collection of ten separate songs. In each the range is generally moderate for the voice type indicated. Entrance pitches usually relate closely to the instrumental material and some doubling occurs throughout. Some meter changes appear, but rhythmic figures are mostly simple.

508. WEIGL, Vally. Soon. New York: American Composers Alliance, 1975.

Text: Edith Segal.
Instrumentation: Voice Flute (or Volin), Piano.

The vocal line moves mostly by steps and small leaps. The range is moderate except for the first phrase which is low. Frequent doublings of pitches occur. The tempo and meter are constant.

509. WEIGL, Vally. In Sprigntime. New York: American Composers Alliance, n.d.

Instrumentation: Medium Voice, Soprano Recorder (or Flute), Piano.

Score not available for review.

510. WEIGL, Vally. Summer Grass. New York: American Composers Alliance, n.d.

Text: Carl Sandburg.
Instrumentation: Mezzo-Soprano (or Soprano), String Quartet.

The vocal line lies within a limited range (d - f') and moves mostly by steps and small leaps. Entrance pitches relate closely to the previous instrumental material and doubling is common.

511. WEIGL, Vally. Summer Stars. New York: American posers Alliance, n.d.

Text: Carl Sandburg.
Instrumentation: Male Voice, Violin, Piano.

The composer indicates her preference for a tenor or high baritone. Entrance pitches relate closely to the previous instrumental material, with a good bit of doubling throughout. A few tempo and meter changes appear, but rhythmic figures are not complex.

512. WEIGL, Vally. Swiftly Along Flows the River. New York American Composers Alliance, n.d.

Text: Vally Weigl.
Instrumentation: Voice, French Horn (or Viola), Piano.

Vocal entrance pitches relate closely to the previous instrumental material and doubling is frequent throughout. The range is moderate. Tempo and meter remain constant.

513. WEIGL, Vally. _Thistle, Yarrow, Clover_. New York: American Composers Alliance, n.d.

Text: K. Porter.
Instrumentation: Medium Voice, Flute, Clarinet, Bassoon.

Score not available for review.

514. WEIGL, Vally. _Thoughts About Grasshoppers_. New York: American Composers Alliance, n.d.

Text: F.P. Jacques.
Instrumentation: Medium Voice, Flute (or Violin or Clarinet), Piano.

Score not available for review.

515. WEIGL, VAlly. _When the Vision Dies ("Perhaps")_. New York: American Composers Alliance, n.d.

Text: Vera Brittain.
Instrumentation: Medium Voice, Flute (or Violin or Clarinet), Piano.

Score not available for review.

516. WEIGL, Vally. _Where Go the Boats_. New York: American Composers Alliance, n.d.

Text: R.L. Stevenson.
Instrumentation: Medium Voice, Recorder, Piano.

Score not available for review.

517. WEIGL, Vally. _Winter Night_. New York: American Composers Alliance, n.d.

Text: Mary F. Butts.
Instrumentation: Medium Voice, Soprano Recorder, Piano.

Score not available for review.

518. WEIGL, Vally. _Wynken, Blynken and Nod_. New York: American Composers Alliance, n.d.

Text: Eugene Field.
Instrumentation: Voice (1 or 2), Recorder, Piano.

Score not available for review.

519. WEISGALL, Hugo. End of Summer. Bryn Mawr, PA: Theodore Presser, 1977.

I. After Lunch (Po Chü-i)
II. Quasi Fantasia
III. Hearing Someone Sing a Poem by Yuan Chen (Po Chu-i)
IV. Presto
V. De Senectute (George Boas)

Text: Po Chü-i (English version by the composer). George Boas.
Instrumentation: Tenor, Oboe, Violin, Viola, Cello.
Commissioned by the New York Chamber Soloists.
Dedication: Randolph S. Rothschild.

Some tempo changes occur in number I; munber II is free; and frequent meter chages appear in number III. Otherwise the tempo and meter remain fairly constant. The string trio most often moves as a unit with similar rhythmic figures. The oboe is occasionally integrated into the ensemble but usually functions as a solo instrument. Number II is written for unaccompanied oboe. The vocal part often moves in steps and small leaps, with many chromatic alterations. Sometimes it is angular with larger leaps. Pitch reference is often remote. The instruments occassionally double isolated pitches or two or three pitches in a row. End of Summer is published in score form. Instrumental parts are available on rental.

520. WEISGALL, Hugo. Fancies and Inventions. Bryn Mawr, PA: Theodore Presser, 1974.

1. To Criticks
2. Soft Musick
3. To Daffadils
4. To His Mistress Objecting To Him Neither Toying Or Talking
5. To Cherry-Blossoms
6. To The Detracter
7. The Voice And Violl
8. The Frozen Heart
9. I Call And I Call
10. To Musick, A Song

Text: Robert Herrick, from The Hesperides.
Instrumentation: Baritone, Flute, Clarinet, Viola, Cello, Piano.
Commissioned by the Baltimore Chamber Music Society. First performed, 1970.

The tempo and meter remain fairly constant throughout each movement except the following: #4 and #9 which have frequently changing meter, and #7 which is marked "quasi recitativo, sempre molto rubato e liberamente." The superimposition of non-similar subdivisions of beats appears in various parts. The vocal line often moves by 1/2 steps, including many chromatic alterations. Many 1/2 tone relationships occur between the vocal line and instruments.

521. WERNICK, Richard. <u>A Prayer for Jerusalem</u>. Bryn Mawr, PA: Theodore Presser, 1975.

Text: Portions of Psalm 122.
Instrumentation: Mezzo-Soprano, Percussion.
Composed: 1971.
Dedication: Jan DeGaetani West.
A recipient of the Naumburg Recording Award, 1975.

The piece is constructed in bars of varying length, identifed as "senza misura." The composer expects the time values and their relationsips to each other to remain constant. He also specifically indicates extremes in dynamics: pppp - fff. The singer's pitch references are extremely remote. Doublings, even of isolated notes, appear infrequently. When a passing half tone relationship occurs, the instrument usually sounds after the voice. The angular vocal line includes many grace notes. The singer also uses a dark stage whisper and plays the chimes. The text is set in Hebrew.

522. WHEAR, Paul. <u>From Thoreau</u>. Champaign, IL: Media Press, 1971.

In Four Movements
- not in strict rhythm
- very freely
- flowing
- like a dirge

Instrumentation: Soprano, Violin.

The vocal line moves by steps, small leaps and chromaticism within a moderate range. Entrance pitches (as well as many others) relate to the violin by consonant intervals. Number two is scored for voice alone. The meter changes fairly frequently.

523. WHITE, Louie, <u>This Son so Young</u>. New York: H.W. Gray, 1954.

I. Antiphon
II. Recitative
III. Air - This Son so Young
IV. Recitative
V. Air - Rise, My Son
VI. Antiphon

Text: Frederick H. Miesel.
Instrumentation: High Voice, Harp (or Piano), Organ.
Dedication: Russell Oberlin.

The lyric vocal line encompasses a moderate range (for a high voice) and contains some short coloratura passages. Instruments frequently double the vocal part. Meter changes sometimes occur frequently and some tempo changes appear within each piece. A few extremes of dynamics are required.

524. WITTENBERG, Charles. Even Though the World Keeps Changing. New York: American Composers Alliance, n.d.

Text: Rainer Maria Rilke, From Sonnets to Orpheus.
Instrumentation: Baritone, Flute, Vibraphone, Viola.
Composed: 1961.
Duration: ca. 4 Minutes.

Rhythmic coordination of the ensemble is complex. Irregular subdivisions of beats often occur across more than one beat. (See next listing for an example.) Superimposition of non-similar rhythmic figures is common. The tempo and meter change frequently. The vocal part often relates to the instrumental parts by a half tone, but little doubling occurs. Some spoken parts are required.

525. WHITTENBERG, Charles. Two Dylan Thomas Songs. New York: American Composers Alliance, 1964.

1. I Have Longed to Move Away
2. Now (Say Nay)

Instrumentation: Soprano, Flute (Alto Flute), Piano.
Dedication: Mary.

Rhythmic coordination of the ensemble is complex. Irregular subdivisions of beats often occur across more than one beat. E.g.

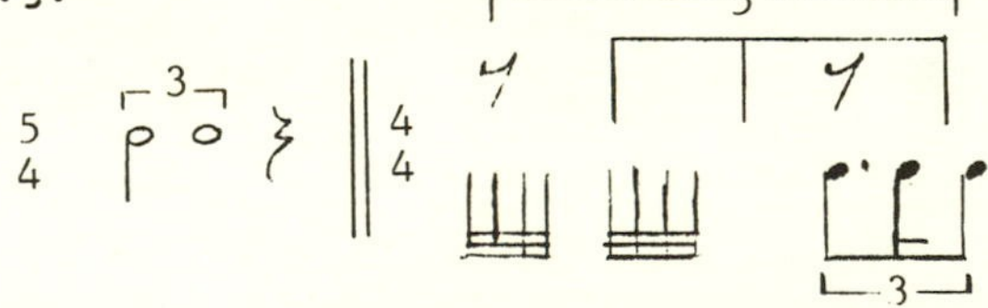

Superimposition of non-similar rhythmic figures is common. The tempo and meter change frequently. Much of the angular vocal line lies above the treble staff, but the range encompasses B - c''. Entrance pitches usually relate to the previous instrumental material by a small or consonant interval. Some doubling occurs.

526. WHITTENBERG, Charles. *Vocalise*. New York: American Composers Alliance, n.d.

Instrumentation: Soprano, Viola, Percussion.
Composed: 1963.

The composer explains the phonetic syllables and "New Articulation Signs" used in this piece. The pitches of the very angular vocal line relate remotely to the instrumental parts. The tempo and meter change frequently.

527. WILDER, Alec. *Phyllis McGinley Song Cycle*. Newton Centre, MA: Margun Music, n.d.

Instrumentation: Soprano, Bassoon, Harp.
Composed: 1979.
Duration: 8 Minutes.

Score not available for review.

528. WILLIAMS, Ronald Ray. "Suite of Six Texts." *ASUC Journal of Music* (1974):67-89.

An Argument of His Book (Herrick)
An Epitaph upon a Virgin (Herrick)
Epigram (Pope)
Echo (Christina Rossetti)
Mercury's Song to Phaedra (Dryden)
Music, when soft voices die (Shelly)

Instrumentation: Tenor, String Quartet.

The modest vocal range lies entirely on the treble staff. Though vocal pitches generally relate to the quartet, little doubling occurs. The quartet usually moves as a rhythmically homogeneous unit in contrast to the voice. The meter changes frequently.

529. WILSON, Donald. *Five Haiku*. n.p.: Higate Press, 1966.

I. Bell Tones (Bashō)
II. Evening Shadows (Buson)
III. The Sudden Chillness (Buson)
IV. The Morning Haze (Buson)
V. A Cove at the "Lake of the Views" (Bashō)

Texts: Bashō and Buson, translated by Harold Henderson.
Instrumentation: Tenor, English Horn, Guitar, String Quartet.
Duration: 8 Minutes.
Composed: 1962.

The vocal pitches relate clearly to the instrumental parts but often in half tone relationships. In addition to singing the tenor performs a falsetto hum and some spoken passages. The range is cb - b'. The meter and tempo remain constant throughout each movement.

530. WILSON, Donald. Sett. New York: Composers Facsimile Edition, n.d.

I. Symphonie
II. Ayre
III. Madrigal
IV. Chacon
V. Fuge

Instrumentation: 1-3 Low Voices (Optional), 3 Low Instruments.
Duration: 9 Minutes
Composed: 1962-63. Revised: 1965-67.
1974 Award winning Composition of the Jacksonville Delius Festival.
Dedication: Robert Palmer.

The composer includes no text in the score and gives no specific indications of where or how the voice is used. The following notes appear: "This 'sett' of pieces might be described as an homage to an ancient time. The forms are archaic, the titles purposefully antiquated. An Elizabethan poem, 'The Lady and her Viol' by John Donne, has been used for the third movement, a madrigal wich may be sung by three male voices, played by three instruments, or both"... or a combination of voices and instruments.

531. WILSON, Olly. Sometimes. Newton Centre, MA Margun Music, n.d.

Instrumentation: Tenor, Tape.
Composed: 1976.
Duration: 16 Minutes.

Score not available for review.

532. WINSOR, Philip. The Fly. New York: American Composers Alliance, n.d.

Text: William Blake.
Instrumentation: Baritone, Flute, Bass Clarinet, Violin, Cello.

Score not available for review.

533. WINSOR, Philip. <u>The Sick Rose</u>. New York: American Composers Alliance, n.d.

Text: William Blake.
Instrumentation: Soprnao, Flute, Bass Clarinet, Volin, Cello.

Score not available for review.

534. WOLPE, Stefan. <u>Quintet with Voice</u>. n.p.: Southern Music Publishing, 1977.

I. Of Festive Grace
II. Here the sun, violet (Hilda Morley)
III. Variations

Instrumentation: Voice (in second movement only), Clarinet, French Horn, Cello, Harp, Piano.
Composed: 1956-57.

The voice part, notated in the bass clef, relates only remotely to the instrumental parts. Very little doubling, even of isolated pitches, occurs. The meter and tempo change frequently. <u>Quintet</u> is published in a very difficult to read manuscript score.

535. WRIGHT, Maurice. <u>Cantata</u>. Hillsdale, NY: Mobart, 1976.

I. To Music, to Becalm His Fever (Robert Herrick)
II. To Lucia Playing on her Lute (Samuel Pardage)
III. The Commendation of Music (William Strode)
IV. Wit Predominant (Thomas Rymer)
V. To Music, To Becalm His Fever (continued)

Instrumentation: Tenor, Percussion, Tape.
Duration: 17 Minutes.

The tempo remains fairly steady throughout each movement, but frequent meter changes occur in some sections. The tape is continuous in all movements. According to the score indications, many of the tenor's isolated pitches are doubled by the tape. However, these doublings are usually at a half step relationship with another pitch on the tape. The angular tenor line includes a high c.

536. WUORINEN, Charles. <u>A Message to Denmark Hill</u>. New York: C.F. Peters, 1976.

Text: from Untitled Subjects by Richard Howard and made into a Cantata by Charles Wuorinen.

Instrumentation: Baritone, Flute, Cello, Piano.
Duration: 26 Minutes.
Composed: 1970.

This piece consists of recitatives, arias, spoken sections, an instrumental symphony and several instrumental laments. The vocal line is angular. Irregular subdivisions of the beats and meter changes occur frequently. The superimposition of non-similar rhythmic figures contributes to the complexity of the ensemble coordination.

537. WYNER, Yehudi. Memorial Music I: Man Comes from Dust (Ki K'shimcho). Memoral Music II: Lord, let Me Know My End. New York: Associated Music Publishers, 1975.

Text: Psalm 39; Isaiah 40.
Instrumentation: Soprano, Flute (2, 1 with B extention), Alto Flute in G.
Completed: I in 1971; II in 1973.

The vocal line is somewhat angular and includes some octave displacement. Entrance pitches relate cearly to the flute parts. Some tempo changes appear, especially in number II. The flute part requires some use of flutter tongue.

538. YANNATOS, James. Priere Dans L'Arche. New York: American Composers Alliance, n.d.

Text: de Gazstold.
Instrumentation: Soprano, Flute, Clarinet, Oboe, Bassoon, Trumpet, Trombone, French Horn, Violin (2), Viola, Cello, Contrabass.

Score not available for review.

539. Yannatos, James. Three Songs. New York: American Composers Alliance, n.d.

Instrumentation: Soprano (or Tenor), String Quartet.

Score not available for review.

540. YANNY, Yehuda. At The End of the Parade. New York: American Composers Alliance, n.d.

Text: William C. Williams.
Instrumentation: Baritone, Violin (Viola), Contrabass, Keyboard, Percussion (2).

Score not available for review.

541. YTTREHUS, Rolv. Angstwagen. New York: American Composers Alliance. n.d.

Instrumentation: Soprano, Percussion (3).
Composed: 1971.
Dedication: Clare Holsten.

The following appears in the prefatory material: "The text and its retrograde are used as source materials for textual and timbral interplay between the voice and percussion. Especially important are [certain] voice sounds and their instrumental analogues." The angular vocal line includes a wide range, F# - bb'. Wide leaps often plunge below the staff. Pitch references are remote at best.

542. YTTREHUS, Rolv. Six Haiku. New York: American Composers Alliance, 1972.

Instrumentation: Voice Flute, Harpsichord, Cello.
Composed: 1960.

The somewhat angular vocal line does not exploit the extremes of the range. Many entrance pitches appear in the previous instrumental materal. Much doubling occurs, but half tone relationships with the instruments are also common. The meter changes frequently.

543. ZONN, Paul. Shadows of an Orange Leaf. New York: American Composers Alliance, n.d.

Text: Composer's adaptations of Ancient Chinese verse.
Instrumentation: Voice, Oboe, Trombone, Piano, Percussion, Cello, Contrabass.
Composed: 1971.

The vocal range encomposses E - b', and includes many slides, glissandi and wide intervals. Pitch reference is remote at best. Some sections are free, some are indicated in seconds and some are metered. In the latter, meter changes occur frequently. The piece is constructed in seven parts; several do not include voice. It is printed in a very large score which causes difficulty in seeing one's own part and other parts at the same time. Symbols for quarter tones appear, but "these are used for expressive purpose and need not be tuned absolutely."

544. ZUR, Menachem. The Affairs. New York: Seesaw Music, 1971.

Instrumentation: Soprano, Flute, Clarinet, Trumpet, Tuba, Viola, Piano, Percussion (2).

The composer states that this is "a theatrical piece for soprano, conductor and eight musicians." He further comments that "*Affairs* is a series of attempts at communication between a singer and an ensemble." He provides specific stage set up for each of the two acts. The performance notes include a page of instructions as well as a page which explains the notaion. Following are some excerpts from the instructions:

"Each phrase lasts 5"."

"After being cued...the group plays from the score while standing around the piano."

"Improvise syllables into the microphone."

"Read your newspaper. Gradually become aware of violinist's presence."

The vocal part requires extensive whistling. When specific vocal pitches are indicated, the pitch reference is sometimes fairly easy, with some doublings, and is sometimes remote.

Appendix I

CLASSIFIED BY VOICE AND INSTRUMENTS

A. VOICE

SOPRANO

ADLER, Canto V
ALBERT, To Wake the Dead
AMATO, Two Together
AMES, Among the Gods.
ANDERSON, Variations on a Theme by M.B. Tolson
AUSTIN, Homecoming
AVSHALOMOV, Two Little Birds
BABBIT, Vision & Prayer
BEALE, Lamentations
BEALE, Three Songs
BEERMAN, Consort and Song
BENSON, Nara
BIALOSKY, Three Songs
BISCARDI, Turning
BLACKWOOD, Voyage à Cythère, Un
BLANK, Being: Three Vignettes
BLANK, Coalitions
BLANK, Esther's Monologue
BLANK, Finale: Mélange
BLANK, Four Dream Poems
BLANK, Four Poems by Emily Dickinson
BLANK, I Missed His Book, But I Read His Name
BLANK, Recital
BLANK, Zulus Live in Land Without a Square
BLICKHAN, Speak Softly
BOEHNLEIN, From the J.C. Penney Catalog
BOND, Cornography
BOTTJE, In a word
BOTTJE, In Praise of Music
BREHM, Cycle of Six Songs, A

BRINGS, Tre Madrigali Concertati
BRINGS, Tre Sonetti di Michelangelo Buonarroti
CACIOPPO, Bestiary I: Eingang
CARTER, Mirror on Which to Dwell, A
CHANCE, Dark Song
CHANCE, Duos I
CHANCE, Edensong
CHANCE, Three Poems by Rilke
CHILDS, Lanterns and Candlelight
CHILDS, Seven Epigrams
CIRONE, Five Items
CLARK, Four Elements
CONSOLI, Equinox II
CONSOLI, Isonic
CONSOLI, Tre Canzoni
CORY, Walking
COWELL, Toccanta
CRANE, Cords
CRUMB, Ancient Voices of Children
CRUMB, Lux Aeterna
CRUMB, Madrigals: Book I
CRUMB, Madrigals: Book II
CRUMB, Madrigals: Book III
CRUMB, Madrigals: Book IV
CRUMB, Night Music I
DAILEY, Shell, The
DAVIS, Though Men Call Us Free
DE BOHUN, Songs of Estrangement
DEL TREDICI, I Hear An Army
DEL TREDICI, Night Conjure-Verse
DERR, I Never Saw Another Butterfly
DI DOMENICA, Four Short Songs
DIAMOND, Mad Maid's Song, The
DIAMOND, Vocalises
DIEMENTE, Forms of Flight and Fancy
DIEMER, Four Poems by Alice Meynell
DINERSTEIN, Four Settings
DONOVAN, Five Elizabethan Lyrics
DREW, Aria
DRUCKMAN, Animus II
EDWARDS, Captive, The
EDWARDS, Three Hopkins Songs
EDWARDS, Veined Variety
EHLE, Algorhythms
FARBERMAN, Evolution
FELDMAN, For Franz Kline
FELDMAN, Four Songs to e e cummings
FELDMAN, Journey to the End of the Night
FELDMAN, Rabbi Akiba
FELDMAN, Vertical Thoughts III
FELDMAN, Vertical Thoughts V
FERRITTO, Oggi
FLANAGAN, Good-Bye, My Fancy
FOSS, Thirteen Ways of Looking at a Blackbird
FOSS, Time Cycle
FOX, Time Excursions

FRANCO, Lord Commeth, The
FRANCO, Song of Life, The
FRANCO, Songs of the Spirit
FRANCO, Tempset, Incidental Music, The
GABURO, Cantilena 4
GIDEON, Condemned Playground, The
GODFREY, Wedding Airs, The
GRATZ, Earthbound
HAINES, Four Loves
HAMPTON, Labyrinth
HARTWAY, Three Ways of Looking at a Blackbird
HELLERMANN, Poem for Soprano and Four Instruments
HENRY, The Sons of Martha
HIBBARD, Ménage
HOVHANESS, Canticle
HOVHANESS, Hercules
HOVHANESS, Saturn
HOVHANNISSIAN, Plea
HUGGLER, Bittere Nüsse
HUGGLER, For Coloratura, Clarinet, Viola, Cello
IMBRIE, Tell me where is fancy bred
IVEY, Solstice
IVEY, Three Songs of Night
JAMES, Four Poems of Michael Fried
JOHNSTON, Three Chinese Lyrics
KARLINS, Quartet
KARLINS, Songs for Soprano
KARLINS, Three Songs
KARLINS, Three Songs from 16th and 17th Century
KAVANAUGH, Jubal
KOLB, Chanson Bas
KOLB, Songs before an Adieu
KUPFERMAN, Conceptual Wheel, The
LANG, Three Puerto Rican Songs
LERDAHL, Wake
LEVI, Truth, The
LOMBARDO, Frosted Window: Variations on White
LUENING, Soundless Song, The
LUENING, Suite for Soprano and Flute
LYBBERT, Leopardi Canti
LYBBERT, Lines for The Fallen
MAMLOCK, Five Songs
MATTHEWS, Paysage
MAYER, Eight Miniatures
MAYER, Barbara -- what have you done?
MAYER, Two News Items
MELBY, Due Canti di Leopardi
MELBY, Men that Are Falling, The
MELBY, Two Stevens Songs
MELBY, Valedictory
MILLER, Bashō Songs
MILLER, Mists and Waters
MOLLICONE, Kyrie Eleison
MONOD, Passacaille
MORTON, Tears, Idle Tears
MORYL, Lied, Das

MORYL, de morte cantoris
MOSS, Unseen Leaves
MYERS, Mini-Song Cycle, A
MYROW, Four Songs In Spring
MYROW, Songs From the Japanese
McBRIDE, Nonsense Syllables
McBRIDE, Vocalise
McNIEL, Three Preludes To The Aureate Earth
NOWAK, Maiden's Song
OLIVE, Mar-ri-ia-a
ORREGO-SALAS, Garden Songs
PARRIS, Dreams
PASATIERI, Far from Love
PASATIERI, Heloise and Abelard
PECK, Automobile
PENN, Three Songs on Three Teton Sioux Poems
PINKHAM, Two Motets
PLESKOW, Motet and Madrigal
PLESKOW, On Two Ancient Texts
PLOG, Four Sierra Scenes
PLOG, Two Scenes
POWELL, Settings
POWELL, Three Poems of Paul Zelanske
RANDALL, Improvisations
RECK, Night sounds (and Dream)
REYNOLDS, Again
RHODES, Autumn Settings
RILEY, Five Songs on Japanese Haiku
ROCHBERG, String Quartet No. 2 with Soprano
ROOSEVELT, American Sampler, An
ROOSEVELT, Four Songs for Soprano and Viola
ROOSEVELT, Three Songs from Poe
ROREM, Ariel
ROSEN, Serenade
ROUSE, Ecstasis Mane Eburnei
ROUSE, First Stratum of Empyrean
ROUSE, Nox Aeris Temporis
ROVICS, Haunted Object
ROVICS, Hunter, The
SACCO, Three Psalms
SCHICKELE, Lowest Trees Have Tops, The
SCHRAMM, Songs of Tāyumānavar
SCHWANTNER, Wild Angels of the Open Hills
SEMEGEN, Lieder auf der Flucht
SEREBRIER, Erotica
SHAPEY, Incantations
SHIELDS, Wildcat Songs
SHIFRIN, A Renaissance Garland
SHIFRIN, Satires of Circumstance
SILSBEE, Scroll
SIMS, Elegie
SOWERBY, God Mounts His Throne
SOWERBY, Happy the Nation
STEARNS, Five Lyrics from "The Prophet"
STEARNS, Three Love Songs
STEARNS, Three Sacred Songs

STEIN, String Quartet No. 5 - Ekloge
STEINER, Dream Dialogue 1974
STEWART, D., Wait
STOCK, Scat
STOUT, Allegory: Pride, An
STOUT, Christmas Antiphon
STOUT, Commentary of T'ung Jen
STOUT, Engel, Die
STOUT, Two Songs of Ariel, 1957
SYDEMAN, Four Japanese Songs
SYDEMAN, Jabberwocky
SYDEMAN, Three Songs
SYDEMAN, Three Songs of Elizabethan Texts
TANENBAUM, Images III
TANENBAUM, Peter Quince At the Clavier
TAUB, Of Things Past
TAUB, O Sweet Spontaneous Earth
TAYLOR, Two Songs
THOMAS, Dirge in the Woods
THOMSON, Five Phrases from the Song of Solomon
TRIMBLE, Four Fragments From the Canterbury Tales
TUBB, Five Haiku
UDOW, Eight American Indian Children's Poems
UNG, Tall Wind
VAN NOSTRAND, Earth Manual - 1976
VAN NOSTRAND, Lunar Possession Manual - 1973, A Winter Ceremonial
VERRAL, Rose of the World, The
WARREN, Sonnets for Soprano and String Quartet
WEBER, Concert Aria after Solomon
WEBER, Four Songs
WEBER, Three Songs
WEIGL, K., Five Songs
WEIGL, V., Requiem for Allison
WEIGL, V., Summer Grass
WHEAR, From Thoreau
WHITTENBERG, Two Dylan Thomas Songs
WHITTENBERG, Vocalise
WILDER, Phyllis McGinley Song Cycle
WINSOR, Sick Rose, The
WYNER, Memorial Music
YANNATOS, Priere Dans L'Arche
YANNATOS, Three Songs
YTTREHUS, Angstwagen
ZUR, Affairs, The

MEZZO-SOPRANO, CONTRALTO

BINKERD, Portrait Intérieur
BINKERD, Three Songs
CLAFLIN, Finale
CLARK, Rondeau Redouble
COLGRASS, New People
CONSOLI, Equnox I
CONSOLI, Vuci Siculani

DEL TREDICI, Night Conjure-Verse
DRUCKMAN, Dark upon the Harp
ECKERT, Sea-Changes
FARBERMAN, New York Times, Aug. 30, 1964
FOSS, Thirteen Ways of Looking at a Blackbird
FRANCO, Two Duets for Voice and Flute
GABURO, Two
HARRIS, Abraham Lincoln Walks at Midnight
HAUBIEL, Threnody for Love, A
HOSKINS, Romance, Who Loves to Nod and Sing
IVEY, Terminus
JENKINS, Three Carols from the Quiet Wars
JOHNSTON, Sea Dirge, A
KARLINS, Four Inventions and a Fugue
LEICHTLING, Psalm 37
LEICHTLING, Two Proverbs
LERDAHL, Eros
LOMON, Five Songs after Poems by William Blake
LORA, At Sunset Time
MOLINEUX, Crystals
MOLLICONE, Murali
MOORE, Dorothy, From the Dark Tower
MOORE, Dorothy, Songs
MORYL, de morte cantoris
NOWAK, Five Songs
ORGAD, Leave Out My Name
PERERA, Three Poems of Günter Grass
PINKHAM, Man that is born of a woman
POPE, At that hour
PRESSER, Songs of Death
PUSZTAI, Requiem Profana
RAN, O The Chimneys
RANDALL, Improvisations
REALE, Three Songs from the Chinese
RILEY, Cantata I
ROUSE, Aphrodite Cantos
SAMUEL, Relativity of Icarus, The
SIMS, Cantata 3
STOUT, Landscape
STRAVINSKY, Three Songs from William Sakespeare
THOMSON, Four Songs to Poems of Thomas Campion
UNG, Mohori
WEIGL, K., Three Songs
WEIGL, V., Brief Encounters
WEIGL, V., Challenge
WEIGL, V., Christ Child's Lullaby
WEIGL, V., Do Not Wake Me
WEIGL, V., Five Songs of Remembrance
WEIGL, V., Glimpse of Hope
WEIGL, V., Lyrical Suite
WEIGL, V., Requiem for Allison
WEIGL, V., Seal Lullaby
WEIGL, V., Summer Grass
WERNICK, Prayer for Jerusalem, A

TENOR

ANDERSON, Beyond Silence
BEERMAN, Mass
CHOU, Seven Poems of T'ang Dynasty
CORY, Aria Viva
DIEMER, Four Poems by Alice Meynell
DRUCKMAN, Animus IV
FELCIANO, Glossolalia
FRANCO, Lord Commeth, The
FRANCO, Song of Life, The
FRANCO, Songs of the Spirit
GIDEON, Condemned Playground, The
JENNI, Get Hence Foule Griefe
MOLLICONE, Two Love Songs
McBRIDE, Commentary
McBRIDE, Vocalise No. 3 On Nonsense Syllables
PICCOLO, Found in Machaut's Chamber
PINKHAM, Two Motets
PLESKOW, Motet and Madrigal
PLESKOW, Three Songs
POWELL, Two Prayer Settings
PUSZTAI, Requiem Profana
REALE, Traveler, The
REYNOLDS, Compass
SACCO, Three Psalms
SCHULLER, Six Renaissance Lyrics
SHIFRIN, A Renaissance Garland
STOUT, Christmas Antiphon
STOUT, Commentary of T'ung Jen
STRAVINSKY, In memoriam Dylan Thomas
SYDEMAN, Jabberwocky
SYDEMAN, Malediction
SYDEMAN, Three Songs of Elizabethan Texts
TAYLOR, Two Songs
WEBER, Four Songs
WEBER, Three Songs
WEISGALL, End of Summer
WILLIAMS, Suite of Six Texts
WILSON, D., Five Haiku
WILSON, O., Sometimes
WRIGHT, Cantata
YANNATOS, Three Songs

BARITONE, BASS

ADLER, Passionate Sword The
AMRAM, Three Songs for America
BABBIT, Two Sonnets
BEALE, Proverbs
BLANK, Finale: Mélange
BLANK, I Missed His Book, But I Read His Name
BROOKS, Last Night I Was the Wind
CLARK, Rondeau Redoublé
CLARKE, Suite of Changes

COWELL, Sonatina
CRUMB, Songs Drones, and Refrains of Death
CUSTER, Cartagena Songs
EVETT, Billy in the Darbies
FELDMAN, Intervals
FELDMAN, O'Hara Songs, The
FERRITTO, Quattro Madrigali
FLANAGAN, Weeping Pleiads, The
FRANCO, Two Duets for Voice and Flute
HARRISON, Alma Redemptoris Mater
LEICHTLING, Rubáiyát Fragments
LEICHTLING, Three Songs by Emily Dickinson
MOORE, Dorothy, Weary Blues
MOORE, Douglas, Ballad of William Sycamore, The
NELHYBEL, House that Jack Built, The
PASATIERI, Heloise and Abelard
PINKHAM, Eight Poems of Gerard Manley Hopkins
PLESKOW, For Five Players and Baritone
REALE, Pange Lingua
REIF, Artist, The
REYNOLDS, Compass
ROUSE, Kiss, The
SAMUEL, Relativity of Icarus, The
SCHWANTNER, Shadows II, Consortium IV
SEYFRIT, Winter's Warmth
SIMONS, Trialogue
SIMS, Owl and the Pussycat, The
SOWERBY, God Mounts His Throne
SOWERBY, Happy the Nation
ST. JOHN, Her Drifting from Me These Days
SYDEMAN, Encounters
UDOW, Electric Silence
WEIGL, V., Challenge
WEIGL, V., Glimpse of Hope
WEISGALL, Fancies and Inventions
WHITTENBERG, Even Though the World Keeps Changing
WINSOR, Fly, The
WUORINEN, Message to Denmark Hill, A
YANNY, At The End of the Parade

VOICE

ADOLPHYS, Lilacs
AVSHALOMOV, Little Clay Cart, The
BALLOU, 5-4-3
BARAB, Moments Macabres
BENVENUTI, Cantus, Gemellus
BERGER, A., Three Poems of Yeats
BERGER, J., Six Rondeau
BIALOSKY, Six Riddles from Symphosius
BINKERD, Secret-Love
BLANK, Don't let that horse eat that violin
BLANK, Pennycandystore beyond the El, The
BLANK, Poem
BLANK, Two Parables by Franz Kafka

CAGE, Forever and Sunsmell
CARTER, Tell Me where is Fancy Bred
CHAJES, By the Rivers of Babylon
CLARK, Life in Ghana
CLARK, Lord Is My Shepherd, The
CLARK, Woman of Viture, A
COWELL, Vocalise
CROUNCE, Slumber did my Spirit Seal, A
CUCINOTTA, Beasts
DE JONG, hist wist
DIEMENTE, 3 - 31 - '70
DIEMER, Four Chinese Love Poems
EBERHARD, Parody
FARBERMAN, Greek Scene
FELDMAN, I met heine on the rue fürstenberg
FINE, Confession, The
FINE, Great Wall of China, The
FRANCO, Little Lamb
FRANCO, Sonnet
GIDEON, Adorable Mouse, The
GIDEON, Hound of Heaven, The
GIDEON, Little Ivory Figures
GIDEON, Questions on Nature
GIDEON, Rhymes from the Hill
GIDEON, Sonnets from Shakespeare
GRUNDMAN, Zoo Illogical
HARDIN, Moondog on the Streets of New York
HARRISON, Air
HEILNER, Democracy
HEILNER, Gift of Fire, The
HEILNER, Henry at the Grating
HEILNER, Letters from the Draft Board
HEILNER, Rock-'n'-Roll Session
HEILNER, Wild Anemone, The
HOVHANESS, O Lady Moon
IVES, Sunrise
IVES, Vote for Names
KAUDER, Song from "Dierdre"
KAUDER, Two Songs
LESSARD, Five Poems by Robert Herrick
LEWIS, Song
MESTRES-QUADRENY, Invecions Movils II
MONOD, Chamber Aria
MOURANT, Two Songs
NELHYBEL, Concerto Spirituoso No.1
NELHYBEL, Concerto Spirtuoso No. 2
ORLAND, Love and Pity
PASATIERI, Rites de Passage
PERERA, Dove sta amore
PINKHAM, Safe in their Alabaster Chambers
PISK, Waning Moon, The
POWELL, Faces
PRESSER, Hymne to God the Father, A
REIF, Reverence for Life
RIEGGER, Music for Voice and Flute
ROCHBERG, Blake Songs

ROREM, Four Dialogues
ROREM, Last Poems of Wallace Stevens
ROREM, Mourning Scene
ROREM, Serenade on Five English Poems
ROVICS, Echo
RUSSEL, Ballad with Epitaphs
SCHUMAN, In Sweet Music
SCHWARTZ, Septet
SEIGMEISTER, Songs of Experience
SIMONS, Songs for Wendy
SIMS, Celebration of Dead Ladies
SMIT, Four Motets
STEINER, New Poems
STEINER, Three Poems
STEVENS, Two Shakespeare Songs
STEVENS, When Icicles Hang by the Wall
STEWART, F., The First Joy of Marriage
SWACK, Psalm VIII
WEIGL, V., City Birds
WEIGL, V., Nightfall in the Mountains
WEIGL, V., Pippa's Song
WEIGL, V., Rabbles of Scattered Leaves
WEIGL, V., Salvation of the Dawn, The
WEIGL, V., Sea Moves Always, The
WEIGL, V., Songs for a Child
WEIGL, V., Soon
WEIGL, V., Swiftly Along Flows the River
WEIGL, V., Wynken, Blynken and Nod
WOLPE, Quintet with Voice
YTTREHUS, Six Haiku
ZONN, Shadows of an Orange Leaf

HIGH VOICE

ARGENTO, Letters from Composers
ARGENTO, To Be Sung Upon The Water
BALAZS, Sonnets after Elizabeth Barrett Browning
BARAB, Bagatelles
BRANT, Encephalograms
CUMMING, As Dew in April
FRANCO, Ariel's Four Songs
GIDEON, Nocturnes
GIDEON, Seasons of Time, The
GIDEON, Sonnets from Fatal Interview
KIM, Earthlight
PINKHAM, Letters from Saint Paul
PINKHAM, Now the Trumpet Summons Us Again
ROE, Hot Sun, Cool Fire
STUCKEY, Schneemusik
WEIGL, V., Beyond Time
WEIGL, V., Birds in Springtime
WEIGL, V., Cardinal in March
WEIGL, V., Nature Moods
WHITE, This Son so Young

MEDIUM VOICE

ADLER, Whitman Serenade
ANDERSON, Block Songs
BEESON, Creole Mystery, A
BEESON, Day's No Rounder Than Its Angles Are, The
BERGER, J., Five Songs
BERGER, J., Tres Canciones
CALDWELL, Christmas Triptych, A
CALDWELL, Lute Caroll, A
CLARK, Emily Dickinson Canons
CLARK, Puget Sound Cinquain
CLARK, Song to a Young Pianist
FENNELLY, Songs with improvisation
FERGUSON, Two Spanish Songs
HARTLEY, Psalm Cycle, A
HAUFRECHT, Let's Play Maccabees, Children's Songs
HEILNER, Every Day is Friday to a Seal
HEILNER, Peace is a Lovely Word
HEILNER, Stevenson
HEILNER, What Were They Like?
JOHNSTON, Five Fragments
MORYL, Corridors
PLESKOW, On Three Old English Rhymes
SARGON, Patterns in Blue
STEINER, Four Songs for Medium Voice and Vibraphone
STEINER, Interlude
STEVENS, Three Japanese Folksongs
TAYLOR, Quattro Liriche from "Mattino Domenicale"
TRIMBLE, Petit Concert
WEIGL, V., Along the Moving Darkness
WEIGL, V., Dear Earth: A Quintet of Poems
WEIGL, V., Drums of War, The
WEIGL, V., Echoes
WEIGL, V., Huntsmen, The
WEIGL, V., I Saw Two Birds
WEIGL, V., In Springtime
WEIGL, V., Little Singers, The
WEIGL, V., Long, Long Ago
WEIGL, V., Rock-A-By Lady, The
WEIGL, V., Seeking You
WEIGL, V., Silver
WEIGL, V., Songs from "Native Island"
WEIGL, V., Songs from "No Boundary"
WEIGL, V., Thistle, Yarrow, Clover
WEIGL, V., Thoughts About Grasshoppers
WEIGL, V., When the Vision Dies ("Perhaps")
WEIGL, V., Where Go the Boats
WEIGL, V., Winter Night

LOW VOICE

NOWAK, Summer is Away
WEIGL, V., Rain at Night

FEMALE VOICE

BENTON, Love Song
GABER, Voce II
HILLER, Avalanche, An
KAM, Nocturnes
SHAPEY, Walking Upright
TANENBAUM, Image
TANENBAUM, Mirage and Incantation

MALE VOICE

LEICHTLING, Trial and Death of Socrates
WEIGL, V., Summer Stars

BOY SOPRANO

CRUMB, Ancient Voices of Children

RECITER, SPEAKER, NARRATOR

FOX, Time Excursions
HILLER, Avalanche, An
ROVICS, Haunted Object

B. STRINGS

VIOLIN

ADLER, Passionate Sword The
ADLER, Whitman Serenade
ALBERT, To Wake the Dead
AMES, Among the Gods.
AMRAM, Three Songs for America
ANDERSON, Variations on a Theme by M.B. Tolson
BALAZS, Sonnets after Elizabeth Barrett Browning
BARAB, Moments Macabres
BEALE, Three Songs
BEESON, Creole Mystery, A
BEESON, Day's No Rounder Than Its Angles Are, The
BINKERD, Portrait Intérieur
BINKERD, Three Songs
BISCARDI, Turning
BLANK, Don't let that horse eat that violin
BLANK, Two Parables by Franz Kafka
BOEHNLEIN, From the J.C. Penney Catalog
BOTTJE, In Praise of Music
BREHM, Cycle of Six Songs, A
BRINGS, Tre Sonetti di Michelangelo Buonarroti
CALDWELL, Lute Caroll, A

CARTER, Mirror on Which to Dwell, A
CLAFLIN, Finale
CONSOLI, Equinox II
CONSOLI, Vuci Siculani
CORY, Walking
COWELL, Sonatina
DE BOHUN, Songs of Estrangement
DEL TREDICI, I Hear An Army
DEL TREDICI, Night Conjure-Verse
DI DOMENICA, Four Short Songs
DINERSTEIN, Four Settings
DONOVAN, Five Elizabethan Lyrics
DRUCKMAN, Animus IV
EBERHARD, Parody
ECKERT, Sea-Changes
EDWARDS, Captive, The
EDWARDS, Veined Variety
EVETT, Billy in the Darbies
FELDMAN, For Franz Kline
FELDMAN, I met heine on the rue fürstenberg
FELDMAN, O'Hara Songs, The
FELDMAN, Vertical Thoughts III
FELDMAN, Vertical Thoughts V
FINE, Confession, The
FLANAGAN, Weeping Pleiads, The
FOX, Time Excursions
FRANCO, Sonnet
GIDEON, Condemned Playground, The
GIDEON, Hound of Heaven, The
GIDEON, Nocturnes
GIDEON, Sonnets from Fatal Interview
GIDEON, Sonnets from Shakespeare
HAINES, Four Loves
HARRIS, Abraham Lincoln Walks at Midnight
HARRISON, Air
HARRISON, Alma Redemptoris Mater
HAUBIEL, Threnody for Love, A
HIBBARD, Ménage
HOVHANESS, Canticle
HOVHANESS, Hercules
HUGGLER, Bittere Nüsse
IVES, Sunrise
JAMES, Four Poems of Michael Fried
JENKINS, Three Carols from the Quiet Wars
JOHNSTON, Sea Dirge, A
JOHNSTON, Three Chinese Lyrics
KAM, Nocturnes
KARLINS, Quartet
KARLINS, Three Songs from 16th and 17th Century
KIM, Earthlight
LEICHTLING, Psalm 37
LERDAHL, Wake
LESSARD, Five Poems by Robert Herrick
LEVI, Truth, The
LEWIS, Song
LORA, At Sunset Time

LUENING, Soundless Song, The
MAYER, Eight Miniatures
MAYER, Two News Items
MILLER, Mists and Waters
MYROW, Songs From the Japanese
NOWAK, Maiden's Song
OLIVE, Mar-ri-ia-a
PARRIS, Dreams
PASATIERI, Far from Love
PASATIERI, Rites de Passage
PERERA, Three Poems of Günter Grass
PERRY, Stabat Mater
PINKHAM, Letters from Saint Paul
PINKHAM, Now the Trumpet Summons Us Again
PISK, Waning Moon, The
PLESKOW, For Five Players and Baritone
PLESKOW, Motet and Madrigal
PLESKOW, Three Songs
POPE, At that hour
POPE, Rain
POWELL, Two Prayer Settings
POWELL, Three Poems of Paul Zelanske
PRESSER, Songs of Death
PUSZTAI, Requiem Profana
REIF, Artist, The
REIF, Reverence for Life
RHODES, Autumn Settings
RILEY, Five Songs on Japanese Haiku
ROCHBERG, Blake Songs
ROCHBERG, String Quartet No. 2 with Soprano
ROREM, Mourning Scene
ROREM, Serenade on Five English Poems
ROUSE, First Stratum of Empyrean
ROUSE, Nox Aeris Temporis
SAMUEL, Relativity of Icarus, The
SCHULLER, Six Renaissance Lyrics
SCHWANTNER, Shadows II, Consortium IV
SEMEGEN, Lieder auf der Flucht
SEYFRIT, Winter's Warmth
SHAPEY, Walking Upright
SHIFRIN, Satires of Circumstance
SILSBEE, Scroll
SIMS, Elegie
SMIT, Four Motets
STEARNS, Three Love Songs
STEIN, String Quartet No. 5 - Ekloge
STEVENS, Three Japanese Folksongs
STOCK, Scat
STOUT, Engel, Die
STOUT, Two Songs of Ariel, 1957
STRAVINSKY, In memoriam Dylan Thomas
SYDEMAN, Four Japanese Songs
SYDEMAN, Encounters
SYDEMAN, Malediction
TANENBAUM, Mirage and Incantation
TAUB, Of Things Past

TRIMBLE, Petit Concert
TUBB, Five Haiku
UDOW, Electric Silence
VAN NOSTRAND, Earth Manual - 1976
VAN NOSTRAND, Lunar Possession Manual - 1973, A Winter Ceremonial
WARREN, Sonnets for Soprano and String Quartet
WEBER, Concert Aria after Solomon
WEBER, Three Songs
WEIGL, K., Five Songs
WEIGL, K., Three Songs
WEIGL, V., Along the Moving Darkness
WEIGL, V., Beyond Time
WEIGL, V., Brief Encounters
WEIGL, V., Dear Earth: A Quintet of Poems
WEIGL, V., Do Not Wake Me
WEIGL, V., Echoes
WEIGL, V., Five Songs of Remembrance
WEIGL, V., Glimpse of Hope
WEIGL, V., Nature Moods
WEIGL, V., Nightfall in the Mountains
WEIGL, V., Rabbles of Scattered Leaves
WEIGL, V., Requiem for Allison
WEIGL, V., Salvation of the Dawn, The
WEIGL, V., Sea Moves Always, The
WEIGL, V., Seeking You
WEIGL, V., Songs from "No Boundary"
WEIGL, V., Soon
WEIGL, V., Summer Grass
WEIGL, V., Summer Stars
WEIGL, V., Thoughts About Grasshoppers
WEIGL, V., When the Vision Dies ("Perhaps")
WEISGALL, End of Summer
WHEAR, From Thoreau
WILLIAMS, Suite of Six Texts
WILSON, D., Five Haiku
WINSOR, Fly, The
WINSOR, Sick Rose, The
YANNATOS, Priere Dans L'Arche
YANNATOS, Three Songs
YANNY, At The End of the Parade

VIOLA

ADLER, Whitman Serenade
AMES, Among the Gods.
AMRAM, Three Songs for America
ANDERSON, Beyond Silence
AVSHALOMOV, Little Clay Cart, The
BABBIT, Two Sonnets
BALAZS, Sonnets after Elizabeth Barrett Browning
BALLOU, 5-4-3
BARAB, Moments Macabres
BEALE, Three Songs
BEESON, Creole Mystery, A

BEESON, Day's No Rounder Than Its Angles Are, The
BERGER, J., Five Songs
BERGER, J., Six Rondeau
BERGER, J., Tres Canciones
BINKERD, Three Songs
BLANK, Esther's Monologue
BLANK, Two Holy Sonnets by John Donne
BLANK, Two Parables by Franz Kafka
BOEHNLEIN, From the J.C. Penney Catalog
BOTTJE, In Praise of Music
BREHM, Cycle of Six Songs, A
CARTER, Mirror on Which to Dwell, A
CLAFLIN, Finale
CLARK, Emily Dickinson Canons
COLGRASS, New People
CONSOLI, Vuci Siculani
CORY, Walking
DE BOHUN, Songs of Estrangement
DE JONG, hist wist
DEL TREDICI, I Hear An Army
DEL TREDICI, Night Conjure-Verse
DI DOMENICA, Four Short Songs
DIAMOND, Vocalises
DINERSTEIN, Four Settings
DONOVAN, Five Elizabethan Lyrics
ECKERT, Sea-Changes
EDWARDS, Captive, The
EVETT, Billy in the Darbies
FELDMAN, I met heine on the rue fürstenberg
FELDMAN, O'Hara Songs, The
FELDMAN, Vertical Thoughts III
FINE, Confession, The
FOX, Time Excursions
FRANCO, Sonnet
GIDEON, Condemned Playground, The
GIDEON, Sonnets from Fatal Interview
GIDEON, Sonnets from Shakespeare
HAINES, Four Loves
HOSKINS, Romance, Who Loves to Nod and Sing
HOVHANESS, Canticle
HUGGLER, Bittere Nüsse
HUGGLER, For Coloratura, Clarinet, Viola, Cello
IVEY, Three Songs of Night
JAMES, Four Poems of Michael Fried
JENKINS, Three Carols from the Quiet Wars
KARLINS, Quartet
LEICHTLING, Psalm 37
LERDAHL, Eros
LERDAHL, Wake
LEVI, Truth, The
LOMBARDO, Frosted Window: Variations on White
LOMON, Five Songs after Poems by William Blake
LORA, At Sunset Time
LUENING, Soundless Song, The
LYBBERT, Leopardi Canti
MOLLICONE, Two Love Songs

MYROW, Four Songs In Spring
MYROW, Songs From the Japanese
ORLAND, Love and Pity
ORREGO-SALAS, Garden Songs
PASATIERI, Rites de Passage
PERERA, Three Poems of Günter Grass
PERRY, Stabat Mater
PINKHAM, Eight Poems of Gerard Manley Hopkins
PINKHAM, Letters from Saint Paul
PINKHAM, Now the Trumpet Summons Us Again
PLESKOW, Three Songs
POPE, At that hour
POWELL, Two Prayer Settings
PRESSER, Hymne to God the Father, A
PRESSER, Songs of Death
REIF, Reverence for Life
RHODES, Autumn Settings
ROCHBERG, Blake Songs
ROCHBERG, String Quartet No. 2 with Soprano
ROOSEVELT, Four Songs for Soprano and Viola
ROREM, Mourning Scene
ROREM, Serenade on Five English Poems
ROUSE, Aphrodite Cantos
ROUSE, Ecstasis Mane Eburnei
ROUSE, First Stratum of Empyrean
ROVICS, Hunter, The
SAMUEL, Relativity of Icarus, The
SCHICKELE, Lowest Trees Have Tops, The
SCHULLER, Six Renaissance Lyrics
SCHUMAN, In Sweet Music
SCHWANTNER, Shadows II, Consortium IV
SEIGMEISTER, Songs of Experience
SEYFRIT, Winter's Warmth
SIMONS, Songs for Wendy
SIMONS, Trialogue
SIMS, Celebration of Dead Ladies
SIMS, Elegie
ST. JOHN, Her Drifting from Me These Days
STEARNS, Five Lyrics from "The Prophet"
STEARNS, Three Love Songs
STEIN, String Quartet No. 5 - Ekloge
STRAVINSKY, In memoriam Dylan Thomas
STRAVINSKY, Three Songs from William Sakespeare
SYDEMAN, Malediction
TANENBAUM, Peter Quince At the Clavier
TAUB, Of Things Past
THOMSON, Four Songs to Poems of Thomas Campion
TUBB, Five Haiku
WARREN, Sonnets for Soprano and String Quartet
WEBER, Three Songs
WEIGL, K., Five Songs
WEIGL, K., Three Songs
WEIGL, V., Five Songs of Remembrance
WEIGL, V., Nightfall in the Mountains
WEIGL, V., Rain at Night
WEIGL, V., Requiem for Allison

WEIGL, V., Songs from "No Boundary"
WEIGL, V., Summer Grass
WEIGL, V., Swiftly Along Flows the River
WEISGALL, End of Summer
WEISGALL, Fancies and Inventions
WHITTENBERG, Even Though the World Keeps Changing
WHITTENBERG, Vocalise
WILLIAMS, Suite of Six Texts
WILSON, D., Five Haiku
YANNATOS, Priere Dans L'Arche
YANNATOS, Three Songs
YANNY, At The End of the Parade
ZUR, Affairs, The

CELLO

ADLER, Canto V
ADLER, Passionate Sword The
ADLER, Whitman Serenade
ALBERT, To Wake the Dead
AMES, Among the Gods.
AMRAM, Three Songs for America
ANDERSON, Beyond Silence
ANDERSON, Variations on a Theme by M.B. Tolson
AVSHALOMOV, Little Clay Cart, The
BABBIT, Two Sonnets
BALAZS, Sonnets after Elizabeth Barrett Browning
BARAB, Moments Macabres
BEESON, Creole Mystery, A
BEESON, Day's No Rounder Than Its Angles Are, The
BERGER, A., Three Poems of Yeats
BERGER, J., Five Songs
BERGER, J., Tres Canciones
BIALOSKY, Six Riddles from Symphosius
BINKERD, Portrait Interiéur
BINKERD, Secret-Love
BINKERD, Three Songs
BISCARDI, Turning
BLANK, Esther's Monologue
BLANK, Poem
BOEHNLEIN, From the J.C. Penney Catalog
BOTTJE, In Praise of Music
BREHM, Cycle of Six Songs, A
BRINGS, Tre Madrigali Concertati
BRINGS, Tre Sonetti di Michelangelo Buonarroti
CARTER, Mirror on Which to Dwell, A
CHAJES, By the Rivers of Babylon
CHANCE, Edensong
CHANCE, Three Poems by Rilke
CLAFLIN, Finale
CLARK, Four Elements
CLARK, Rondeau Redoublé
CONSOLI, Equnox I
CONSOLI, Equinox II
CONSOLI, Tre Canzoni

CONSOLI, Vuci Siculani
CORY, Walking
COWELL, Toccanta
CRUMB, Night of the Four Moons
DE BOHUN, Songs of Estrangement
DEL TREDICI, I Hear An Army
DEL TREDICI, Night Conjure-Verse
DIEMER, Four Poems by Alice Meynell
DINERSTEIN, Four Settings
DONOVAN, Five Elizabethan Lyrics
EBERHARD, Parody
ECKERT, Sea-Changes
EDWARDS, Captive, The
EDWARDS, Veined Variety
EVETT, Billy in the Darbies
FELDMAN, For Franz Kline
FELDMAN, Four Songs to e e cummings
FELDMAN, Intervals
FELDMAN, O'Hara Songs, The
FELDMAN, Rabbi Akiba
FELDMAN, Vertical Thoughts III
FINE, Confession, The
FINE, Great Wall of China, The
FLANAGAN, Weeping Pleiads, The
FOSS, Time Cycle
FOX, Time Excursions
FRANCO, Sonnet
GIDEON, Condemned Playground, The
GIDEON, Hound of Heaven, The
GIDEON, Nocturnes
GIDEON, Rhymes from the Hill
GIDEON, Seasons of Time, The
GIDEON, Sonnets from Fatal Interview
GIDEON, Sonnets from Shakespeare
HAINES, Four Loves
HARRIS, Abraham Lincoln Walks at Midnight
HAUBIEL, Threnody for Love, A
HELLERMANN, Poem for Soprano and Four Instruments
HOVHANESS, Canticle
HUGGLER, Bittere Nüsse
HUGGLER, For Coloratura, Clarinet, Viola, Cello
IVEY, Three Songs of Night
JAMES, Four Poems of Michael Fried
JENKINS, Three Carols from the Quiet Wars
JOHNSTON, Five Fragments
KARLINS, Quartet
KARLINS, Songs for Soprano
KARLINS, Three Songs from 16th and 17th Century
LEICHTLING, Psalm 37
LEICHTLING, Three Songs by Emily Dickinson
LERDAHL, Wake
LEVI, Truth, The
LEWIS, Song
LORA, At Sunset Time
LUENING, Soundless Song, The
MAMLOCK, Five Songs

MATTHEWS, Paysage
MAYER, Eight Miniatures
MAYER, Two News Items
MOORE, Dorothy, From the Dark Tower
MOORE, Dorothy, Weary Blues
MYROW, Four Songs In Spring
MYROW, Songs From the Japanese
NOWAK, Five Songs
NOWAK, Summer is Away
OLIVE, Mar-ri-ia-a
PARRIS, Dreams
PASATIERI, Far from Love
PASATIERI, Rites de Passage
PERRY, Stabat Mater
PICCOLO, Found in Machaut's Chamber
PINKHAM, Letters from Saint Paul
PINKHAM, Now the Trumpet Summons Us Again
PISK, Waning Moon, The
PLESKOW, For Five Players and Baritone
PLESKOW, Motet and Madrigal
PLESKOW, On Three Old English Rhymes
PLESKOW, On Two Ancient Texts
PLESKOW, Three Songs
POPE, At that hour
POPE, Rain
POWELL, Two Prayer Settings
POWELL, Faces
PRESSER, Hymne to God the Father, A
PRESSER, Songs of Death
PUSZTAI, Requiem Profana
RAN, O The Chimneys
REALE, Pange Lingua
REIF, Reverence for Life
REYNOLDS, Compass
RHODES, Autumn Settings
RILEY, Cantata I
RILEY, Five Songs on Japanese Haiku
ROCHBERG, Blake Songs
ROCHBERG, String Quartet No. 2 with Soprano
ROREM, Last Poems of Wallace Stevens
ROREM, Mourning Scene
ROUSE, Aphrodite Cantos
ROUSE, First Stratum of Empyrean
ROUSE, Nox Aeris Temporis
SAMUEL, Relativity of Icarus, The
SCHULLER, Six Renaissance Lyrics
SCHWANTNER, Shadows II, Consortium IV
SEMEGEN, Lieder auf der Flucht
SEYFRIT, Winter's Warmth
SHAPEY, Incantations
SHIFRIN, Satires of Circumstance
SIMS, Celebration of Dead Ladies
SIMS, Elegie
STEARNS, Three Love Songs
STEARNS, Three Sacred Songs
STEIN, String Quartet No. 5 - Ekloge

STEVENS, Three Japanese Folksongs
STOCK, Scat
STOUT, Allegory: Pride, An
STOUT, Christmas Antiphon
STOUT, Two Songs of Ariel, 1957
STRAVINSKY, In memoriam Dylan Thomas
SYDEMAN, Encounters
SYDEMAN, Jabberwocky
SYDEMAN, Malediction
SYDEMAN, Three Songs
TANENBAUM, Mirage and Incantation
TAUB, Of Things Past
TUBB, Five Haiku
UDOW, Electric Silence
UNG, Mohori
UNG, Tall Wind
VAN NOSTRAND, Earth Manual - 1976
VAN NOSTRAND, Lunar Possession Manual - 1973, A Winter Ceremonial
WARREN, Sonnets for Soprano and String Quartet
WEBER, Concert Aria after Solomon
WEBER, Four Songs
WEBER, Three Songs
WEIGL, K., Five Songs
WEIGL, K., Three Songs
WEIGL, V., Dear Earth: A Quintet of Poems
WEIGL, V., Five Songs of Remembrance
WEIGL, V., Lyrical Suite
WEIGL, V., Requiem for Allison
WEIGL, V., Summer Grass
WEISGALL, End of Summer
WEISGALL, Fancies and Inventions
WILLIAMS, Suite of Six Texts
WILSON, D., Five Haiku
WINSOR, Fly, The
WINSOR, Sick Rose, The
WOLPE, Quintet with Voice
WUORINEN, Message to Denmark Hill, A
YANNATOS, Priere Dans L'Arche
YANNATOS, Three Songs
YTTREHUS, Six Haiku
ZONN, Shadows of an Orange Leaf

VIOLS

NEUMANN, Sephardic Kiddush
ROE, Hot Sun, Cool Fire
SHIFRIN, A Renaissance Garland

CONTRABASS

AMRAM, Three Songs for America
AUSTIN, Homecoming
BARAB, Moments Macabres

BLACKWOOD, Voyage á Cythere, Un
BREHM, Cycle of Six Songs, A
BRINGS, Tre Sonetti di Michelangelo Buonarroti
CARTER, Mirror on Which to Dwell, A
CLARK, Lord Is My Shepherd, The
CORY, Walking
CRANE, Cords
CRUMB, Madrigals: Book I
CRUMB, Madrigals: Book IV
CRUMB, Songs Drones, and Refrains of Death
DIEMENTE, 3 - 31 - '70
EDWARDS, Captive, The
EHLE, Algorhythms
FELDMAN, Rabbi Akiba
GABURO, Two
GRATZ, Earthbound
HOVHANESS, Canticle
MORYL, Lied, Das
MYROW, Songs From the Japanese
McBRIDE, Commentary
McBRIDE, Vocalise No. 3 On Nonsense Syllables
PARRIS, Dreams
PECK, Automobile
PINKHAM, Letters from Saint Paul
PINKHAM, Now the Trumpet Summons Us Again
PUSZTAI, Requiem Profana
RECK, Night sounds (and Dream)
REYNOLDS, Again
REYNOLDS, Compass
SCHULLER, Six Renaissance Lyrics
SHIFRIN, Satires of Circumstance
SILSBEE, Scroll
VAN NOSTRAND, Lunar Possession Manual - 1973, A Winter Ceremonial
YANNY, At The End of the Parade
ZONN, Shadows of an Orange Leaf

HARP

BALLOU, 5-4-3
BEERMAN, Consort and Song
BEERMAN, Mass
BENTON, Love Song
BINKERD, Secret-Love
BLANK, Poem
BLANK, Two Holy Sonnets by John Donne
BRANT, Encephalograms
CHANCE, Edensong
CRUMB, Ancient Voices of Children
CRUMB, Madrigals: Book III
CRUMB, Madrigals: Book IV
DIEMER, Four Chinese Love Poems
DIEMER, Four Poems by Alice Meynell
ECKERT, Sea-Changes
HARRISON, Air

HAUFRECHT, Let's Play Maccabees, Children's Songs
HOVHANESS, Canticle
JENNI, Get Hence Foule Griefe
KAUDER, Song from "Dierdre"
KAUDER, Two Songs
LEICHTLING, Psalm 37
LEICHTLING, Trial and Death of Socrates
LERDAHL, Eros
LERDAHL, Wake
MOLLICONE, Murali
MORTON, Tears, Idle Tears
MORYL, de morte cantoris
MOURANT, Two Songs
NELHYBEL, House that Jack Built, The
ORREGO-SALAS, Garden Songs
PUSZTAI, Requiem Profana
ROCHBERG, Blake Songs
ROUSE, Kiss, The
SCHICKELE, Lowest Trees Have Tops, The
SCHUMAN, In Sweet Music
SCHWANTNER, Wild Angels of the Open Hills
SEYFRIT, Winter's Warmth
STEARNS, Three Love Songs
STOUT, Landscape
STOUT, Two Songs of Ariel, 1957
THOMAS, Dirge in the Woods
THOMSON, Four Songs to Poems of Thomas Campion
UNG, Mohori
WHITE, This Son so Young
WILDER, Phyllis McGinley Song Cycle
WOLPE, Quintet with Voice

GUITAR (OTHER PLUCKED)

ARGENTO, Letters from Composers
AVSHALOMOV, Little Clay Cart, The
BARAB, Bagatelles
CARTER, Tell Me where is Fancy Bred
CHANCE, Dark Song
CONSOLI, Vuci Siculani
CRUMB, Ancient Voices of Children
CRUMB, Lux Aeterna
CRUMB, Night of the Four Moons
CRUMB, Songs Drones, and Refrains of Death
CUCINOTTA, Beasts
DAILEY, Shell, The
DIEMENTE, 3 - 31 - '70
FLANAGAN, Good-Bye, My Fancy
FRANCO, Little Lamb
GIDEON, Little Ivory Figures
HEILNER, Democracy
HEILNER, Every Day is Friday to a Seal
HEILNER, Gift of Fire, The
HEILNER, Henry at the Grating
HEILNER, Letters from the Draft Board

HEILNER, Peace is a Lovely Word
HEILNER, Rock-'n'-Roll Session
HEILNER, Stevenson
HEILNER, Wild Anemone, The
IMBRIE, Tell me where is fancy bred
KAM, Nocturnes
KOLB, Songs before an Adieu
LERDAHL, Eros
MESTRES-QUADRENY, Invecions Movils II
PICCOLO, Found in Machaut's Chamber
PINKHAM, Man that is born of a woman
PINKHAM, Two Motets
RANDALL, Improvisations
SCHWANTNER, Shadows II, Consortium IV
SHIFRIN, A Renaissance Garland
SIMS, Owl and the Pussycat, The
TANENBAUM, Peter Quince At the Clavier
UNG, Mohori
UNG, Tall Wind
WEIGL, V., Drums of War, The
WILSON, D., Five Haiku

C. WINDS

RECORDER

BARAB, Bagatelles
GODFREY, Wedding Airs, The
ROUSE, Ecstasis Mane Eburnei
SHIFRIN, A Renaissance Garland
WEIGL, V., Huntsmen, The
WEIGL, V., In Springtime
WEIGL, V., Little Singers, The
WEIGL, V., Long, Long Ago
WEIGL, V., Pippa's Song
WEIGL, V., Rock-A-By Lady, The
WEIGL, V., Seal Lullaby
WEIGL, V., Silver
WEIGL, V., Songs for a Child
WEIGL, V., Where Go the Boats
WEIGL, V., Winter Night
WEIGL, V., Wynken, Blynken and Nod

FLUTE, PICCOLO

ADLER, Canto V
ADLER, Passionate Sword The
ALBERT, To Wake the Dead
AMRAM, Three Songs for America
AVSHALOMOV, Little Clay Cart, The
BARAB, Moments Macabres
BEALE, Lamentations

BEERMAN, Mass
BENSON, Nara
BENTON, Love Song
BENVENUTI, Cantus, Gemellus
BERGER, A., Three Poems of Yeats
BERGER, J., Five Songs
BLACKWOOD, Voyage à Cythère, Un
BLANK, Four Poems by Emily Dickinson
BLICKHAN, Speak Softly
BOEHNLEIN, From the J.C. Penney Catalog
BREHM, Cycle of Six Songs, A
BRINGS, Tre Sonetti di Michelangelo Buonarroti
BROOKS, Last Night I Was the Wind
CALDWELL, Christmas Triptych, A
CALDWELL, Lute Caroll, A
CARTER, Mirror on Which to Dwell, A
CHANCE, Dark Song
CHANCE, Duos I
CHANCE, Edensong
CHANCE, Three Poems by Rilke
CHOU, Seven Poems of T'ang Dynasty
CLARK, Life in Ghana
CLARK, Lord Is My Shepherd, The
CLARK, Song to a Young Pianist
CLARKE, Suite of Changes
CONSOLI, Equnox I
CONSOLI, Equinox II
CONSOLI, Isonic
CONSOLI, Tre Canzoni
CONSOLI, Vuci Siculani
CORY, Aria Viva
COWELL, Toccanta
COWELL, Vocalise
CROUNCE, Slumber did my Spirit Seal, A
CRUMB, Lux Aeterna
CRUMB, Madrigals: Book II
CRUMB, Madrigals: Book IV
CRUMB, Night of the Four Moons
DE JONG, hist wist
DEL TREDICI, Night Conjure-Verse
DI DOMENICA, Four Short Songs
DIAMOND, Mad Maid's Song, The
DIEMER, Four Poems by Alice Meynell
EBERHARD, Parody
ECKERT, Sea-Changes
EDWARDS, Captive, The
EDWARDS, Veined Variety
FELDMAN, I met heine on the rue fürstenberg
FELDMAN, Journey to the End of the Night
FELDMAN, Rabbi Akiba
FELDMAN, Vertical Thoughts III
FERRITTO, Quattro Madrigali
FINE, Confession, The
FINE, Great Wall of China, The
FLANAGAN, Good-Bye, My Fancy
FLANAGAN, Weeping Pleiads, The

FOSS, Thirteen Ways of Looking at a Blackbird
FOX, Time Excursions
FRANCO, Songs of the Spirit
FRANCO, Two Duets for Voice and Flute
GABER, Voce II
GABURO, Two
GIDEON, Adorable Mouse, The
GIDEON, Condemned Playground, The
GIDEON, Nocturnes
GIDEON, Seasons of Time, The
GRATZ, Earthbound
GRUNDMAN, Zoo Illogical
HAINES, Four Loves
HARRISON, Air
HARTLEY, Psalm Cycle, A
HARTWAY, Three Ways of Looking at a Blackbird
HAUBIEL, Threnody for Love, A
HELLERMANN, Poem for Soprano and Four Instruments
HOVHANNISSIAN, Plea
HUGGLER, Bittere Nüsse
IVEY, Solstice
IVEY, Three Songs of Night
JAMES, Four Poems of Michael Fried
JOHNSTON, Sea Dirge, A
KAM, Nocturnes
KARLINS, Songs for Soprano
KARLINS, Three Songs
KARLINS, Three Songs from 16th and 17th Century
KAUDER, Song from "Dierdre"
KOLB, Songs before an Adieu
LEICHTLING, Trial and Death of Socrates
LERDAHL, Eros
LEVI, Truth, The
LUENING, Soundless Song, The
LYBBERT, Leopardi Canti
MAMLOCK, Five Songs
MATTHEWS, Paysage
MAYER, Eight Miniatures
MAYER, Two News Items
MONOD, Chamber Aria
MONOD, Passacaille
MOORE, Douglas, Ballad of William Sycamore, The
MYERS, Mini-Song Cycle, A
MYROW, Four Songs In Spring
MYROW, Songs From the Japanese
McBRIDE, Nonsense Syllables
McBRIDE, Vocalise
NELHYBEL, Concerto Spirituoso No.1
NELHYBEL, House that Jack Built, The
NEUMANN, Sephardic Kiddush
NOWAK, Summer is Away
OLIVE, Mar-ri-ia-a
ORGAD, Leave Out My Name
ORREGO-SALAS, Garden Songs
PARRIS, Dreams
PECK, Automobile

PERERA, Three Poems of Günter Grass
PICCOLO, Found in Machaut's Chamber
PINKHAM, Two Motets
PLESKOW, For Five Players and Baritone
PLESKOW, Motet and Madrigal
PLESKOW, On Three Old English Rhymes
PLESKOW, On Two Ancient Texts
POPE, At that hour
RAN, O The Chimneys
REALE, Traveler, The
REIF, Artist, The
REYNOLDS, Again
RIEGGER, Music for Voice and Flute
ROCHBERG, Blake Songs
ROUSE, First Stratum of Empyrean
ROVICS, Echo
SAMUEL, Relativity of Icarus, The
SCHICKELE, Lowest Trees Have Tops, The
SCHRAMM, Songs of Tāyumānavar
SCHULLER, Six Renaissance Lyrics
SCHUMAN, In Sweet Music
SCHWANTNER, Shadows II, Consortium IV
SCHWANTNER, Wild Angels of the Open Hills
SEREBRIER, Erotica
SEMEGEN, Lieder auf der Flucht
SHIELDS, Wildcat Songs
SHIFRIN, Satires of Circumstance
SILSBEE, Scroll
SIMS, Celebration of Dead Ladies
SIMS, Elegie
SMIT, Four Motets
STEARNS, Five Lyrics from "The Prophet"
STEVENS, Two Shakespeare Songs
STEVENS, When Icicles Hang by the Wall
STEWART, D., Wait
STOCK, Scat
STOUT, Engel, Die
STOUT, Landscape
STRAVINSKY, Three Songs from William Sakespeare
SYDEMAN, Jabberwocky
SYDEMAN, Three Songs of Elizabethan Texts
TANENBAUM, Peter Quince At the Clavier
TAUB, O Sweet Spontaneous Earth
TRIMBLE, Four Fragments From the Canterbury Tales
UDOW, Electric Silence
UNG, Mohori
UNG, Tall Wind
VAN NOSTRAND, Earth Manual - 1976
VAN NOSTRAND, Lunar Possession Manual - 1973, A Winter Ceremonial
VERRAL, Rose of the World, The
WEBER, Concert Aria after Solomon
WEIGL, V., Along the Moving Darkness
WEIGL, V., Birds in Springtime
WEIGL, V., Cardinal in March
WEIGL, V., Challenge

WEIGL, V., Christ Child's Lullaby
WEIGL, V., City Birds
WEIGL, V., Glimpse of Hope
WEIGL, V., In Springtime
WEIGL, V., Little Singers, The
WEIGL, V., Long, Long Ago
WEIGL, V., Lyrical Suite
WEIGL, V., Nature Moods
WEIGL, V., Sea Moves Always, The
WEIGL, V., Seeking You
WEIGL, V., Songs for a Child
WEIGL, V., Soon
WEIGL, V., Thistle, Yarrow, Clover
WEIGL, V., Thoughts About Grasshoppers
WEIGL, V., When the Vision Dies ("Perhaps")
WEISGALL, Fancies and Inventions
WHITTENBERG, Even Though the World Keeps Changing
WHITTENBERG, Two Dylan Thomas Songs
WINSOR, Fly, The
WINSOR, Sick Rose, The
WUORINEN, Message to Denmark Hill, A
WYNER, Memorial Music
YANNATOS, Priere Dans L'Arche
YTTREHUS, Six Haiku
ZUR, Affairs, The

CLARINET

ADLER, Passionate Sword The
ADOLPHYS, Lilacs
ALBERT, To Wake the Dead
AMES, Among the Gods.
AMRAM, Three Songs for America
ANDERSON, Beyond Silence
ARGENTO, To Be Sung Upon The Water
AVSHALOMOV, Little Clay Cart, The
AVSHALOMOV, Two Little Birds
BABBIT, Two Sonnets
BARAB, Moments Macabres
BEERMAN, Consort and Song
BERGER, A., Three Poems of Yeats
BIALOSKY, Three Songs
BLACKWOOD, Voyage à Cythère, Un
BLANK, Being: Three Vignettes
BLANK, Coalitions
BLANK, Four Dream Poems
BLANK, Four Poems by Emily Dickinson
BLANK, Poem
BOEHNLEIN, From the J.C. Penney Catalog
BREHM, Cycle of Six Songs, A
BRINGS, Tre Sonetti di Michalengelo Buonarroti
BROOKS, Last Night I Was the Wind
CARTER, Mirror on Which to Dwell, A
CHANCE, Dark Song
CHANCE, Edensong

CHILDS, Seven Epigrams
CHOU, Seven Poems of T'ang Dynasty
CLARK, Rondeau Redoublé
CLARKE, Suite of Changes
CONSOLI, Equinox II
CONSOLI, Vuci Siculani
CORY, Walking
DAVIS, Though Men Call Us Free
DEL TREDICI, Night Conjure-Verse
DI DOMENICA, Four Short Songs
EBERHARD, Parody
ECKERT, Sea-Changes
EDWARDS, Captive, The
EDWARDS, Veined Variety
EHLE, Algorhythms
EVETT, Billy in the Darbies
FELDMAN, I met heine on the rue fürstenberg
FELDMAN, Journey to the End of the Night
FENNELLY, Songs with improvisation
FERRITTO, Oggi
FERRITTO, Quattro Madrigali
FLANAGAN, Weeping Pleiads, The
FOSS, Time Cycle
FOX, Time Excursions
FRANCO, Lord Commeth, The
FRANCO, Song of Life, The
FRANCO, Songs of the Spirit
GIDEON, Adorable Mouse, The
GIDEON, Rhymes from the Hill
GRUNDMAN, Zoo Illogical
HAUBIEL, Threnody for Love, A
HAUFRECHT, Let's Play Maccabees, Children's Songs
HELLERMANN, Poem for Soprano and Four Instruments
HOVHANESS, O Lady Moon
HOVHANESS, Saturn
HUGGLER, Bittere Nüsse
HUGGLER, For Coloratura, Clarinet, Viola, Cello
IMBRIE, Tell me where is fancy bred
IVEY, Three Songs of Night
JAMES, Four Poems of Michael Fried
KUPFERMAN, Conceptual Wheel, The
LEICHTLING, Rubáiyát Fragments
LEICHTLING, Trial and Death of Socrates
LEICHTLING, Two Proverbs
LEVI, Truth, The
LUENING, Soundless Song, The
LYBBERT, Leopardi Canti
MATTHEWS, Paysage
MILLER, Mists and Waters
MONOD, Chamber Aria
MONOD, Passacaille
MYROW, Songs From the Japanese
NELHYBEL, House that Jack Built, The
NOWAK, Maiden's Song
NOWAK, Summer is Away
OLIVE, Mar-ri-ia-a

ORLAND, Love and Pity
PARRIS, Dreams
PASATIERI, Far from Love
PERERA, Three Poems of Günter Grass
PISK, Meadow-Saffrons
PLESKOW, For Five Players and Baritone
PLESKOW, Motet and Madrigal
PLESKOW, On Three Old English Rhymes
PLESKOW, On Two Ancient Texts
PLESKOW, Three Songs
POPE, At that hour
POPE, Rain
PUSZTAI, Requiem Profana
RAN, O The Chimneys
RANDALL, Improvisations
REALE, Pange Lingua
REIF, Artist, The
RILEY, Five Songs on Japanese Haiku
ROCHBERG, Blake Songs
ROOSEVELT, Three Songs from Poe
ROREM, Ariel
ROUSE, Aphrodite Cantos
ROUSE, Kiss, The
SAMUEL, Relativity of Icarus, The
SARGON, Patterns in Blue
SCHWANTNER, Shadows II, Consortium IV
SEMEGEN, Lieder auf der Flucht
SEREBRIER, Erotica
SEYFRIT, Winter's Warmth
SHIFRIN, Satires of Circumstance
SIMS, Celebration of Dead Ladies
SIMS, Elegie
STEARNS, Three Love Songs
STEVENS, Two Shakespeare Songs
STOCK, Scat
STOUT, Allegory: Pride, An
STOUT, Two Songs of Ariel, 1957
STRAVINSKY, Three Songs from William Sakespeare
SWACK, Psalm VIII
TANENBAUM, Mirage and Incantation
TANENBAUM, Peter Quince At the Clavier
TAYLOR, Two Songs
THOMSON, Four Songs to Poems of Thomas Campion
TRIMBLE, Four Fragments From the Canterbury Tales
UDOW, Electric Silence
VAN NOSTRAND, Earth Manual - 1976
VAN NOSTRAND, Lunar Possession Manual - 1973, A Winter Ceremonial
WEBER, Concert Aria after Solomon
WEIGL, V., Birds in Springtime
WEIGL, V., Cardinal in March
WEIGL, V., Christ Child's Lullaby
WEIGL, V., I Saw Two Birds
WEIGL, V., Lyrical Suite
WEIGL, V., Nature Moods
WEIGL, V., Salvation of the Dawn, The

WEIGL, V., Sea Moves Always, The
WEIGL, V., Songs from "Native Island"
WEIGL, V., Thistle, Yarrow, Clover
WEIGL, V., Thoughts About Grasshoppers
WEIGL, V., When the Vision Dies ("Perhaps")
WEISGALL, Fancies and Inventions
WINSOR, Fly, The
WINSOR, Sick Rose, The
WOLPE, Quintet with Voice
YANNATOS, Priere Dans L'Arche
ZUR, Affairs, The

SAXOPHONE

ANDERSON, Variations on a Theme by M.B. Tolson
AUSTIN, Homecoming
CORY, Walking
DERR, I Never Saw Another Butterfly
DIEMENTE, 3 - 31 - '70
HAMPTON, Labyrinth
NELHYBEL, Concerto Spirtuoso No. 2
RANDALL, Improvisations
RILEY, Cantata I
ROSEN, Serenade
SHAPEY, Incantations
TAYLOR, Quattro Liriche from "Mattino Domenicale"

OBOE, ENGLISH HORN, HEKELPHONE

AMRAM, Three Songs for America
BARAB, Moments Macabres
BEALE, Proverbs
BLACKWOOD, Voyage à Cythère, Un
BLANK, Esther's Monologue
BLANK, Two Holy Sonnets by John Donne
BOEHNLEIN, From the J.C. Penney Catalog
BOTTJE, In a word
BREHM, Cycle of Six Songs, A
BROOKS, Last Night I Was the Wind
CARTER, Mirror on Which to Dwell, A
CHOU, Seven Poems of T'ang Dynasty
CORY, Aria Viva
CRUMB, Ancient Voices of Children
CUMMING, As Dew in April
CUSTER, Cartagena Songs
DEL TREDICI, Night Conjure-Verse
EDWARDS, Captive, The
FELDMAN, Rabbi Akiba
FRANCO, Lord Commeth, The
FRANCO, Song of Life, The
FRANCO, Songs of the Spirit
GIDEON, Hound of Heaven, The
GIDEON, Nocturnes
GIDEON, Questions on Nature

HAINES, Four Loves
HAUFRECHT, Let's Play Maccabees, Children's Songs
HOVHANESS, Canticle
JOHNSTON, Five Fragments
JOHNSTON, Sea Dirge, A
MONOD, Chamber Aria
MONOD, Passacaille
MOORE, Dorothy, Songs
MOORE, Dorothy, Weary Blues
MORTON, Tears, Idle Tears
MORYL, Lied, Das
MORYL, de morte cantoris
MOSS, Unseen Leaves
PARRIS, Dreams
POWELL, Two Prayer Settings
PUSZTAI, Requiem Profana
REALE, Pange Lingua
REALE, Three Songs from the Chinese
RIEGGER, Music for Voice and Flute
ROUSE, Nox Aeris Temporis
ROVICS, Haunted Object
SAMUEL, Relativity of Icarus, The
SCHULLER, Six Renaissance Lyrics
SEREBRIER, Erotica
STEARNS, Three Sacred Songs
STOUT, Commentary of T'ung Jen
STOUT, Engel, Die
STOUT, Landscape
STOUT, Two Songs of Ariel, 1957
TRIMBLE, Petit Concert
UDOW, Eight American Indian Children's Poems
UNG, Mohori
UNG, Tall Wind
WEBER, Concert Aria after Solomon
WEIGL, V., Brief Encounters
WEIGL, V., Seal Lullaby
WEIGL, V., Songs from "Native Island"
WEISGALL, End of Summer
WILSON, D., Five Haiku
YANNATOS, Priere Dans L'Arche
ZONN, Shadows of an Orange Leaf

BASSOON

AMRAM, Three Songs for America
BIALOSKY, Six Riddles from Symphosius
BLACKWOOD, Voyage á Cythére, Un
BLANK, Don't let that horse eat that violin
BLANK, Pennycandystore beyond the El, The
BOEHNLEIN, From the J.C. Penney Catalog
BOND, Cornography
BREHM, Cycle of Six Songs, A
BROOKS, Last Night I Was the Wind
CHOU, Seven Poems of T'ang Dynasty
CLARK, Rondeau Redoublé

CORY, Aria Viva
CORY, Walking
DEL TREDICI, Night Conjure-Verse
FELDMAN, Journey to the End of the Night
FRANCO, Songs of the Spirit
GIDEON, Adorable Mouse, The
GIDEON, Condemned Playground, The
GRUNDMAN, Zoo Illogical
JOHNSTON, Five Fragments
KARLINS, Four Inventions and a Fugue
LEVI, Truth, The
LOMBARDO, Frosted Window: Variations on White
MONOD, Chamber Aria
MONOD, Passacaille
NELHYBEL, House that Jack Built, The
NOWAK, Summer is Away
PUSZTAI, Requiem Profana
REIF, Artist, The
ROVICS, Haunted Object
SEREBRIER, Erotica
SEYFRIT, Winter's Warmth
UDOW, Eight American Indian Children's Poems
UDOW, Electric Silence
WEBER, Concert Aria after Solomon
WEIGL, V., I Saw Two Birds
WEIGL, V., Thistle, Yarrow, Clover
WILDER, Phyllis McGinley Song Cycle
YANNATOS, Priere Dans L'Arche

TRUMPET

ANDERSON, Variations on a Theme by M.B. Tolson
AUSTIN, Homecoming
BLACKWOOD, Voyage á Cythére, Un
BLANK, Four Dream Poems
BOEHNLEIN, From the J.C. Penney Catalog
BOTTJE, In a word
CHOU, Seven Poems of T'ang Dynasty
CORY, Walking
DIEMENTE, Forms of Flight and Fancy
DIEMENTE, 3 - 31 - '70
DRUCKMAN, Dark upon the Harp
ECKERT, Sea-Changes
FELDMAN, Rabbi Akiba
FELDMAN, Vertical Thoughts III
GIDEON, Sonnets from Shakespeare
GRUNDMAN, Zoo Illogical
HIBBARD, Ménage
MAYER, Eight Miniatures
MAYER, Two News Items
MESTRES-QUADRENY, Invecions Movils II
MONOD, Chamber Aria
MONOD, Passacaille
McBRIDE, Commentary
PINKHAM, Now the Trumpet Summons Us Again

PLOG, Four Sierra Scenes
PLOG, Two Scenes
PUSZTAI, Requiem Profana
RANDALL, Improvisations
REIF, Artist, The
SACCO, Three Psalms
SHAPEY, Incantations
SILSBEE, Scroll
STEARNS, Three Love Songs
STOUT, Engel, Die
SWACK, Psalm VIII
YANNATOS, Priere Dans L'Arche
ZUR, Affairs, The

FRENCH HORN

AMRAM, Three Songs for America
BLACKWOOD, Voyage à Cythère, Un
BOEHNLEIN, From the J.C. Penney Catalog
BOND, Cornography
BOTTJE, In a word
BRANT, Encephalograms
BREHM, Cycle of Six Songs, A
BROOKS, Last Night I Was the Wind
CHANCE, Dark Song
CHANCE, Three Poems by Rilke
CHOU, Seven Poems of T'ang Dynasty
CUSTER, Cartagena Songs
DEL TREDICI, Night Conjure-Verse
DIEMENTE, Forms of Flight and Fancy
DRUCKMAN, Dark upon the Harp
ECKERT, Sea-Changes
FARBERMAN, Evolution
FELDMAN, For Franz Kline
FELDMAN, Rabbi Akiba
FRANCO, Songs of the Spirit
GIDEON, Adorable Mouse, The
KAUDER, Two Songs
LEICHTLING, Rubáiyát Fragments
MELBY, Due Canti di Leopardi
MOLLICONE, Murali
MONOD, Chamber Aria
MONOD, Passacaille
NELHYBEL, House that Jack Built, The
OLIVE, Mar-ri-ia-a
PLOG, Four Sierra Scenes
PUSZTAI, Requiem Profana
REALE, Pange Lingua
REIF, Artist, The
ROOSEVELT, American Sampler, An
SACCO, Three Psalms
SEMEGEN, Lieder auf der Flucht
SEREBRIER, Erotica
SHAPEY, Incantations
STEARNS, Three Sacred Songs

WEBER, Concert Aria after Solomon
WEIGL, V., Brief Encounters
WEIGL, V., Dear Earth: A Quintet of Poems
WEIGL, V., Swiftly Along Flows the River
WOLPE, Quintet with Voice
YANNATOS, Priere Dans L'Arche

TROMBONE

ANDERSON, Beyond Silence
ANDERSON, Variations on a Theme by M.B. Tolson
BIALOSKY, Six Riddles from Symphosius
BLACKWOOD, Voyage à Cythère, Un
BLANK, Coalitions
BLANK, I Missed His Book, But I Read His Name
BOEHNLEIN, From the J.C. Penney Catalog
CHOU, Seven Poems of T'ang Dynasty
DIEMENTE, Forms of Flight and Fancy
DIEMENTE, 3 - 31 - '70
DRUCKMAN, Animus IV
DRUCKMAN, Dark upon the Harp
EBERHARD, Parody
FELDMAN, Intervals
FELDMAN, Rabbi Akiba
FELDMAN, Vertical Thoughts III
GABURO, Cantilena 4
GRUNDMAN, Zoo Illogical
HARRISON, Alma Redemptoris Mater
MOLLICONE, Kyrie Eleison
MOORE, Douglas, Ballad of William Sycamore, The
McBRIDE, Commentary
PLOG, Four Sierra Scenes
PUSZTAI, Requiem Profana
REYNOLDS, Again
SACCO, Three Psalms
STEARNS, Three Love Songs
STOUT, Engel, Die
STRAVINSKY, In memoriam Dylan Thomas
TANENBAUM, Peter Quince At the Clavier
UDOW, Electric Silence
YANNATOS, Priere Dans L'Arche
ZONN, Shadows of an Orange Leaf

TUBA, EUPHONIUM, BARITONE HORN

AMATO, Two Together
BLANK, Finale: Mélange
BLANK, Recital
CLARKE, Suite of Changes
DIEMENTE, Forms of Flight and Fancy
DRUCKMAN, Dark upon the Harp
FELDMAN, Rabbi Akiba
FELDMAN, Vertical Thoughts III
FELDMAN, Vertical Thoughts V

SACCO, Three Psalms
STOUT, Engel, Die
ZUR, Affairs, The

D. KEYBOARD

PIANO

ADOLPHYS, Lilacs
ALBERT, To Wake the Dead
ANDERSON, Beyond Silence
ANDERSON, Variations on a Theme by M.B. Tolson
ARGENTO, To Be Sung Upon The Water
AUSTIN, Homecoming
AVSHALOMOV, Two Little Birds
BEALE, Lamentations
BEALE, Proverbs
BENSON, Nara
BLANK, Coalitions
BLANK, Finale: Mélange
BLANK, Four Dream Poems
BLANK, I Missed His Book, But I Read His Name
BLANK, Recital
BLANK, Zulus Live in Land Without a Square
BOTTJE, In a word
BRANT, Encephalograms
BRINGS, Tre Sonetti di Michelangelo Buonarroti
CACIOPPO, Bestiary I: Eingang
CALDWELL, Christmas Triptych, A
CALDWELL, Lute Caroll, A
CARTER, Mirror on Which to Dwell, A
CHAJES, By the Rvers of Babylon
CHANCE, Dark Song
CHOU, Seven Poems of T'ang Dynasty
CLARK, Life in Ghana
COLGRASS, New People
CONSOLI, Equnox I
CONSOLI, Equinox II
CONSOLI, Isonic
CORY, Walking
COWELL, Sonatina
COWELL, Toccanta
COWELL, Vocalise
CRUMB, Ancient Voices of Children
CRUMB, Night Music I
CRUMB, Songs Drones, and Refrains of Death
CUMMING, As Dew in April
CUSTER, Cartagena Songs
DAVIS, Though Men Call Us Free
DERR, I Never Saw Another Butterfly
DIAMOND, Mad Maid's Song, The
DIEMER, Four Chinese Love Poems
DRUCKMAN, Animus IV

EBERHARD, Parody
EDWARDS, Three Hopkins Songs
EHLE, Algorhythms
FARBERMAN, Greek Scene
FARBERMAN, New York Times, Aug. 30, 1964
FELDMAN, For Franz Kline
FELDMAN, Four Songs to e e cummings
FELDMAN, I met heine on the rue fürstenberg
FELDMAN, O'Hara Songs, The
FELDMAN, Rabbi Akiba
FELDMAN, Vertical Thoughts III
FENNELLY, Songs with improvisation
FERGUSON, Two Spanish Songs
FERRITTO, Oggi
FINE, Confession, The
FINE, Great Wall of China, The
FLANAGAN, Weeping Pleiads, The
FOSS, Thirteen Ways of Looking at a Blackbird
FOSS, Time Cycle
FOX, Time Excursions
GIDEON, Questions on Nature
GIDEON, Seasons of Time, The
GRATZ, Earthbound
GRUNDMAN, Zoo Illogical
HAINES, Four Loves
HARRIS, Abraham Lincoln Walks at Midnight
HARRISON, Air
HARRISON, Alma Redemptoris Mater
HARTLEY, Psalm Cycle, A
HARTWAY, Three Ways of Looking at a Blackbird
HAUBIEL, Threnody for Love, A
HOSKINS, Romance, Who Loves to Nod and Sing
HOVHANESS, O Lady Moon
HOVHANESS, Saturn
IVES, Sunrise
IVES, Vote for Names
IVEY, Solstice
IVEY, Three Songs of Night
JENKINS, Three Carols from the Quiet Wars
KARLINS, Four Inventions and a Fugue
KARLINS, Three Songs
KIM, Earthlight
KUPFERMAN, Conceptual Wheel, The
LEICHTLING, Psalm 37
LEICHTLING, Rubáiyát Fragments
LERDAHL, Eros
LESSARD, Five Poems by Robert Herrick
LEVI, Truth, The
LUENING, Soundless Song, The
LYBBERT, Lines for The Fallen
MATTHEWS, Paysage
MAYER, Eight Miniatures
MAYER, Barbara -- what have you done?
MAYER, Two News Items
MELBY, Due Canti di Leopardi
MELBY, Men that Are Falling, The

MILLER, Mists and Waters
MONOD, Chamber Aria
MONOD, Passacaille
MOORE, Dorothy, From the Dark Tower
MOORE, Douglas, Ballad of William Sycamore, The
MORYL, Lied, Das
MORYL, de morte cantoris
MYROW, Songs From the Japanese
McBRIDE, Commentary
McBRIDE, Vocalise
McBRIDE, Vocalise No. 3 On Nonsense Syllables
NOWAK, Five Songs
NOWAK, Maiden's Song
NOWAK, Summer is Away
PARRIS, Dreams
PASATIERI, Far from Love
PASATIERI, Heloise and Abelard
PENN, Three Songs on Three Teton Sioux Poems
PERERA, Three Poems of Günter Grass
PISK, Waning Moon, The
PLESKOW, For Five Players and Baritone
PLESKOW, Motet and Madrigal
PLESKOW, On Three Old English Rhymes
PLESKOW, On Two Ancient Texts
PLESKOW, Three Songs
POPE, At that hour
POPE, Rain
PRESSER, Hymne to God the Father, A
PUSZTAI, Requiem Profana
RAN, O The Chimneys
RANDALL, Improvisations
REALE, Traveler, The
REIF, Reverence for Life
RILEY, Cantata I
ROOSEVELT, American Sampler, An
ROOSEVELT, Three Songs from Poe
ROREM, Ariel
ROREM, Four Dialogues
ROREM, Last Poems of Wallace Stevens
ROREM, Serenade on Five English Poems
ROUSE, Aphrodite Cantos
ROUSE, Ecstasis Mane Eburnei
ROUSE, First Stratum of Empyrean
ROUSE, Kiss, The
ROUSE, Nox Aeris Temporis
ROVICS, Echo
SAMUEL, Relativity of Icarus, The
SARGON, Patterns in Blue
SCHULLER, Six Renaissance Lyrics
SCHWARTZ, Septet
SEIGMEISTER, Songs of Experience
SEMEGEN, Lieder auf der Flucht
SHAPEY, Incantations
SHIFRIN, Satires of Circumstance
SILSBEE, Scroll
STEVENS, Three Japanese Folksongs

STEVENS, When Icicles Hang by the Wall
STEWART, D., Wait
STOUT, Allegory: Pride, An
STOUT, Commentary of T'ung Jen
STOUT, Engel, Die
STUCKEY, Schneemusik
SWACK, Psalm VIII
SYDEMAN, Encounters
TANENBAUM, Image
TANENBAUM, Mirage and Incantation
TAUB, Of Things Past
TAYLOR, Quattro Liriche from "Mattino Domenicale"
TAYLOR, Two Songs
UDOW, Eight American Indian Children's Poems
UDOW, Electric Silence
UNG, Mohori
VAN NOSTRAND, Earth Manual - 1976
VAN NOSTRAND, Lunar Possession Manual - 1973, A Winter Ceremonial
VERRAL, Rose of the World, The
WEBER, Concert Aria after Solomon
WEIGL, V., Along the Moving Darkness
WEIGL, V., Beyond Time
WEIGL, V., Birds in Springtime
WEIGL, V., Cardinal in March
WEIGL, V., Challenge
WEIGL, V., Christ Child's Lullaby
WEIGL, V., City Birds
WEIGL, V., Dear Earth: A Quintet of Poems
WEIGL, V., Do Not Wake Me
WEIGL, V., Echoes
WEIGL, V., Glimpse of Hope
WEIGL, V., Huntsmen, The
WEIGL, V., In Springtime
WEIGL, V., Little Singers, The
WEIGL, V., Long, Long Ago
WEIGL, V., Lyrical Suite
WEIGL, V., Nightfall in the Mountains
WEIGL, V., Pippa's Song
WEIGL, V., Rabbles of Scattered Leaves
WEIGL, V., Rain at Night
WEIGL, V., Rock-A-By Lady, The
WEIGL, V., Salvation of the Dawn, The
WEIGL, V., Sea Moves Always, The
WEIGL, V., Seal Lullaby
WEIGL, V., Seeking You
WEIGL, V., Silver
WEIGL, V., Songs for a Child
WEIGL, V., Songs from "Native Island"
WEIGL, V., Songs from "No Boundary"
WEIGL, V., Soon
WEIGL, V., Summer Stars
WEIGL, V., Swiftly Along Flows the River
WEIGL, V., Thoughts About Grasshoppers
WEIGL, V., When the Vision Dies ("Perhaps")
WEIGL, V., Where Go the Boats

WEIGL, V., Winter Night
WEIGL, V., Wynken, Blynken and Nod
WEISGALL, Fancies and Inventions
WHITE, This Son so Young
WHITTENBERG, Two Dylan Thomas Songs
WOLPE, Quintet with Voice
WUORINEN, Message to Denmark Hill, A
YANNY, At The End of the Parade
ZONN, Shadows of an Orange Leaf
ZUR, Affairs, The

CELESTA

CONSOLI, Equnox I
CONSOLI, Equinox II
ECKERT, Sea-Changes
FELDMAN, Vertical Thoughts V
FRANCO, Tempset, Incidental Music, The
HOVHANESS, Canticle
PARRIS, Dreams
PINKHAM, Now the Trumpet Summons Us Again
ROCHBERG, Blake Songs
ROUSE, Kiss, The
STOUT, Two Songs of Ariel, 1957

HARPSICHORD

BRINGS, Tre Madrigali Concertati
CHANCE, Dark Song
DIAMOND, Mad Maid's Song, The
DIEMER, Four Poems by Alice Meynell
EDWARDS, Captive, The
FRANCO, Tempset, Incidental Music, The
GIDEON, Adorable Mouse, The
HAINES, Four Loves
LEVI, Truth, The
NELHYBEL, Concerto Spirituoso No.1
NELHYBEL, Concerto Spirtuoso No. 2
TRIMBLE, Four Fragments From the Canterbury Tales
TRIMBLE, Petit Concert
YTTREHUS, Six Haiku

ORGAN, HARMONIUM

ALBERT, To Wake the Dead
DRUCKMAN, Animus IV
FELCIANO, Glossolalia
MAYER, Eight Miniatures
PLOG, Two Scenes
SOWERBY, God Mounts His Throne
SOWERBY, Happy the Nation
STOUT, Christmas Antiphon
WHITE, This Son so Young

E. PERCUSSION

ADLER, Canto V
ADLER, Passionate Sword The
AUSTIN, Homecoming
AVSHALOMOV, Little Clay Cart, The
BEALE, Proverbs
BEERMAN, Consort and Song
BEERMAN, Mass
BENSON, Nara
BLANK, Coalitions
BLANK, Finale: Mélange
BLANK, I Missed His Book, But I Read His Name
BLANK, Zulus Live in Land Without a Square
BLICKHAN, Speak Softly
BOEHNLEIN, From the J.C. Penney Catalog
BRANT, Encephalograms
BRINGS, Tre Sonetti di Michelangelo Buonarroti
CACIOPPO, Bestiary I: Eingang
CAGE, Forever and Sunsmell
CARTER, Mirror on Which to Dwell, A
CHANCE, Dark Song
CHANCE, Edensong
CHILDS, Lanterns and Candlelight
CHOU, Seven Poems of T'ang Dynasty
CIRONE, Five Items
CLARK, Lord Is My Shepherd, The
CLARK, Woman of Viture, A
CONSOLI, Equnox I
CONSOLI, Equinox II
CONSOLI, Isonic
CORY, Walking
CRUMB, Ancient Voices of Children
CRUMB, Lux Aeterna
CRUMB, Madrigals: Book I
CRUMB, Madrigals: Book II
CRUMB, Madrigals: Book III
CRUMB, Madrigals: Book IV
CRUMB, Night Music I
CRUMB, Night of the Four Moons
CRUMB, Songs Drones, and Refrains of Death
CUCINOTTA, Beasts
DAILEY, Shell, The
DE JONG, hist wist
DIEMENTE, 3 - 31 - '70
DREW, Aria
DRUCKMAN, Animus II
DRUCKMAN, Animus IV
DRUCKMAN, Dark upon the Harp
EBERHARD, Parody
EDWARDS, Captive, The
FARBERMAN, Evolution
FARBERMAN, Greek Scene
FARBERMAN, New York Times, Aug. 30, 1964
FELCIANO, Glossolalia

FELDMAN, For Franz Kline
FELDMAN, I met heine on the rue fürstenberg
FELDMAN, Intervals
FELDMAN, O'Hara Songs, The
FELDMAN, Rabbi Akiba
FELDMAN, Vertical Thoughts III
FELDMAN, Vertical Thoughts V
FOSS, Thirteen Ways of Looking at a Blackbird
FOSS, Time Cycle
FOX, Time Excursions
FRANCO, Tempset, Incidental Music, The
GABER, Voce II
GIDEON, Adorable Mouse, The
GIDEON, Nocturnes
GIDEON, Questions on Nature
GIDEON, Rhymes from the Hill
GRATZ, Earthbound
GRUNDMAN, Zoo Illogical
HARDIN, Moondog on the Streets of New York
HARTWAY, Three Ways of Looking at a Blackbird
HAUFRECHT, Let's Play Maccabees, Children's Songs
HENRY, The Sons of Martha
HILLER, Avalanche, An
HOVHANESS, Canticle
IVEY, Solstice
KOLB, Chanson Bas
LANG, Three Puerto Rican Songs
LEICHTLING, Psalm 37
LERDAHL, Eros
LERDAHL, Wake
LOMBARDO, Frosted Window: Variations on White
MATTHEWS, Paysage
MAYER, Eight Miniatures
MAYER, Two News Items
MILLER, Bashō Songs
MOLINEUX, Crystals
MOLLICONE, Murali
MORYL, Corridors
MORYL, Lied, Das
MORYL, de morte cantoris
MYROW, Songs From the Japanese
McBRIDE, Commentary
McBRIDE, Vocalise No. 3 On Nonsense Syllables
NELHYBEL, House that Jack Built, The
OLIVE, Mar-ri-ia-a
PARRIS, Dreams
PECK, Automobile
PENN, Three Songs on Three Teton Sioux Poems
PINKHAM, Now the Trumpet Summons Us Again
PUSZTAI, Requiem Profana
RAN, O The Chimneys
REALE, Three Songs from the Chinese
RECK, Night sounds (and Dream)
REIF, Artist, The
REYNOLDS, Again
RILEY, Cantata I

ROUSE, Aphrodite Cantos
ROUSE, Ecstasis Mane Eburnei
ROUSE, First Stratum of Empyrean
ROUSE, Kiss, The
ROUSE, Nox Aeris Temporis
ROUSE, Subjectives V
RUSSEL, Ballad with Epitaphs
SAMUEL, Relativity of Icarus, The
SCHULLER, Six Renaissance Lyrics
SEMEGEN, Lieder auf der Flucht
SHAPEY, Incantations
SHIFRIN, A Renaissance Garland
SILSBEE, Scroll
SIMS, Celebration of Dead Ladies
ST. JOHN, Her Drifting from Me These Days
STEINER, Dream Dialogue 1974
STEINER, Four Songs for Medium Voice and Vibraphone
STEINER, Interlude
STEINER, New Poems
STEINER, Three Poems
STEWART, F., The First Joy of Marriage
STOUT, Allegory: Pride, An
STOUT, Christmas Antiphon
STOUT, Commentary of T'ung Jen
STOUT, Engel, Die
STOUT, Landscape
STOUT, Two Songs of Ariel, 1957
TANENBAUM, Image
THOMAS, Dirge in the Woods
THOMSON, Five Phrases from the Song of Solomon
UDOW, Electric Silence
UNG, Mohori
VAN NOSTRAND, Earth Manual - 1976
VAN NOSTRAND, Lunar Possession Manual - 1973, A Winter Ceremonial
WERNICK, Prayer for Jerusalem, A
WHITTENBERG, Even Though the World Keeps Changing
WHITTENBERG, Vocalise
WRIGHT, Cantata
YANNY, At The End of the Parade
YTTREHUS, Angstwagen
ZONN, Shadows of an Orange Leaf
ZUR, Affairs, The

F. TAPE, SYNTHESIZED TAPE, SYNTHESIZER

BABBIT, Vision & Prayer
BEERMAN, Consort and Song
BEERMAN, Mass
DRUCKMAN, Animus II
DRUCKMAN, Animus IV
FELCIANO, Glossolalia

IVEY, Terminus
IVEY, Three Songs of Night
MELBY, Men that Are Falling, The
MELBY, Two Stevens Songs
MELBY, Valedictory
MOSS, Unseen Leaves
McBRIDE, Commentary
OLIVE, Mar-ri-ia-a
PERERA, Dove sta amore
PERERA, Three Poems of Günter Grass
PINKHAM, Safe in their Alabaster Chambers
RAN, O The Chimneys
REYNOLDS, Again
REYNOLDS, Compass
ROVICS, Haunted Object
SCHWANTNER, Shadows II, Consortium IV
SYDEMAN, Malediction
TANENBAUM, Image
TANENBAUM, Images III
TANENBAUM, Mirage and Incantation
WILSON, O., Sometimes
WRIGHT, Cantata

G. MULTIMEDIA: LIGHTS, DANCERS, ETC.

BLANK, Zulus Live in Land Without a Square
FRANCO, Tempset, Incidental Music, The
HILLER, Avalanche, An
KIM, Earthlight
MOSS, Unseen Leaves
REYNOLDS, Again
REYNOLDS, Compass
VAN NOSTRAND, Lunar Possession Manual - 1973, A Winter Ceremonial

Appendix II

CLASSIFIED BY NUMBER OF PERFORMERS

1 PERFORMERS

KAVANAUGH, Jubal
SIMS, Cantata 3

2 PERFORMERS

AMATO, Two Together
ARGENTO, Letters from Composers
BABBIT, Vision & Prayer
BENVENUTI, Cantus, Gemellus
BERGER, J., Six Rondeau
BIALOSKY, Three Songs
BLANK, Being: Three Vignettes
BLANK, Pennycandystore beyond the El, The
CARTER, Tell Me where is Fancy Bred
CHANCE, Duos I
CHILDS, Lanterns and Candlelight
CHILDS, Seven Epigrams
CLARK, Emily Dickinson Canons
CLARK, Four Elements
CLARK, Puget Sound Cinquain
CLARK, Song to a Young Pianist
CROUNCE, Slumber did my Spirit Seal, A
DIAMOND, Vocalises
DIEMER, Four Chinese Love Poems
FRANCO, Ariel's Four Songs
FRANCO, Little Lamb
FRANCO, Two Duets for Voice and Flute
GABURO, Cantilena 4
GIDEON, Little Ivory Figures
GODFREY, Wedding Airs, The
HARDIN, Moondog on the Streets of New York

HEILNER, Democracy
HEILNER, Every Day is Friday to a Seal
HEILNER, Gift of Fire, The
HEILNER, Henry at the Grating
HEILNER, Letters from the Draft Board
HEILNER, Peace is a Lovely Word
HEILNER, Rock-'n'-Roll Session
HEILNER, Stevenson
HEILNER, What Were They Like?
HEILNER, Wild Anemone, The
HOVHANESS, Hercules
HOVHANNISSIAN, Plea
IVEY, Terminus
JENNI, Get Hence Foule Griefe
LEICHTLING, Three Songs by Emily Dickinson
LOMON, Five Songs after Poems by William Blake
LUENING, Suite for Soprano and Flute
MELBY, Two Stevens Songs
MELBY, Valedictory
MOLLICONE, Kyrie Eleison
MOLLICONE, Two Love Songs
MOORE, Dorothy, Songs
MORYL, Corridors
MOURANT, Two Songs
MYERS, Mini-Song Cycle, A
McBRIDE, Nonsense Syllables
NEUMANN, Sephardic Kiddush
ORGAD, Leave Out My Name
PERERA, Dove sta amore
PINKHAM, Eight Poems of Gerard Manley Hopkins
PINKHAM, Man that is born of a woman
PINKHAM, Safe in their Alabaster Chambers
POWELL, Faces
RIEGGER, Music for Voice and Flute
ROOSEVELT, Four Songs for Soprano and Viola
ROSEN, Serenade
ROUSE, Subjectives V
ROVICS, Hunter, The
SCHRAMM, Songs of Tāyumānavar
SHAPEY, Walking Upright
SHIELDS, Wildcat Songs
SIMONS, Songs for Wendy
STEINER, Dream Dialogue 1974
STEINER, Four Songs for Medium Voice and Vibraphone
STEINER, Interlude
STEINER, New Poems
STUCKEY, Schneemusik
SYDEMAN, Three Songs
SYDEMAN, Three Songs of Elizabethan Texts
TANENBAUM, Images III
TAUB, O Sweet Spontaneous Earth
THOMSON, Five Phrases from the Song of Solomon
WEBER, Four Songs
WEIGL, V., Drums of War, The
WHEAR, From Thoreau
WILSON, O., Sometimes

3 PERFORMERS

ADOLPHYS, Lilacs
ARGENTO, To Be Sung Upon The Water
AVSHALOMOV, Two Little Birds
BALLOU, 5-4-3
BARAB, Bagatelles
BEALE, Lamentations
BEALE, Three Songs
BENTON, Love Song
BERGER, J., Tres Canciones
BIALOSKY, Six Riddles from Symphosius
BINKERD, Portrait Interiéur
BINKERD, Secret-Love
BLANK, Don't let that horse eat that violin
BLANK, Four Poems by Emily Dickinson
BLANK, Recital
BLANK, Two Parables by Franz Kafka
BLICKHAN, Speak Softly
BOND, Cornography
BRINGS, Tre Madrigali Concertati
CAGE, Forever and Sunsmell
CALDWELL, Christmas Triptych, A
CALDWELL, Lute Caroll, A
CHAJES, By the Waters of Babylon
CLARK, Life in Ghana
CLARK, Lord Is My Shepherd, The
CLARK, Woman of Viture, A
COLGRASS, New People
CONSOLI, Tre Canzoni
COWELL, Sonatina
COWELL, Vocalise
CRANE, Cords
CRUMB, Madrigals: Book I
CRUMB, Madrigals: Book II
CRUMB, Madrigals: Book III
CUMMING, As Dew in April
DAILEY, Shell, The
DAVIS, Though Men Call Us Free
DERR, I Never Saw Another Butterfly
DIAMOND, Mad Maid's Song, The
DREW, Aria
FARBERMAN, Greek Scene
FARBERMAN, New York Times, Aug. 30, 1964
FELDMAN, Four Songs to e e cummings
FENNELLY, Songs with improvisation
FERGUSON, Two Spanish Songs
FERRITTO, Oggi
FERRITTO, Quattro Madrigali
FLANAGAN, Good-Bye, My Fancy
GABER, Voce II
GABURO, Two
HARTLEY, Psalm Cycle, A
HIBBARD, Ménage
HOSKINS, Romance, Who Loves to Nod and Sing

HOVHANESS, O Lady Moon
HOVHANESS, Saturn
IMBRIE, Tell me where is fancy bred
IVES, Sunrise
JOHNSTON, Three Chinese Lyrics
KARLINS, Four Inventions and a Fugue
KARLINS, Songs for Soprano
KARLINS, Three Songs
KAUDER, Song from "Dierdre"
KAUDER, Two Songs
KOLB, Songs before an Adieu
KUPFERMAN, Conceptual Wheel, The
LESSARD, Five Poems by Robert Herrick
LYBBERT, Lines for The Fallen
MAMLOCK, Five Songs
MAYER, Barbara -- what have you done?
MELBY, Due Canti di Leopardi
MELBY, Men that Are Falling, The
MESTRES-QUADRENY, Invecions Movils II
MOLLICONE, Murali
MOORE, Dorothy, From the Dark Tower
MOORE, Dorothy, Weary Blues
MORTON, Tears, Idle Tears
McBRIDE, Vocalise
NOWAK, Five Songs
ORLAND, Love and Pity
PASATIERI, Heloise and Abelard
PINKHAM, Two Motets
PISK, Meadow-Saffrons
PLOG, Two Scenes
POWELL, Three Poems of Paul Zelanske
PRESSER, Hymne to God the Father, A
REALE, Traveler, The
RECK, Night sounds (and Dream)
ROOSEVELT, American Sampler, An
ROOSEVELT, Three Songs from Poe
ROREM, Ariel
ROREM, Last Poems of Wallace Stevens
ROVICS, Echo
SARGON, Patterns in Blue
SCHWANTNER, Wild Angels of the Open Hills
SEIGMEISTER, Songs of Experience
SIMONS, Trialogue
SIMS, Owl and the Pussycat, The
SOWERBY, God Mounts His Throne
SOWERBY, Happy the Nation
STEARNS, Five Lyrics from "The Prophet"
STEINER, Three Poems
STEVENS, Two Shakespeare Songs
STEWART, D., Wait
STEWART, F., The First Joy of Marriage
SWACK, Psalm VIII
SYDEMAN, Four Japanese Songs
SYDEMAN, Jabberwocky
TAYLOR, Quattro Liriche from "Mattino Domenicale"
TAYLOR, Two Songs

THOMAS, Dirge in the Woods
VERRAL, Rose of the World, The
WEIGL, V., Along the Moving Darkness
WEIGL, V., Beyond Time
WEIGL, V., Birds in Springtime
WEIGL, V., Brief Encounters
WEIGL, V., Cardinal in March
WEIGL, V., Challenge
WEIGL, V., Christ Child's Lullaby
WEIGL, V., City Birds
WEIGL, V., Do Not Awake Me
WEIGL, V., Echoes
WEIGL, V., Glimpse of Hope
WEIGL, V., Huntsmen, The
WEIGL, V., I Saw Two Birds
WEIGL, V., In Springtime
WEIGL, V., Little Singers, The
WEIGL, V., Long, Long Ago
WEIGL, V., Nature Moods
WEIGL, V., Nightfall in the Mountains
WEIGL, V., Pippa's Song
WEIGL, V., Rabbles of Scattered Leaves
WEIGL, V., Rain at Night
WEIGL, V., Rock-A-By Lady, The
WEIGL, V., Salvation of the Dawn, The
WEIGL, V., Sea Moves Always, The
WEIGL, V., Seal Lullaby
WEIGL, V., Seeking You
WEIGL, V., Silver
WEIGL, V., Songs for a Child
WEIGL, V., Songs from "No Boundary"
WEIGL, V., Soon
WEIGL, V., Summer Stars
WEIGL, V., Thoughts About Grasshoppers
WEIGL, V., When the Vision Dies ("Perhaps")
WEIGL, V., Where Go the Boats
WEIGL, V., Winter Night
WEIGL, V., Wynken, Blynken and Nod
WHITE, This Son so Young
WHITTENBERG, Two Dylan Thomas Songs
WHITTENBERG, Vocalise
WILDER, Phyllis McGinley Song Cycle
WRIGHT, Cantata

4 PERFORMERS

BABBIT, Two Sonnets
BEALE, Proverbs
BERGER, A., Three Poems of Yeats
BERGER, J., Five Songs
BLANK, Esther's Monologue
BLANK, Four Dream Poems
BLANK, Poem
BLANK, Two Holy Sonnets by John Donne
BLANK, Zulus Live in Land Without a Square

CHANCE, Three Poems by Rilke
CLARK, Rondeau Redoublé
COWELL, Toccanta
CRUMB, Night Music I
CUCINOTTA, Beasts
CUSTER, Cartagena Songs
DE JONG, hist wist
DRUCKMAN, Animus II
EDWARDS, Three Hopkins Songs
EHLE, Algorhythms
FELCIANO, Glossolalia
FINE, Great Wall of China, The
FOSS, Thirteen Ways of Looking at a Blackbird
FRANCO, Lord Commeth, The
FRANCO, Song of Life, The
GIDEON, Rhymes from the Hill
GIDEON, Seasons of Time, The
GIDEON, Sonnets from Fatal Interview
HARRIS, Abraham Lincoln Walks at Midnight
HARRISON, Alma Redemptoris Mater
HARTWAY, Three Ways of Looking at a Blackbird
HUGGLER, For Coloratura, Clarinet, Viola, Cello
IVES, Vote for Names
IVEY, Solstice
JOHNSTON, Five Fragments
JOHNSTON, Sea Dirge, A
KAM, Nocturnes
KARLINS, Three Songs from 16th and 17th Century
KIM, Earthlight
KOLB, Chanson Bas
LEICHTLING, Rubáiyát Fragments
LEICHTLING, Trial and Death of Socrates
LEICHTLING, Two Proverbs
LEWIS, Song
LOMBARDO, Frosted Window: Variations on White
LYBBERT, Leopardi Canti
MILLER, Bashō Songs
MILLER, Mists and Waters
MOORE, Douglas, Ballad of William Sycamore, The
McBRIDE, Vocalise No. 3 On Nonsense Syllables
NOWAK, Maiden's Song
ORREGO-SALAS, Garden Songs
PECK, Automobile
PICCOLO, Found in Machaut's Chamber
PISK, Waning Moon, The
REALE, Three Songs from the Chinese
RILEY, Five Songs on Japanese Haiku
ROREM, Four Dialogues
ROREM, Serenade on Five English Poems
RUSSEL, Ballad with Epitaphs
SCHICKELE, Lowest Trees Have Tops, The
SCHUMAN, In Sweet Music
SMIT, Four Motets
STEARNS, Three Sacred Songs
STEVENS, Three Japanese Folksongs
STEVENS, When Icicles Hang by the Wall

STOUT, Commentary of T'ung Jen
STRAVINSKY, Three Songs from William Sakespeare
SYDEMAN, Encounters
TANENBAUM, Image
THOMSON, Four Songs to Poems of Thomas Campion
TRIMBLE, Four Fragments From the Canterbury Tales
TRIMBLE, Petit Concert
UDOW, Eight American Indian Children's Poems
WEIGL, V., Lyrical Suite
WEIGL, V., Requiem for Allison
WEIGL, V., Songs from "Native Island"
WEIGL, V., Thistle, Yarrow, Clover
WHITTENBERG, Even Though the World Keeps Changing
WUORINEN, Message to Denmark Hill, A
WYNER, Memorial Music
YTTREHUS, Angstwagen
YTTREHUS, Six Haiku

5 PERFORMERS

ADLER, Whitman Serenade
BALAZS, Sonnets after Elizabeth Barrett Browning
BEERMAN, Consort and Song
BEERMAN, Mass
BEESON, Creole Mystery, A
BEESON, Day's No Rounder Than Its Angles Are, The
BENSON, Nara
BINKERD, Three Songs
BISCARDI, Turning
BLANK, Finale: Mélange
BLANK, I Missed His Book, But I Read His Name
BOTTJE, In a word
BOTTJE, In Praise of Music
CLAFLIN, Finale
CLARKE, Suite of Changes
CRUMB, Lux Aeterna
CRUMB, Madrigals: Book IV
CRUMB, Night of the Four Moons
DE BOHUN, Songs of Estrangement
DEL TREDICI, I Hear An Army
DI DOMENICA, Four Short Songs
DIEMER, Four Poems by Alice Meynell
DONOVAN, Five Elizabethan Lyrics
EDWARDS, Veined Variety
FELDMAN, Intervals
FELDMAN, Journey to the End of the Night
FELDMAN, O'Hara Songs, The
FELDMAN, Vertical Thoughts V
FOSS, Time Cycle
FRANCO, Sonnet
GIDEON, Hound of Heaven, The
GIDEON, Questions on Nature
GRATZ, Earthbound
HAMPTON, Labyrinth
HAUFRECHT, Let's Play Maccabees, Children's Songs

HELLERMANN, Poem for Soprano and Four Instruments
HENRY, The Sons of Martha
KARLINS, Quartet
LORA, At Sunset Time
MYROW, Four Songs In Spring
PASATIERI, Far from Love
PASATIERI, Rites de Passage
PENN, Three Songs on Three Teton Sioux Poems
PERRY, Stabat Mater
PLESKOW, On Three Old English Rhymes
PLESKOW, On Two Ancient Texts
POPE, Rain
POWELL, Two Prayer Settings
PRESSER, Songs of Death
REALE, Pange Lingua
RHODES, Autumn Settings
RILEY, Cantata I
ROCHBERG, String Quartet No. 2 with Soprano
ROE, Hot Sun, Cool Fire
ROREM, Mourning Scene
ST. JOHN, Her Drifting from Me These Days
STEIN, String Quartet No. 5 - Ekloge
STOCK, Scat
STOUT, Allegory: Pride, An
STOUT, Landscape
TUBB, Five Haiku
UNG, Tall Wind
WARREN, Sonnets for Soprano and String Quartet
WEBER, Three Songs
WEIGL, K., Five Songs
WEIGL, K., Three Songs
WEIGL, V., Dear Earth: A Quintet of Poems
WEIGL, V., Five Songs of Remembrance
WEIGL, V., Summer Grass
WEISGALL, End of Summer
WILLIAMS, Suite of Six Texts
WINSOR, Fly, The
WINSOR, Sick Rose, The
YANNATOS, Three Songs

6 PERFORMERS

ADLER, Canto V
ADLER, Passionate Sword The
AMES, Among the Gods.
ANDERSON, Beyond Silence
AUSTIN, Homecoming
BROOKS, Last Night I Was the Wind
CIRONE, Five Items
CONSOLI, Isonic
CORY, Aria Viva
CRUMB, Songs Drones, and Refrains of Death
DIEMENTE, Forms of Flight and Fancy
EVETT, Billy in the Darbies
FELDMAN, For Franz Kline

FINE, Confession, The
FLANAGAN, Weeping Pleiads, The
FRANCO, Songs of the Spirit
FRANCO, Tempset, Incidental Music, The
GIDEON, Nocturnes
GIDEON, Sonnets from Shakespeare
HAUBIEL, Threnody for Love, A
HILLER, Avalanche, An
HUGGLER, Bittere Nüsse
JENKINS, Three Carols from the Quiet Wars
LANG, Three Puerto Rican Songs
MATTHEWS, Paysage
MORYL, Lied, Das
MOSS, Unseen Leaves
NOWAK, Summer is Away
PLESKOW, For Five Players and Baritone
PLOG, Four Sierra Scenes
RAN, O The Chimneys
RANDALL, Improvisations
REIF, Reverence for Life
REYNOLDS, Compass
ROUSE, Aphrodite Cantos
ROUSE, Ecstasis Mane Eburnei
ROUSE, Kiss, The
SACCO, Three Psalms
SEREBRIER, Eritica
SHIFRIN, A Renaissance Garland
SIMS, Elegie
SYDEMAN, Malediction
TANENBAUM, Mirage and Incantation
TAUB, Of Things Past
WEISGALL, Fancies and Inventions
WOLPE, Quintet with Voice
YANNY, At The End of the Parade

7 PERFORMERS

ALBERT, To Wake the Dead
ANDERSON, Variations on a Theme by M.B. Tolson
AVSHALOMOV, Little Clay Cart, The
BLANK, Coalitions
FELDMAN, I met heine on the rue fürstenberg
GIDEON, The adorable Mouse
HARRISON, Air
IVEY, Three Songs of Night
JAMES, Four Poems of Michael Fried
MAYER, Two News Items
MORYL, de morte cantoris
McNIEL, Three Preludes To The Aureate Earth
NELHYBEL, House that Jack Built, The
PERERA, Three Poems of Günter Grass
PLESKOW, Motet and Madrigal
PLESKOW, Three Songs
POPE, At that hour
ROVICS, Haunted Object

SCHWARTZ, Septet
SEYFRIT, Winter's Warmth
SHIFRIN, Satires of Circumstance
SILSBEE, Scroll
SIMS, Celebration of Dead Ladies
STOUT, Christmas Antiphon
TANENBAUM, Peter Quince At the Clavier
VAN NOSTRAND, Earth Manual - 1976
WILSON, D., Five Haiku
ZONN, Shadows of an Orange Leaf

8 PERFORMERS

BRINGS, Tre Sonetti di Michelangelo Buonarroti
CACIOPPO, Bestiary I: Eingang
CONSOLI, Equnox I
CONSOLI, Vuci Siculani
DRUCKMAN, Animus IV
DRUCKMAN, Dark upon the Harp
GIDEON, Condemned Playground, The
HAINES, Four Loves
LERDAHL, Wake
LUENING, Soundless Song, The
MAYER, Eight Miniatures
MONOD, Chamber Aria
MONOD, Passacaille
OLIVE, Mar-ri-ia-a
VAN NOSTRAND, Lunar Possession Manual - 1973, a Winter Ceremonial

9 PERFORMERS

BARAB, Moments Macabres
CONSOLI, Equinox II
CRUMB, Ancient Voices of Children
EBERHARD, Parody
FARBERMAN, Evolution
GRUNDMAN, Zoo Illogical
LERDAHL, Eros
McBRIDE, Commentary
PINKHAM, Letters from Saint Paul
REIF, Artist, The
ROCHBERG, Blake Songs
ROUSE, First Stratum of Empyrean
ROUSE, Nox Aeris Temporis
SAMUEL, Relativity of Icarus, The
SCHULLER, Six Renaissance Lyrics
SEMEGEN, Lieder auf der Flucht
SHAPEY, Incantations
STEARNS, Three Love Songs
STRAVINSKY, In memoriam Dylan Thomas
UNG, Mohori
WEBER, Concert Aria after Solomon
ZUR, Affairs, The

10 PERFORMERS

CARTER, Mirror on Which to Dwell, A
CHANCE, Edensong
FOX, Time Excursions
HOVHANESS, Canticle
PARRIS, Dreams
SCHWANTNER, Shadows II, Consortium IV
STOUT, Two Songs of Ariel, 1957
UDOW, Electric Silence

11 PERFORMERS

AMRAM, Three Songs for America
BLACKWOOD, Voyage à Cythère, Un
BREHM, Cycle of Six Songs, A
CHOU, Seven Poems of T'ang Dynasty
CORY, Walking
DIEMENTE, 3 - 31 - '70
FELDMAN, Rabbi Akiba
FELDMAN, Vertical Thoughts III
LEICHTLING, Psalm 37
PINKHAM, Now the Trumpet Summons Us Again

12 PERFORMERS

ECKERT, Sea-Changes
REYNOLDS, Again

13 PERFORMERS

DEL TREDICI, Night Conjure-Verse
EDWARDS, Captive, The
LEVI, Truth, The
YANNATOS, Priere Dans L'Arche

14 PERFORMERS

NELHYBEL, Concerto Spirituoso No.1
NELHYBEL, Concerto Spirtuoso No. 2
PUSZTAI, Requiem Profana
STOUT, Engel, Die

15 PERFORMERS

BRANT, Encephalograms
CHANCE, Dark Song

Appendix III

CLASSIFIED BY ENSEMBLE

A. POPULAR ENSEMBLE COMBINATIONS

STRING QUARTET WITH ONE VOICE:

Adler, A Whitman Serenade (Medium Voice)
Balazs, Sonnets After Elizabeth Barrett Browning (High Voice)
Beeson, A Creole Mystery (Medium Voice)
The Day's No Rounder Than Its Angles Are (Middle Voice)
Binkerd, Three Songs (Mezzo-Soprano)
Bottje, In Praise of Music (Soprano)
Claflin, Finale (Contralto)
de Bohun, Songs of Estrangement (Soprano)
Del Tredici, I Hear An Army (Soprano)
Dinerstein, Four Settings (Soprano)
Donovan, Five Elizabethian Lyrics (Soprano)
Franco, Sonnet (Voice)
Karlins, Quartet (Soprano)
Lora, At Sunset Time (Mezzo-Soprano)
Pasatieri, Rites de Passage (Voice)
Perry, Stabat Mater (Contralto)
Presser, Songs of Death (Mezzo-Soprano)
Rhodes, Autumn Settings (Soprano)
Rochberg, String Quartet No. 2 (Soprano)
Rorem, Mourning Scene (Voice)
Stein, String Quartet No. 5 - Ekloge (Soprano)
Tubb, Five Haiku (Soprano)
Warren, Sonnets (Soprano)
Weber, Three Songs (Soprano or Tenor)
Weigl, K., Five Songs (Soprano)
Three Songs (Mezzo-Soprano)
Weigl, V., Five Songs of Remembrance (Contralto)
Requiem for Allison (Mezzo-Soprano)
Summer Grass (Mezzo-Soprano)
Williams, Suite of Six Texts (Tenor)
Yannatos, Three Songs (Soprano or Tenor)

PIANO & ONE OTHER INSTRUMENT WITH ONE VOICE:

BASSOON

Karlins, Four Inventions and a Fugue (Alto)

CELLO

Chajes, By the rivers of Babylon (Voice)
Feldman, Four Songs to e e cummings (Soprano)
Moore, D., From the Dark Tower (Mezzo-Soprano)
Nowak, Five Songs (Mezzo-Soprano)
Presser, A Hymn to God the Father (Voice)
Rorem, Last Poems of Wallace Stevens (Voice)

CLARINET

Adolphys, Lilacs (Voice)
Argento, To Be Sung Upon The Water (High Voice)
Avshalomov, Two Little Birds (Soprano)
Cummings, As Dew in April (High Voice)
Davis, Though Men Call Us Free (Soprano)
Fennelly, Songs with improvisation (Medium Voice)
Ferritto, Oggi (Soprano)
Hovhaness, O Lady Moon (Voice)
Saturn (Soprano)
Kupferman, The Conceptual Wheel (Soprano)
Roosevelt, Three Songs from Poe (Soprano)
Rorem, Ariel (Soprano)
Sargon, Patterns in Blue (Medium Voice)
Swack, Psalm VIII (Voice)
Taylor, Two Songs (Soprano or Tenor)
Weigl, V., Birds in Springtime (High Voice)
Cardinal in March (High Voice)
Christ Child's Lullaby (Mezzo-Soprano)
Do Not Awake Me (Mezzo-Soprano)
The Salvation of the Dawn (Voice)
The Sea Moves Always (Voice)
Thoughts about Grasshoppers (Medium Voice)
When the Vision Dies ("Perhaps") (Medium Voice)

FLUTE

Beale, Lamentations (Soprano)
Caldwell, A Christmas Triptych (Medium Voice)
A Lute Caroll (Medium Voice)
Clark, Life in Ghana (Voice)
Cowell, Vocalise (Voice)
Diamond, The Mad Maid's Song (Soprano)
Hartley, A Psalm Cycle (Medium High Voice)
Karlins, Three Songs (Soprano)
McBride, Vocalise (Soprano)
Reale, The Traveler (Tenor)
Rovics, Echo (Voice)
Stewart, Wait (Soprano)
Verral, The Rose of the World (Soprano)
Weigl, V., Along the Moving Darkness (Medium High Voice)
Birds in Springtime (High Voice)
Cardinal in March (High Voice)
Challenge (Mezzo-Soprano)
Christ Child's Lullaby (Mezzo-Soprano)

City Birds (Voice)
Do Not Awake Me (Mezzo-Soprano)
Glimpse of Hope (Mezzo-Soprano or Baritone)
The Little Singers (Medium Voice)
Long, Long Ago (Medium Voice)
The Sea Moves Always (Voice)
Seeking You (Medium Voice)
Songs for a Child (Voice)
Soon (Voice)
In Springtime (Medium Voice)
Thoughts About Grasshoppers (Medium Voice)
When the Vision Dies ("Perhaps") (Medium Voice)

Whittenberg, Two Dylan Thomas Songs (Soprano)

FRENCH HORN

Melby, Due Canti di Leopardi (Soprano or Tenor)
Roosevelt, An American Sampler (Soprano)
Weigl, V., Swiftly Along Flows the River (Voice)

OBOE

Cummings, As Dew in April (High Voice)
Weigl, V., Seal Lullaby (Mezzo-Soprano)

PERCUSSION

Blank, Zulus Live in Land Without a Square (Soprano)
Farberman, Greek Scene (Voice)
New York Times (Mezzo-Soprano)

RECORDER

Weigl, V., The Huntsmen (Medium Voice)
The Little Singers (Medium Voice)
Long, Long Ago (Medium Voice)
Pippa's Song (Voice)
The Rock-A-By Lady (Medium Voice)
Seal Lullaby (Mezzo-Soprano)
Silver (Medium Voice)
Songs for a Child (Voice)
In Springtime
Where Go the Boats (Medium Voice)
Winter Night (Medium Voice)
Wynken, Blynken and Nod (Voice)

SAXOPHONE

Derr, I Never Saw Another Butterfly (Soprano)
Taylor, Quattro Liriche from "Mattino Domenicale" (Medium Voice)

TAPE

Melby, The Men that Are Falling (Soprano)

TRUMPET

Swack, Psalm VIII (Voice)

TUBA

Blank, Recital (Soprano)

VIOLA

Colgrass, New People (Mezzo-Soprano)
Hoskins, Romance, Who Loves to Nod and Sing (Mezzo-Soprano)
Presser, A Hymn to God the Father (Voice)
Seigmeister, Songs of Experience (Voice)

Weigl, V., Rain at Night (Low Voice)
Songs from "No Boundary"
Swiftly Along Flows the River (Voice)

VIOLIN

Cowell, Sonatina (Baritone)
Cumming, As Dew in April (High Voice)
Ives, Sunrise (Voice)
Lessard, Five Poems by Robert Herrick (Voice)
Weigl, V., Along the Moving Darkness (Medium High Voice)
Beyond Time (High Voice)
Do Not Awake Me (Mezzo-Soprano)
Echoes (Medium Voice)
Glimpse of Hope (Mezzo-Soprano or Baritone)
Nightfall in the Mountains (Voice)
Rabbles of Shattered Leaves (Voice)
The Salvation of the Dawn (Voice)
The Sea Moves Always (Voice)
Seeking You (Medium Low Voice)
Songs from "No Boundary"
Soon (Voice)
Summer Stars (Male Voice)
Thoughts About Grasshoppers (Medium Voice)
When the Vision Dies (Medium Voice)

B. OTHER STANDARD ENSEBLES

BRASS QUINTET:

Diemente, Forms of Flight and Fancy (Soprano)
Plog, Four Sierra Scenes (Soprano)
Sacco, Three Psalms (Tenor)

WOODWIND QUINTET:

Brooks, Last Night I Was the Wind (Baritone)
Franco, Songs of the Spirit (Soprano or Tenor)
Serebrier, Erotica (Soprano)

PIANO QUINTET:

Jenkins, Three Carols from the Queit Wars
Rief, Reverence for Life (Voice)
Taub, "...of Things Past" (Soprano)

PIANO TRIO:

Sydeman, Encounters (Baritone)

STRING TRIO:

Lewis, Song (Voice)

C. INSTRUMENTS (Two or More) OF ONE GENRE:

CLARINET:
- Pisk, Meadow Safrons (Contralto)

CONTRABASS:
- Crane, Cords (Soprano)

FLUTE:
- Wyner, Memorial Music (Soprano)

PERCUSSION:
- Cage, Forever and Sunsmell (Voice)
- Cirone, Five Items (Soprano)
- Henry, The Sons of Martha (Soprano)
- Lang, Three Puerto Rican Songs (Soprano)
- Miller, Basho Songs (Soprano)
- Molineux, Crystals (Mezzo-Soprano)
- Russell, Ballad with Epitaphs (Voice, 2)
- Steiner, Three Poems (Voice)
- Stewart, The First Joys of Marriage (Voice)
- Yttrehus, Angstwagen (Soprano)

PIANO:
- Edwards, Three Hopkins Songs (Soprano, 2)
- Ferguson, Two Spanish Songs (Medium Voice)
- Ives, Vote for Names (Voice)
- Lybbert, Lines for the Fallen (Soprano)
- Rorem, Four Dialogues (Voice, 2)

SAXOPHONE:
- Hampton, Labyrinth (Soprano)

VOIL:
- Roe, Hot Sun, Cool Fire (High Voice)

VIOLIN:
- Johnston, Three Chinese Lyrics (Soprano)
- Powell, Three Poems (Soprano)
- Sydeman, Four Japanese Songs (Soprano)

Index of Titles

(Numerical references are entry numbers)

General Index

(Numerical references are entry numbers)

ABOUT THE COMPILER

PATRICIA LUST is Associate Professor of Music at Longwood College, Farmville, Virginia. She has published articles in *Keeping Up with Experimental Music in the Schools.*